SPIRITUAL

SECOND
EDITION

FROM INSPIRATION TO PUBLICATION

Deborah Levine Herman

Soul Odyssey Books
a division of Micro Publishing Media
Stockbridge, Massachusetts

Spiritual Writing: From Inspiration to Publication
Deborah Levine Herman

Copyright © 2002, 2022 by Deborah Levine Herman

ISBN 978-1-953321-12-1 (Pbk.)

Herman, Deborah, 1958–
Spiritual Writing: from Inspiration to Publication / Deborah Levine Herman
The book Includes resources and an index.

Book and cover design by Jane McWhorter

Published by

Soul Odyssey Books
A Division of Micro Publishing Media, Inc
PO Box 1522
Stockbridge, MA 01262

I dedicate this book to all writers awakened by a Divine voice with the courage to heed the call.

Other Books Published By MPM

These books and more may be found wherever books are sold or at Debsbookparadise.com

TABLE OF CONTENTS

Acknowledgments

Many remarkable people contributed love and Spirit to my writer's journey sharing my spiritual path. My husband, Jeff Herman, is a twin flame and partner in every sense of the word. He has helped me on my journey through raising my three children, Shana, Joshua, and Jessica, and traveled by my side through the ups and downs of life. He has always supported my dreams.

Shana, Joshua, and Jessica are my loves and have taught me more than they can imagine. They have brought new family members through their Soul partnerships who have expanded our love for each other. My grandson Solomon is my greatest hope for the future of humankind as I know if God is bringing such light-bearing Souls into the planet, there must be more on their way.

I want to give a special acknowledgment to my sister, Brenda, without whom this new edition of this book might not have happened. She knows why.

My brother, Larry, is always a wonderful friend, advisor, and source of constant laughter.

My father, Stuart Ava Shalom, is lovingly remembered for always cheering me on and teaching me about business and sales despite myself. Since the first edition of this book, he has been joined in Spirit by my mother, who was and will always be an inspiration.

I want to acknowledge my sister on the journey, Rebecca Briggs, who has been loyal, loving, and kind. And Dianne Lake, who opened me up to new potential as a writer, helped me achieve one of my dreams, and has provided me with lasting friendship. I also send love to my recent friends, whom I value more than they will ever know. And I want to acknowledge my friend and mentor, Jane McWhorter, who reminds me to protect my energy and use my time wisely. And a special thank you to my angel, William Stevenson who has believed in me and supported my work.

Thank you to my distributor, Tom Doherty, and Cardinal Publishers Group's excellent staff. Tom has been a great source of advice and guidance; his team has helped me grow my Indie publishing vision.

And a special thank you to Cynthia Black, who was called back to the other side, for shepherding the first edition of this book. Thank you for believing in me.

A sad and final wish for Shaun Royer. I would have shared this book with you, but you were called back home. You will always be remembered.

To anyone I didn't include, I haven't forgotten you. I could go on forever in gratitude.

PREFACE

The spiritual path and the writer's journey are inextricably linked. At least they have been for me. At the age of ten, I decided that I would become a lawyer. I never wavered in my devotion to this plan, which structured a path for me as an idealistic do-gooder to save the world. I had images of Gregory Peck in *To Kill a Mockingbird*. My heroes were people like Abraham Lincoln, one of the most outstanding lawyers ever, and every television lawyer who shouted, "I object."

Skipping ahead a few years in between, I did go to law school at The Ohio State University College of Law. I had completed my undergraduate degree there in an Honor's Contract Interdisciplinary, which meant I could take courses that might be relevant to a future as a lawyer, including English and Political Science. Everything was going according to plan until I was in the middle of my first year of Law School. Suffice it to say, it wasn't the scintillating experience I thought it would be, or I didn't have the discipline at this point to stay focused.

Whatever the reason, I helped my boredom by going to a comedy club in the evenings where my brother was performing as an amateur comedian. My brother is only ten months older than me, which automatically gave him a foundation for his humor. I was his official laugher because since we were little brats together, I always thought he was hysterical.

After a while, the club owner said, "Deborah, you are here almost every night; I am going to put you to work."

He said he wanted me to interview the comedians and write articles for a local magazine. He offered me a free cover charge, which I got from the doorman anyway, but it seemed like a fun idea. Then the magazine owner asked me to write articles about other types of events like concerts and movies, and I had no idea what I was doing. But I knew it was much more fun than my law classes.

When I was supposed to be studying law, I was also taking vocal training. I liked theater and always wanted to learn to sing. But to be honest, I was getting desperate for distraction. The vocal training put me on a trajectory that genuinely changed my life. My vocal trainer was a retired jazz singer named Michelle Horsefield. The few times I would arrive early, I would wait in her living room and see her husband in the background. He was an older man in a wheelchair, having lost both legs to diabetes. He had very engaging eyes, but I never spoke to him.

One day he rolled his chair over to me and said hello. Then all he said, with a gleam, was, "I have something for you." He showed me a book he had self-published titled *Llanimai*. It meant "I am in All." It was a book of what looked to be his poetry. He opened the book to a particular page and asked me to read it. It was awkward having him watch me read, but I felt an opening in my heart. I looked into his eyes and knew that something was changing in me. I wasn't sure what it was. Finally, he gave me the book and said, "it is really for you. I want you to keep it."

The following week I was scheduled to come in for a vocal lesson when I received a call from Michelle. "I have to cancel our lesson, Deborah," she said through tears. "My beloved Eric has died."

I felt my stomach jump. I had only just met him, yet I felt a terrible loss. There was so much I wanted to ask him. Then she surprised me and said, "I want you to write his eulogy for the newspaper. I know Eric would have wanted it that way."

I was so taken aback. I had only met Eric once, yet I felt connected and grief-stricken. This brief conversation was my first experience with what I realized later was a Soul connection. It was my first awareness that there is something amazing beyond the here and now. I believe that Eric Horsefield was my first spiritual teacher. I believe he embodied the saying, "when the student is ready, the teacher appears."

Because of Eric, I realized my calling as a writer. His funeral was a celebration of life. I did not attend but wrote the article from what I knew about him from other people who had spent years basking in his light. He touched many people's lives just as he had touched mine. After I finished the article for the paper about Eric, I also learned about a family secret. But that is a story and book for another time.

This final sign was what I needed to shift my path in a new direction. I went to the college of Journalism at Ohio State University, and they accepted me for a dual degree master's program with the College of Law. Anyone who survives first-year law school would be silly to give it up, and my parents would have been very unhappy. But, looking back, I was not frightened at all to change a direction I had planned since childhood. It felt so right. I didn't stop law; I just added the Journalism Master's and completed both not knowing where they would lead. My life has taken many circuitous turns on the way to this place and time and the book's second edition. Eric and Michelle helped ignite my spiritual and writer's flame. Michelle passed away in 2005. I will always be grateful to them, and know they are now making beautiful music and poetry in Heaven.

Cosmic Measurement
By Eric Horsefield
Excerpt from the book *Llanimai*

How do you measure a man's inner worth?
Not as you measure the size of the earth,
For the earth can be measured and plotted and weighed
 But how will you measure a man unafraid

What is the size of my mind or my Soul?
How many miles to my ultimate goal?
How many times can I fall and still rise?
How can you quench the hope light in my eyes?

The spirit of man is not bound by the rules
 Of science or logic as taught in our schools
The seeker sincere in his hope and his doubt
Finds symbols and clues from within and without.

There is great compensation in holding this course
For all human progress has come from this Source
The glimpses I get of the goal I am seeking
The moments when I hear that still small voice speaking

These are the values the world cannot measure
This is the one incorruptible treasure
Then somehow, I know I have finished my test
And my Soul is serene as I lie down to rest.

INTRODUCTION

When I wrote the first edition of this book, I worked strictly as a literary agent and occasional author. My husband, Jeff Herman, is a nonfiction agent, and I was our official screener. It was in the late 1990s and early 2000s when we received physical submissions. I would go through hundreds of number ten envelopes with eagerly written query letters inside of them. Unfortunately, as much as I was mining for gold, as agents want to find things they can sell, I would only select a small portion to pass on to Jeff for consideration.

We received hundreds of query letters each day as well as unsolicited manuscripts. At one time, we designated a walk-in closet in one of our offices as "ye olde slush room." It was physically impossible to read through these unsolicited submissions even if we dedicated 24 hours daily to that. Sometimes we would grab a box, but it was the luck of the draw, and most times, we had to reject the submissions that writers so lovingly packaged and sent to us. I know what this felt like to these hopeful authors, as I remember sending my first book to a publisher before knowing anything about the industry. I printed out the pages, tied them with a ribbon, said a blessing, placed the manuscript gently in a box, and sent it off into the ethers.

Nothing happened, of course. I know now this may have had nothing to do with the quality of my work or my worthiness of becoming a published author. There is a world of decision-making that leads to representation and a sale. I learned first-hand why agents and editors choose one book over another. Agents want to find books they can sell, and publishers must choose books they can sell to consumers. The good news is that if you understand how agents and editors make these decisions, you can prepare your work in light of the publishing business rather than in a world of wishful manifestation.

One positive change for agents and publishers was the universal use of email. Of course, we don't receive as many pieces of physical mail, and I do miss them. But I am also a person who loves the tactile feel of physical books and have a home filled with them. We still receive tons of queries and attachments that have the same effect in the virtual world.

While working as an agent back when I originally wrote this book, I had seen more book ideas, proposals, and manuscripts than I could count. Submissions tend to fall into similar categories. Many have been about spiritual subjects, including religion, general spirituality, memoir, psychic experiences, channeling, angel communication, and direct prophecy.

But agents and publishers reject over 95 percent of their submissions, spiritual or otherwise. The percentage may be even higher as publishing changes from the inside out. The Publishing conglomerates continue to grow like some absorbing blob, and the delivery systems continue to change. In addition, the economy has been in constant flux, so the mid-list books, the bread and butter, and the types of books most of you are writing are not selling as fast as they used to, or they are not selling at all.

You, as an aspiring spiritual writer, must find a way to increase your odds of being within the five percent who are not only called but who are chosen.

Or it would help if you found other ways to spread your message and find your audience. The greatest thing about the changes in the publishing industry is that it opens many opportunities for writers like you beyond the traditional route.

As writers, we all dream of what we imagine are the good old days when a writer could be the talent. Upon finishing our masterpiece, we would hand it to our literary agent, who would be sitting in a penthouse office in New York City with tons of staff waiting on them at every turn. We could sit back and wait for the call, "we have an auction for your book, and all the major publishers are throwing their hats in the ring." Then we would receive an enormous advance and be able to retire to a beach house where we could sip wine with other literati and write to our heart's content. It is nice to dream, but this publishing world exists only in the movies.

Not only is it not how it is, but I am not sure that it was ever this way, except for the top writers in the country.

Chicken Soup for the Soul is often considered the gold standard for success stories. I will have writers pitch me on their work quoting that *Chicken Soup for the Soul* was rejected 144 times and then was picked up by a publisher, and the rest is history. "My book will be the next *Chicken Soup for the Soul*," they insist. The most amusing thing about this is that we represented *Chicken Soup for the Soul*, it was only 20 to 40 rejections, and I screened and edited the original proposal. The most important thing to learn about the *Chicken Soup* phenomena is that Jack Canfield and Mark Victor Hansen were ahead of their time and worked tirelessly and innovatively to make the book and resulting series successful. They did it without the advantages you have. More about this later.

As spiritual writers, you know that you are in many ways always "ahead of your time." At a minimum, you walk to a different drummer and are not always taken seriously in the traditional publishing world. Since the original writing of this book, my career has taken many directions. The world has changed with the actual advent of the internet. Self-publishing is no longer the illegitimate son or daughter of the traditional publishing model. No matter what direction you follow, you must provide a quality product. If you self-publish, you will be responsible for recreating the advantages you would get if you were housed within the security of the traditional publishing model. Many writers assume that traditional publishing means they hand in the book, and the rest is done for them. As you will learn in this new edition, learning to promote yourself and your book is more important than ever.

In every situation, writers are expected to promote their books. This expectation has always been true and is one of the factors that publishing houses consider in making an offer. In the past, publishers might consider a nonfiction book by its topic or a novel by its writing. The risk threshold is reduced with the large media companies absorbing the big and small publishing houses. In other words, they look for the sure thing. Only the top-tier books will have real support from a publishing house, which will typically only last through the crucial first two months post-publication. There will be a prelaunch promotion plan and then a follow-up. After two months, the traditional house must move on to the next list and their new titles. Suppose you have the good fortune to work with a traditional publishing house that offers you an advance, publishes, and distributes your book to all retail venues, including bookstores. They will give you some attention, but when they move on, you may feel abandoned if you don't understand how the business works. No matter how your book is published, whether by a traditional publisher, an indie/hybrid publisher, or you alone, you will be responsible for its longevity and ultimate success.

If you are interested in finding a "traditional" publisher, there are many opportunities for you to present yourself as an excellent bet that didn't exist when I wrote the original book. I have added a section on platform building using digital marketing and social media strategy. Understanding marketing, promotion, and author branding will help you level the playing field. Don't worry. You can dedicate yourself to writing and find people to help you with the techie stuff. But it helps to know what you are doing and why. Ultimately you are finding ways for people to know who you are and learn why your message is worth their time. This new marketing paradigm is a reality of publishing in today's world. It will help you achieve your goals.

When I began the updating process for this book, I was aware of changes in digital opportunities for writers. I went back to school at Rutgers University in their mini-MBA program and received three graduate certifications in Digital Marketing Strategy, Social Media Strategy, and Entrepreneurship. I saw a significant change in marketing through the internet and felt completely confused. Many options were available online, but they seemed more confusing and like potential scams. The internet in the beginning is the closest thing we have to what it must have been like in the wild west. I felt fortunate to take a more academic approach with leaders in their fields. There is always a lot to learn, and it changes every day; however, the digital marketing mindset is a constant that I have included in this new edition.

There are many ways spiritual writers can build a platform that did not exist in 2002. As you will learn, a platform is simply a way to explain to a prospective agent or editor that there is a market for your book and how you can reach it. I could not have predicted the pandemic as a life changer when I began this update. I planned to bring in the magic of the internet and the joys of technology to give you all more opportunities for success. But I had no idea how important it would be to your future and the future of publishing that writers embrace technology to stay connected during times of uncertainty. Who could have imagined quarantine? Some of you may write about dystopia. Some of you may have had visions of this time in world history. I prefer to live in my spiritual denial waiting for what is next. I stay in my mental bubble and look for ways to remain optimistic while trying to raise the planet's vibration in any little way I can.

I was lucky to have taken the certifications because they became more relevant. As you will learn in the last section of this book, you can level the playing field and build a viable platform right from the comfort of your home. There are ways to use technology that are simple and easy to embrace with the proper marketing mindset. You can sell your book where your customers are, on the internet. People still love physical books, and I hope that will not change any time soon. If I got rid of my esoteric and spiritual library alone, I would stop my house from settling into the ground. However, statistics show that the buying process has moved to the internet and any number of online retailers.

I am pleased to see many box stores reopening and thriving after the early days of the Pandemic, but there will always be uncertainty with that model. On a happier note, more indie bookstores are returning, providing the much-desired in-person buying experience. I have an online bookstore that I designed to mimic the experience of an out-of-the-way treasure hunt called debsbookparadise.com. There I sell the books my company publishes, but mostly it is home to physical and mostly out-of-print like new but used titles. It is the bookstore of my dreams and my dream is to someday open up a physical location. Deb's Book Paradise will have comfortable furniture, wood shelves from floor to ceiling with rolling ladders, and nooks and crannies to hide in, read, and drink tea. And, of course, it will have a resident cat.

Dream bookstore aside, I revised this book because it is imperative that you, as spiritual writers, take the leap of faith that you can utilize technology as a God-given blessing to find your niche reading audience. This book will at least get you started.

Another new addition to this book is a more extensive discussion of the pros and cons of self-publishing. In 2002, self-publishing automatically meant vanity. Now self-publishing is considered a practical alternative if done right. There is also a newer option called indie/hybrid publishing. A hybrid situation is where you have a professional team behind you, which has elements of doing it yourself but with professional help. Some hybrid publishers offer distribution, but many only offer passive placement in wholesale catalogs. I plan to give you enough information so you can make the right decision for your work. You will learn about the business part of publishing. It isn't as daunting as it may seem. As a spiritual being who has spent much of my life feeling as if I have been shoveling smoke, it seemed out of character for me to have embraced the business end of this industry. I have faith that anyone taking the time to read this book can as well.

As in the first edition of this book, I intend to give you the inspiration to write and the tools to help you navigate the book publishing business.

I have designed the four parts of this book to guide you on your journey to publication and beyond.

I. The Spiritual Writer and the Writer's Path
II. From Inspiration to Manuscript
III. From Manuscript to Publication

IV. Promoting your Book in the Digital Age

As a spiritual writer myself, I am with you every step of the way. I hope you will feel my guidance and connection. We are all students and each other's teachers. I happen to have spent many years in the publishing industry. I am beginning to think maybe that was the plan all along. Perhaps part of my mission is to ensure high vibrational voices like yours can break through the barriers in your way. Whether you classify yourself as a mystic, psychic, an evangelical Christian, a religious or non-religious seeker of universal spiritual truths, you, like all spiritual writers, are somewhere along the continuum of the spiritual experience. My list of possible readers is inadequate. If you have a calling by something inside your Soul that stirs you to see something greater than yourself, I hope I answer your questions and this book helps you find your way.

As spiritual writers, we have been blessed with a connection to the Source of all creation. We continuously examine the nature of reality. Our writing is our access to the universal database.

Part one, "The Spiritual Writer's Path," analyzes how the spiritual path is inextricably linked with the writer's journey. The spiritual path transcends our intellect. We can't simply check off a list of spiritual life lessons and presume that we have become enlightened. Our lessons come in ways we can't anticipate. Maybe we don't even realize when we have progressed, but our progress is noted nonetheless. If we figure out that there is an overall plan for our individual Soul's growth, we can become active participants.

We all encounter specific lessons, which I call the "Seven Lessons of Soul Odyssey." I invite you to explore these lessons to co-create with your cosmic curriculum through journal exercises. The lessons can become a starting point for you on your sacred journey.

Part two, "From Inspiration to Manuscript," talks about craft and the creation of your message. Spiritual writers are sometimes so filled with joy and bliss that we want to persuade everyone to see and adopt our point of view. We are well-meaning and believe we are helping others become enlightened, but we risk becoming "God-intoxicated," which will usually interfere with our objective of getting published. In this section, you'll learn how important it is to take a step back so you can present your material in a marketable way that also connects with the reader's desire to learn something beneficial for their own life. For a spiritual writer, objectivity is crucial. Even with enthusiasm and passion, God does not expect you to save the world alone. However, through well-crafted writing, you can influence the consciousness of those people who read your words, and this is a beautiful contribution to the big picture we all share.

In part three, "from manuscript to sale," you will gain insight from the publisher's, agent's, and editor's perspectives. The value of this section is that you will learn to decode how they examine your work to decide what they will represent or choose to publish.

You will learn the players and the protocols of traditional publishing so you do not make easily avoided mistakes that would take your manuscript out of consideration. Traditional publishing is a difficult journey, but by reading this book, you have already acknowledged you are up for a challenge. There are viable avenues to conventional publishing, but there are fewer opportunities. I will share my experience and insider's knowledge, but many things are out of your control and mine.

This reality of publishing as an industry is why I have added an additional chapter to this section dedicated to what was considered non-traditional methods of getting published. Since I first wrote and published this book, the internet has exploded. It has made it easier for people to upload marginal material to see their name on a book. Still, it has paved the way for writer entrepreneurs willing to learn the ropes to succeed even if the conglomerates won't consider your work. You can level the playing field with online platform building and create a professional product that can reach your intended audience. We will discuss platform building in Part Four, but here we will discuss your options for publishing.

You don't need to become a household name to be a successful spiritual writer any more than you need to lead your own cult. If you believe you have a spiritual mission to share important information for the greater good, you can learn how to reach the people who want what you have to say. Some of you will rise above and become bestselling writers. Few of you will make your living as writers. Even those who get significant advances can't sustain their lives until their books reach critical mass. It takes a lot of work to sell books, and many players add to the success. The most important thing to remember is that if you feel called to write, heed the call and learn what it takes to be published or find a workaround away from the traditional players.

I understand it is the dream to be offered representation by a literary agent and have a publisher validate you with a contract. There are many advantages to this route. They will pay you at least a minimal advance, so you are not paying them for services. They will pay for the printing of the books and will distribute them, and they give you the perceived prestige of saying you are a published author. However, any traditional publisher will still expect you to promote your book; typically, they will not want to give you a contract until you don't need them. Publishing is a risk-averse archaic business that tries to stay ahead of trends. The big conglomerates are media companies within which publishing is only a small part. While editors used to have more autonomy, they now have a much higher threshold to meet according to the goals of the dragon they feed.

What Does this Mean for you?

You need to know what it takes to be professional in your submission process. However, there are still advantages to this route, so if you can make it happen, why not? Platform building and book marketing are essential no matter how your book is published. You will learn to believe in yourself enough to find ways to push ahead even if the traditional route closes its doors on you.

A Word of Caution

Competitiveness is a motivator when kept in balance. I recommend you do not look at what other people are doing unless it is to research trends or educate yourself on subjects that interest you. I have found people who have listened to too much advice from self-proclaimed professionals who have not had years in the trenches of publishing. In other words, take what helps you from resources and discern what is true for you.

Do not compare yourself to other writers. Artists are sensitive beings. You can get psyched out this way and may not pursue your goals. Look inward for your inspiration and to the Divine source. People can bring you down. People may not understand you and will be threatened by your different way of thinking. You do not need anyone's validation but your own and God's. Of course, this is not to say you can get away with avoiding the publishing protocols. It is to help you stay safe in your spiritual shield and bubble while accessing your Divine inner voice.

Early on in my journey, I thought I could never write a book. I looked at spiritual writers of the time and felt defeated before I ever put a word on the keyboard. Either I thought they had already said everything I wanted to say or that they knew better than I did. I also had writer "friends" who would see me and ask, "so what are you writing? Have you gotten anything published yet?" And then they would tell me what they were doing. When it is time for you to write, you will write. Or you can take time to put yourself in the right frame of mind to follow your inner voice if the time is already here. Either way, don't give in to detractors. Otherwise, you are prolonging the wait. I firmly believe you cannot blow your destiny. Your inner guidance and Angels will never abandon you. But you can feel frustrated if you avoid bringing your inner voice into the open.

In some ways, social media and writer's groups worldwide can make it worse for you than how I had it. I could avoid the "friend" when I saw her walking toward me. Be conscious of your screen time if it is causing you to doubt yourself. You can learn things from websites and classes, but the place to start is inside you. Your unique message can't be taught in any online course. You can only learn refinement and technique.

We will discuss the structure and how to construct your writing for the end reader. But that is the craft aspect of writing. That is not the essence of spiritual writing. You are, first and foremost, a messenger and can learn the techniques to be effective. You have felt the call and heeded it. You are willing to face the initiations required of one who takes up the mantle of the Divine. You will learn how to put your Ego aside to allow the purity of the message to shine through. You are a vessel; if you treat yourself with love and respect, you will fulfill your mission. Trust your connection to the Divine.

Now to the Practicalities

In part three, we will look at two documents that can open doors: the query letter and the book proposal. We are going to start with the query letter. Please note, while the query letter will be your first introduction to an agent or editor, you will must have your book proposal or partical manuscript ready to go. . As I was considering how to help you navigate the publishing arena, I remembered how many times I received query letters or even (gasp) phone calls at the office where writers were testing the water. They wanted to see if there would be any interest in their topic before doing the hard work of creating the submission package. Don't do that. We assume the project is available and ready to go if we receive a query letter. We will move on if we request it and you do not have one ready. And we do not forget so easily.

A book proposal is an art form; creating one that stands out will increase your credibility tremendously and move your book to the top of the submissions pile. In this section about publishing, you will also learn what happens if you are fortunate enough to get an offer from either an agent or a publisher and will touch upon your role in book marketing and promotion. In this new digital age, I recommend you begin your platform building and promotion plan at the same time your start your book if you can. But don't worry. When you finish the book, you will know what this means.

The fourth section "promoting your book in the digital age," will give you a strong overview of how to get started In the first edition of this book, I could not include the fantastic possibilities you have to market your books and make them successful because most of them didn't exist. The digital world was in its infancy. Instead, I will walk you through some things you can easily do to get your message to the most people and build your brand. Your goal is to find your reader and tribe. With a strategic approach, you can reach the people who will read what you have to say. Never have there been so many opportunities literally at your fingertips.

Let's Define the Spiritual Writer

The reality of the traditional book business is that the bottom line constrains publishers. Most publishing houses look for books that can fit within the mainstream because that's where they can reach the widest audiences possible. When the first edition of this book was released, publishers often overlooked books on the subjects that interest writers like you as not being mainstream enough. If the agents or publishers considered your books, they would categorize them as New Age. That was a catchall and highly limiting.

Christian writers were also limited by subject matter, whereas the more universal messages can now cross over to secular audiences. Although times are changing and a conservative movement is happening in the United States, there is a market for books about progressive topics such as raising consciousness and sustainability. There are also more liberal Christian publishers interested in lifestyle issues beyond a fundamentalist perspective. We can't predict the tides, so I recommend you follow your inner passion and seek like-minded people who want what you have.

As in every era, this is a time of change; no matter your path, spiritual people feel it in their Souls. I want to be very transparent in this updated book that I hope to steer you away from focusing on the "end times." I find it curious that I took extra time to revise this book only to see a worldwide pandemic and drastic changes in the laws that affect people's daily lives. I kept having external delays and the sense that more needed to be said while I had the chance. The times in which we live are unprecedented, chaotic, and frightening. Upheaval is challenging no matter which side of the arguments you find yourself on.

You will find me stating and restating that my intention is not to alienate anyone with my personal opinions. I can't possibly speak for every person and everyone's path. The publishing material is universal. However, I feel it is essential for you, the reader, to know where I stand. I have learned over the years that you can't be all things to all people. I respect that every person has a path to God that may not mean the same thing it means to me. That is why I started the book with the language caveat that when I say God, I expect you to insert any terminology that suits you.

We live in a material world where labels and opinions matter. I hope you resonate with my message, but you may need to know that I fall on the side of pro-choice and all the other rights the Constitution has afforded us through substantive due process for the past 50 years. I believe we have more important things to do for the planet than turn the clock backward for women, minorities, and LGBTQ populations and eroding the right to privacy for personal decisions. I can't remember any time during my life when there was so much apparent divisiveness. My prayer is for an open and respectful society where everyone is free to worship and experience God as they choose. And when I say pro-choice, I do not mean pro-abortion. My energy work has shown me that no woman casually decides to abort a child. She may compartmentalize, but she never forgets. No one is pro-abortion. However, denying a choice that impacts both men and women is not only legislating morals; it is putting women's lives at risk.

So, what is this commentary doing in a book on spiritual writing? I feel compelled to be as authentic as possible. I am not trying to persuade anyone to believe as I believe. However, I have some wisdom of age and experience that you may find helpful in your search for spiritual explanations for material problems.

Now to the issue of "end times." I recommend steering away from the topic. Over the years, I have reviewed numerous manuscripts discussing this subject or referring to it. As a student of esoteric philosophy and religion, I see that every generation has believed it is in the end times. But what does that mean? We can see evidence of the divisiveness of believing one religion has the whole Truth. People have fought too many wars, and too many cults have risen because leaders play on fear and convince their followers that not only are we in the end times, the only way to survive is to follow their path. I don't want to exclude Bible-based or fundamentalist people of any faith. However, perhaps I must, if you believe other people will only survive or get to Heaven if they follow your Truth. You won't resonate with my message of universality.

The Seven Lessons of Soul Odyssey are universal and individual. They came to me as I was teaching spiritual classes and evolved over the past several decades. They were a gift in answer to my prayers to understand more about why we are here and what we can do to improve things. I feel very blessed to have been born with a concept of God. No one had to explain it to me as it was in my Soul. The movie *The Ten Commandments* influenced my conception and showed me the power of cinema and the arts. I admit I loved the burning bush as a symbol of God and can't help but picture Charlton Heston as Moses.

If you find this book's universal message contradictory to your belief system, I hope you will still read the book's sections about publishing and marketing. I want to encourage the free exchange of ideas only achieved by many voices. What I hope to discourage with your understanding of the Seven Lessons is the force-feeding of one's beliefs upon people who have the inalienable right to believe and act otherwise despite what some politicians and judges may espouse. Of course, my philosophy and my publishing knowledge are two different things. Nevertheless, I am confident the practical information will help you succeed.

As I reread the book as it was in 2002, I realized I had not included enough about my story and underlying system to give you the complete picture of the challenges of the spiritual writer and messenger. So, this is my caveat. I present this with love and the hope that you will experience God as a loving being. My experience shows me a universe of God and higher beings who want what is best for us. The lessons I describe in Chapter One are the foundation of my belief system. They are a way to help us use our free will to grow our Souls without direct interference. God and our Guides give us clues through signs, dreams, and the consequences of our actions. But they never usurp our free will. It is a privilege to be on this planet in physical form because it gives each of us the most significant opportunity for growth.

Why are some of our lives so difficult? Some religions and philosophies believe we are sinful and are punished or led astray. My guidance tells me we are imperfect beings expected to make "Miss Takes." I genuinely believe that when I repeat the same "Miss Take," I can hear my Guides groaning, "there, she has done it again." My Guides may be Jewish like I am, so they would say, "Oy, Vey," in a heavy Yiddish accent. My religion and culture are Jewish, where my Soul landed in this incarnation. I am happy about it, but it is certainly not the easiest tribe to be a part of. In every generation, someone tries to destroy us. We often joke that our holidays are the same: "someone tried to destroy us, we survived, let's eat."

Spirituality is not the same as religion. I define it as the Soul's calling to learn and experience a reality beyond the five senses. I am comfortable that my definition does not contradict any basic belief system except those created by humans. I will not focus on the end times as I do not feel equipped to predict when they will be. I leave it up to God. All I know is that if we are all here to make the world a better place, with or without the end around the corner, we should focus on how to fulfill our spiritual missions. We should try to be the best humans we can be and use our platforms and skills to elevate others.

Since I first wrote this book, I have become a de facto cult expert. I collaborated on a bestselling book with Dianne Lake, titled *Member of the Family: My Story of Charles Manson, Life Inside His Cult, and the Darkness that Ended the Sixties* (Harper Collins). Dianne became a member of the Manson family cult at 14 when her parents dropped out of society as hippies, and she was on her own. She did not participate in the crimes but later testified against Manson and the others. She kept her secret, even from her children, for over 30 years. My research into cult behavior for that book and based upon Dianne's first-hand experience with Manson's descent into madness and his brainwashing, allowed me to see some frightening patterns. We will further discuss the potential pitfalls for spiritual writers in the Seven Lessons of the Soul Odyssey section.

Still, I want to make it abundantly clear at the outset that the primary role of any spiritual messenger is to serve the reader and the audience. You are here for the greater good of all people and the planet.

There is a common thread in all cults. Eventually, the followers elevate the personality above the message. The energy goes up to a human being rather than leading the people to a more personal relationship with God. We have the sacred gift of communication to aid people on their path to the Divine Source. Unfortunately, too many cult leaders have led their followers to disaster by believing they are more important and special than the people they serve. The human personality is not equipped to accept adoration on the level created by cults of personality. Invariably the person will believe the hype and succumb to lower impulses like greed and control. The Seven Lessons and the spiritual path will lead us out of shame, guilt, fear, and negative, self-defeating emotions. We are meant to live in a world of hope and love. This is the true nature of God, yet darkness and the lower nature of humankind will use these vulnerabilities to undermine the light.

It is also human nature to want to give away power to those we believe know more than us. While there is brainwashing and control where free will is essentially defeated, there is a point when people willingly give up their path for what they believe will bring them closer to God. Or people want to feel special and part of something with a corner on the Truth. Cult leaders like Jim Jones and Charles Manson convinced people they would only survive a nuclear apocalypse or a race war if they stayed with them in their cult bubble. Part of the spiritual path and the Seven Lessons is to build a strong sense of self and a direct relationship with the Source so people will not look to false prophets for easy answers. It is not easy to do, but it is our challenge as spiritual beings. Perhaps what God meant in the ten commandments by *Thou Shalt Have No Other Gods Before Me* and *Thou Shalt Not Make unto Thee Any Graven Images* was to warn generations of vulnerable humans not to put people and personalities before God.

I am not a religious expert. I can't explain the nuances of various traditions and wouldn't be so arrogant to claim any corner on the Truth at that level. But I am confident that we as spiritual writers must be mindful of the power of our words. Some of you will reach heights of recognition. If I have done my job right, you will learn how to create an author brand and direct attention to your work through digital marketing and word of mouth. However, it is my most profound prayer that you use this power for good. Always remember you work for the universe and not for yourself. There is no reason not to benefit from your work financially. That is a fact of our physical/material world, and tangible success is great. I will never judge you if you use prosperity for fun things. You don't necessarily have to live in poverty to be spiritual. Nor must you be a starving artist to please God. Be healthy and wealthy but above all, be wise. Your words have energy. Please use the wisdom and guidance you learn in this book for the good of others and not for personal aggrandizement.

If you look at the history of cults, some of which have been disguised as mainstream religions, many leaders take advantage of their people for their gain. People want to do good, and if they believe giving up their wealth to support an organization is serving God, they will happily do it. But where is the money going? Gurus and ministers do not need luxuries to bring their people closer to God. We do not need to treat them as pharaohs or royalty.

Some cult leaders become so caught up in their control over other people's lives that they will tell them if they leave, they will be cursed, and all the good they received from God or the god-head figure at the helm will be taken away. This is pure manipulation. I am harping on this point before we move on to other topics because I wish cults were a thing of the past. They are not. The worst part is when people find out about them; they judge the members as being somehow ignorant or stupid. Anyone at a vulnerable time in their life can be a target for a cult and may be far into it before they even realize what has happened. When asked what they want to be when they grow up, I guarantee that no child will reply, "I want to be a member of a cult."

As spiritual writers, the universe will give you lessons to ensure you are up for the task. If people resonate with your work, they may feel they know you. They may look to you for answers, and you may have them. However, people may elevate you beyond what you can do for them. Unless you are a fully enlightened being and prophet of God, not the self-appointed kind, I recommend you always turn to higher guidance with humility.

Does this Conflict with the Idea of Self-Promotion?

Not at all. If your energy is balanced, you should learn to promote and share your message by utilizing all the available tools and avenues. Spiritual writers can learn to tether their camels and straddle the worlds of Spirit and business. Perhaps you already use both sides of the brain and access things like intuition. We are both Spirit and human. Although I prefer flowy clothing, not every one of us should dress like we are just leaving an ashram. Nor do you need to conform to anyone's idea of how spiritual people should look. Spiritual writers come in all shapes and sizes. We come in all colors, cultures, and genders. Aside from learning about publishing, my goal is to help you find your authentic Self. That will lead to an engaging voice that will connect with your reader. So, all is good.

Each of you has a Soul directive to share your piece of the larger picture. No one is more important to the planet's destiny as each of you is a universe. Perhaps it is the butterfly effect. Mathematicians have described flapping a butterfly's wings as changing the weather on the other side of the planet. I think of it as each of us doing one small thing that can change the world. We don't know what that one thing is.

It has become a directive for those called to share their piece of what can help turn around this planet. No matter what faith you are, I think we can all agree that we have not yet made this world a place that reflects the highest vision of the Creator on Earth. Our writing can change things, but we must do it well and with clarity of Spirit. From a business standpoint, this is an area of publishing growing exponentially. We can't predict what the large publishers will do in this arena as they continue to consolidate rapidly. However, the readers are there, and you can find ways to reach them. Your task is to find your passion and the best avenue to bring it to fruition. Your tribe is waiting for you.

In Part four, "promoting your book in the digital age," we will discuss how you can build your platform and reach your targeted audience using the technologies available. Technology changes rapidly; however, the ideas behind promotion and platform building do not.

I will introduce you to what I know and things you may not have considered. I will also give you information so you can ask the right questions of people who may help you implement your goals. Having a platform is not the dirty word many make it out to be. This section will demystify the concept and leave you with many ideas of how you can be proactive in building your brand. Manifestation is ten percent inspiration and 90 percent perspiration. Well, that is not exactly true. Hard work doing something you love and know will be effective is not spinning your wheels even if it does not bring an immediate return. You are always building something that will go where it needs to go. To succeed at writing and disseminating your work, you must show up, put in the time, and learn your craft and the publishing protocols. Then all kinds of things will open for you. Angels can only respond to your action in helping make your dreams come true.

The Spirit within motivates spiritual writers. But if you want your book to reach the greatest possible audience, Spirit is not enough: you are going to have to become a student of the market. This "marketing" effort does not violate the essence of your spirituality. You could live isolated on a mountaintop, but the challenge is to live spiritually in the physical world. So be proud of the challenge you have willingly embraced. It is a privilege to share the walk with you on the path from the journey to sale.

Lastly, watch for the pothole on the spiritual path called "ego." Spiritual Ego will compel some writers to write because they want to be the message and not serve as a conduit for higher truth. We have already discussed how cults happen. You may think it silly that you could be a cult leader, but these people had to start somewhere. You may think, "all I want to do is write a book and publish it." But I believe in each of you and know you have the power for good but also are human beings. That is why the Seven Lessons are my gift to you. The universe will weed out most Ego writers, but many will slip through. It is essential to check your motives as a sincere spiritual writer continuously. You may have a great deal to offer, but this most difficult human vice, Ego, may stand in your way. Hopefully, this revelation and the information in this book will keep you grounded and actively involved in your path and career choices. You can't go wrong if you examine your life and choose to grow. You will always have the guidance you need, even when you least expect it.

A Word About Terminology

I do not assume that spirituality has anything to do with being raised in or adhering to a particular religion. However, many of you do. While I respect your path, as a writer, trying to be all things to all people will drive me to distraction.

While I heartily respect and admire anyone's choice to know the God of their understanding, I prefer to be more generic. I am comfortable with the use of the term God as all-encompassing. I also refer to God as a male, even though I acknowledge that this concept is limiting. In today's world, I hope you will forgive any language missteps. While I recognize the significant changes in inclusive language, I am not well versed enough to do so regularly. Please know that I accept the diverse paths and hope that the energy of this book transcends any limitations that language identification causes. Within these pages, you will also find references to Spirit, the Universe, the Creator, and similarly nonspecific descriptions of what is the Source of Divine creativity.

With joy and blessings on your journey,

— Deborah Levine Herman

Part One
THE SPIRITUAL WRITER'S PATH

1

THE SPIRITUAL WRITER

The calling to write can be a blessing or the bane of your existence. Some of us are driven to write as if we were on a life-or-death mission, and others write as easily and naturally as we breathe. Some of us have no idea why or how we have followed this path. There are certainly easier ways to make a living, many other careers that do not require masochism or guarantee rejection. I have often thought that medical science should recognize a common mental disorder called "writerphrenia"—the obsessive need to remove oneself from reality and human connection for hours. Writerphrenia is characterized by coffee drinking, snacking, hair twisting, handwringing, and postal or email paranoia. I have seen people—OK, I admit it was me—who pray and hold ceremonies over manuscripts before placing them in the hands of the U.S. Postal Service or hitting attach and send.

While writing is difficult, the spiritual writer's journey is always one of rewarding transformation. While the writer shares insight and wisdom with others, the act of writing returns this wisdom to the writer, touching them with an inner light—the Source of all creation. The spiritual writer accesses the inner voice that gives expression to the Spirit.

The Spiritual Path

Your journey as a writer parallels your spiritual path. While the idea of a spiritual path might conjure images of peaceful meditation, incense, wind chimes, gospel choirs, and undying faith, you will likely discover that the spiritual path is not always serene. The process of developing awareness, serenity, and faith is often painful. Our lives are in turmoil as we struggle to understand our place in the universe. Sometimes we don't have any faith at all. If our feelings are too strong or our lives too complicated, we may have to detach from the process altogether until we have the strength to continue exploring.

As human beings, we are on an endless search for our identity. We learn by experience and grow through struggle, but even knowing this, we may not always be ready for the challenges as they come to us.

Choosing to write, for example, can have many unexpected consequences. When you commit to this way of life, no matter what road you take, you may feel that your troubles are worse than before.

What keeps you coming back for more? Perhaps you sense there is a reason for everything, and you want to find out what that reason is and where it will lead you. Living on earth is a spiritual path. Our entire reason for being born is to figure this out; we are students in a perpetual classroom, and everything we experience is part of our spiritual education. You can participate in a fad or live in a culture, but the spiritual path can only draw you in by something inside your Soul. Like a pilot light waiting for a match, your journey begins long before the flame is ignited.

Before we move into the details of spiritual writing, I want to introduce you to the Seven Lessons of Soul Odyssey. In the first edition of this book, I explained them as more of an aside. But, perhaps with a few decades of experience and exploration, I now realize their meaning and the importance they have to spiritual writers and our shared path.

When I first wrote this book, I had already written four or five books, but I was still early in my path. I had not achieved many of the goals I had set and was in the throes of parenting and individuating. I am still first learning how to share my light openly, but I can't ask you to do it if I am unwilling to do it as well.

The Seven Lessons of Soul Odyssey

I came into awareness as a young woman in the mid-1980s. Coming into awareness is a neat spiritual term for opening to a spiritual path. My telepathic and mystical experiences started much earlier, but I didn't associate them with a life path.

I may have shut down my gifts because I made the error of telling a family ghost story in my Hebrew school class. I must have been nine years old at the time. The story was, when my mother was a teenager, she went to a sleepaway camp someplace in upstate New York. She and her closest friends were counselors in training. As teenagers with authority often do, they disobeyed a rule about rowing a boat on the lake at night. It was cold, and my mother said she and her best friend had wrapped their arms around each other to keep warm. They were giddy and happy until the unthinkable happened. A motorboat must not have seen them in the dark water and drove into them, cutting the boat in two. The impact caused my mother and her friend to be thrown out of the rowboat; tragically, the propeller killed her friend. My mother said she felt pulled toward the blades when something pushed her back to safety. Later, while wrapped in a blanket in the back of a car, she saw a woman's concerned but smiling face. She thought someone might be looking in, but no one was there. When her mother and aunts picked her up to bring her home, she described the woman, and they burst into tears. She had described her grandmother, a woman who died two weeks before she was born and for whom she had been named.

I was comfortable with my mother's story and the concept of life after death but learned quickly to keep such things in the home. And I didn't believe her supernatural gifts applied to me. Ironically, it was my father who was fascinated with all things paranormal. He was probably one of the first to buy *Kreskin's ESP Game*. I can remember him trying to test his ESP to no avail. As children, we also had the requisite séance in our unfinished basement and scared the heck out of ourselves. I think my older sister, who later became a professional medium after I pioneered past the community ridicule, must have conjured someone as she never tried it again.

It began with Eric Horsefield, but I didn't have an overnight awakening. It started with seeing people's faces in my mind's eye and then receiving a call from them a few minutes later. I was never sure if I was a sender or a receiver and am not always sure to this day. I know when I think of my son, he calls, but I am not sure if he is the one who starts the psychic telephone or if it is me.

When I was first married, we had to put my fourteen-year-old cat to sleep. Now I like to refer to this as purposeful transitioning. I remember being devastated when I left poor Smokey at the vet's office. We had been through a lot together. He was in tune with me, but I had not yet developed my telepathic abilities with animals on a conscious level. Smokey was a huge Russian blue cat who once scared away a date. I wanted the guy to leave, so Smokey took care of it for me with a few threatening growls. Smokey had been the family cat who traveled from our home on Long Island to

Columbus, Ohio. When I took him to live with me, we became inseparable companions.

I reluctantly left Smokey at the vet's office and forgot about it. We were going to some event, and as I dressed, I saw Smokey, and then he disappeared. I looked at the clock and realized he was likely euthanized at that moment. I felt sad but relieved that he had come to say goodbye. The cat I saw in my vision was the young and healthy cat I would never forget.

These small events didn't catch my attention until my ex-husband's father passed away unexpectedly. I was about four months pregnant with our daughter, which was a tough time for us. It was also the first time I knew I was connecting to people who had passed on. About a week after he passed, I had a vivid dream. He was sitting in the middle of a nondescript room on a stool. There was nothing else there except him. Then he smiled at me and took his teeth out. I woke up with a start.

The following day, I asked my then-husband if his father had all his teeth? The funny thing is he didn't question why I was asking but replied matter-of-factly, "no, he lost them during the war. He wore dentures."

This was all the proof I needed that I was seeing his father's Spirit in my dream. I did not know his tooth situation. And I realized he was showing that to me for a reason. He came into my dreams three more times to show me symbolically that I would be heading for marital discord. He warned me about a shift in family dynamics, but I think it was to soften the blow. After our daughter was born, we had an unusual visit from him. We named our daughter after him, as is the Jewish tradition. While in her bassinet, we noticed something had moved a small toy bear next to her.

The marriage eventually ended, but these dreams started me on my path, as they gave me the confidence to pay attention to what was changing inside me. I had other dreams involving people who had passed, even when I knew nothing of their passing. One was a law professor I saw sitting on a hospital gurney. He said, "this is strange." I found out the next day he had died the night before.

Then I had a dream about one of my father's best friends. They were part of a group of men who regularly met for bagels at a local restaurant. I knew him but not closely. In my dream, he was in the back of a car, asking what had happened. I really couldn't answer him. I found out the next day that he had died on the way to the hospital in the back of a car. He had a massive heart attack and died suddenly.

I was becoming aware of instances of unusual events, such as being next to someone and suddenly feeling pain in my chest. I looked over to see the person coughing. I especially had this sensitivity when I was with my mother. She had angina, a condition where she would get a sudden pain in her chest which could also spread to her shoulders and neck. An inadequate supply of blood causes pain in the heart. Out of nowhere, I would feel the pain and then realize my mother was having an attack. I was glad to be empathic but needed to control it. It was becoming very confusing.

I learned that spiritual gifts don't come alive all at once if you are fortunate. Later, when I formed a partnership in a holistic center in the late 80s, my chakras and gifts popped open all at once. That is a spiritual emergency, and it is not fun. I went from a smattering of experiences to be able to think of something I wanted and knowing exactly where to find it in a store. That may sound like a valuable skill, but I was becoming too separated from my body and this reality. It also made me vulnerable to profound initiations that helped me learn about the Seven Lessons.

The mid to late 1980s is when the "New Age" became popularized. As they did in the 1960s, people were examining new paradigms. Pioneers like Shirley MacLaine wrote books about spiritual awakening that crossed over into the mainstream. I was grateful to have books to explain what was happening to me. Other books helped. I read *Joy's Way* by Dr. Brugh Joy and learned about energy. I read Richard Bach's *Illusions* to help me understand the path and eventually would go into bookstores and have books practically fall on my head. At the time, there was only one bookstore in someone's home on a faraway street that had the types of books I wanted. This access to esoteric information helped me survive the confusion and is one of the reasons I am so adamant about guiding people like you.

Although Shirley MacLaine became what would have been a meme in today's emoji world, she awakened many Souls who were looking for answers. A few years after I graduated from law school, I opened a holistic center with a woman who was a powerful clairvoyant. I had separated from my first husband, left the practice of law, and dedicated myself to what I now call my "Soul Odyssey." We had a popular public access cable television show which had a following. You would think no one was watching, but it caught on, and people started recognizing me wherever I went.

We would begin the show with what people called the "talk to." This is where I discussed aspects of spirituality like alternative health, reincarnation, esoteric philosophy, comparative religion, or Soul progression. Soul Progression was what I called the Seven Lessons at that time. Then we would open the phones. My partner would answer the questions like "will I meet a Soul-mate or win the lottery," and I either did Soul progression readings or responded to questions related to the spiritual path. Soul-progression readings were where I would tell people which of the Seven Lessons were challenging them. In the late 1980s, people were not always ready for this material.

I had law school colleagues leave messages at my office saying how crazy they thought it was that I left the law for nonsense. As many of you may have found in your own lives, I never questioned what I was doing because it felt right. It coincided with my writer's journey, a more straightforward explanation to give people. I didn't leave the law for nonsense. I learned what I needed from it. I felt my change of direction was to meet God's Divine purpose and to follow my Soul mission. There was no other choice. My ex-husband told people I was an extraterrestrial; to this day, I have not corrected him.

Over the years, I taught spirituality based on the Seven Lessons to a group of regular students. When you study law, there is a concept of 'hiding the ball." Law professors don't spoon-feed you the black letter law so you can regurgitate it on the exam. Instead, they are teaching critical thinking through the Socratic method. They call on you at random in such a way as to get you to "think like a lawyer."

I taught the Seven Lessons to students from 1988 until 1996 and integrated them into my books, including *The Complete Idiot's Guide to Motherhood*. The publishing world was different then and was first opening to the idea of spiritual material. I had written the Seven Lessons in a book proposal called "Your Cosmic Curriculum" that made it to the pub board with a top publisher. This means that an editor thought enough of it to take it to the inner sanctum, where editors discuss which books they want to acquire. They ultimately rejected it with helpful suggestions, but I wasn't ready to give it life. As I recommend from experience, your spiritual message will need time to gestate. I needed to grow on my path and move away from the sidelines.

Here goes:

I am finally ready to admit that I have many gifts that I attribute to God. I am not a psychic, but I am a Mystic. I study all religions for the truth they can provide as one would look for puzzle pieces. I find there is a direct link to the Divine Spark that they all have in common. I no longer care if people see me as strange or weird. I embrace this about myself and am grateful to those friends and acquaintances who accept me as I am. In the process, I am learning to accept myself. Like many of you, I connect to the other side, communicate with animals telepathically, use intuition in writing and editing, and have precognitive and lucid dreams. Thankfully, the only thing that has eluded me is seeing dead people with my eyes open. I only see those who have passed in my mind's eye, a dream or through a feeling.

One day I decided I wanted to see beyond the veil with my eyes open. I stared at a candle flame for what seemed like hours. I had read that it was a good way to develop clairvoyant sight. I stared and stared. Nothing. I stared some more. Nothing. Then my cat jumped onto the table, and I jumped three feet in the air and shrieked. I am sure I heard my Guides laughing and saying, "you really don't want to see with your eyes. It would freak you out."

And it would have. I respect people who do this and are not scared by it. I am fine meeting people in my dreams, but even in my dreams, I don't want to see them as Spirits. I don't' know why. We all have limitations, and I suppose I need to firmly grip this reality without adding other dimensions.

Oh, I do automatic drawings with symbolic meanings that I use as a tool to tune into people. Sometimes I can do energy balancing that fixes chakras, and occasionally I see color. I don't know why my brain works this way. I accept these gifts from God and have learned to use them wisely. When I first realized I had abilities, I tried to play roulette. I did a little too well, and then I would lose. Thankfully I knew when to quit. I wound up with the amount I bet. There are rules, and I do my best to follow them.

If you stay grounded in the understanding that we work for a universe trying to rebalance itself toward the positive and bring light to a suffering world. If you are ready to take up your mantle, I hope this information will help you. The next chapter will explain the Seven Lessons of Soul Odyssey as they relate to your writer's journey. Do not think you can check off the list and be done with it. We have been given a clue, nothing more. You can participate as a co-creator, but it is in partnership with God, your Guides, and your own Soul's mission. No matter what religion or faith you may be, you are presumably a human. Our task is to bring our Souls together in love, light, and understanding to make a better world for the next generations. You can do that with your writing. Become your best self, and you will change the energy of everyone around you.

2

THE SEVEN LESSONS OF SOUL ODYSSEY

*T*he spiritual path and the writer's journey are linked. I had lessons to learn just as you do. You will see in this chapter how these lessons may relate to your life. My understanding of them is that they represent our vulnerabilities. If we have circumstances that keep repeating, we can analyze them according to these seven factors and change our thoughts to move ahead despite the challenges and obstacles. The Seven Lessons generally relate to the spiritual path, but we will examine how they influence your journey as a spiritual writer.

A **Soul Odyssey** is a hero's journey with tribulations. Our job on "Classroom Earth" is to discover who we are from the inside out. To transcend human challenges, we can surrender to the Divine essence in each of us and live Spiritual principles in our daily lives. The greatest asset we have are our thoughts. Our perception of a situation can change the outcome. If we begin with the premise God-Loves us unconditionally, we make choices reflecting a positive sense of self. The Seven Lessons of Soul Odyssey provide a systematic way of achieving balance while igniting the Divine spark. We each come into our lives with specific lessons to master. These challenges offer a tool for self-examination. We experience each of the lessons during our lives, but we have some that are more prominent. They may be vulnerabilities that follow us from lifetime to lifetime. What matters is the life you are in and the challenges you face as you develop in Spirit and wholeness.

The descriptions of the following lessons are intentionally minimal, so you will turn to your intuition to define their relevance. At the end of this section, you will find Soul Odyssey journal exercises to use as jumping-off points for self-examination and spiritual exploration.

The Seven Lessons of Soul Odyssey are:

1. Courage
2. Tolerance
3. Self-Protection
4. Self-Love
5. Ego
6. Love of Humanity
7. God-Love

COURAGE

Spiritual Courage is different from bravery. It is difficult to think about courage without conjuring images of the cowardly lion in the classic film *The Wizard of Oz*. In a way, the lion and his discovery that he was always courageous is a good metaphor for the spiritual path. We all have everything we need inside of ourselves.

For our purposes, the lesson of Spiritual Courage is knowing and accepting that your inner truth can guide you on your path even if you are breaking free of your family, your other institutions, and the things that people teach you. If you are willing to follow what you believe is the right path for you, that is the essence of the lesson of Spiritual Courage. Human beings are like herd animals. We want to be the same as other people. We want to think we are on the path of the one Truth to be sure and comfortable in that certainty. But what if your inner voice conflicts with what others say or do? Do you have the strength of a lion to do what is right following your direct link to the Divine Source? True faith comes from within. We each have a Divine spark. Although some may disagree, my experience tells me that God equally loves us and guides us directly.

There are many benefits to belonging to a religion and culture. Community and rituals and sharing human experiences are beneficial for our lives. However, many institutions are human-created, political, and not a reflection of God. No matter what religion you follow, if your community is not elevating the people and their relationship to the Divine, they have missed the mark. If the places of worship cause members to feel unwelcome, condemned, or shamed in the name of God, the community is standing in God's way.

People who are open to true faith in the Source will feel this negative energy. The inclination is to go along to get along. Who wants to feel like an outsider? Attend your institutions as much as you wish. But know that your deepest thoughts belong to you. Not everyone is comfortable taking a public stand. If you are being true to yourself, you don't need to start a revolution to learn the lesson of Spiritual Courage. You will eventually know that your truth is something you can trust.

I am not trying to alienate people who rely on scripture for answers. Although my tradition follows the five books of Moses and not the New Testament, I believe there is great wisdom in the *Bible*. Jewish people consider the Torah a living document; everything we need to guide our lives can be found within its pages. Although I am not an expert on the New Testament, I have studied the teachings of Jesus and particularly love the "Sermon on the Mount." Anything that brings people of faith together lovingly is my understanding of the spirit of Christianity.

Of course, there are so many other traditions throughout the world. I had the opportunity to spend six weeks in Hawaii on the relatively undeveloped island of Molokai and learned about the indigenous beliefs. While working on an author's memoir, I was invited to the inner sanctum of Hawaiian prayer, rarely seen by non-Hawaiians. The author of the book *The Kahuna and I* was married to a powerful Hawaiian healer, then called a medicine man, who had passed away. My experience as her editor gave me the privilege of observing these rituals. I experienced the Mahalo Oli chant, which is a chant of thanks. It felt so powerful as if all the ancestors were in the room with us.

I tend to refer to the Judeo-Christian traditions because they are the ones I am most familiar with. However, a world of faith, ritual, and spirituality comprises the family of humans. If only we could see ourselves through God's eyes.

The lesson of Courage questions our man-made institutions and the human tendency to turn over our will to other people rather than believing we have a direct link to the Source. These lessons come in many forms. One may be brave and yet not have the courage to follow one's heart. The spiritual path leads you to find your true self and connection to the Divine Spark within you. It is an act of courage to believe that you could be right because your inner voice, the direct link to Spirit, is telling you so.

Choosing is Often an Act of Spiritual Courage.

There are many aspects to the lesson of Courage. For example, we often become paralyzed when given the option of moving forward in a direction that seems, as Robert Frost would say, "The road less traveled." So even if our Soul is sending us all the signs supporting our choice, we may simply feel most comfortable standing still. Doing nothing is a choice. We ask for opportunities all the time, even if they are unconscious. Spirit knows what we desire and will lead us on our path.

Getting what you want can be frightening. We may not know what to do or may feel we are not ready. There is nothing wrong with acknowledging that. The opportunity will come again, even if in another form. You can't blow your mission. The purpose of this lesson is to have the courage to go inward with the honesty that you may not be ready for what you desire.

Sometimes one choice is not better than another. This lesson of Courage challenges us to learn to choose rather than be passive in our lives. Rather than living by default, we can move ahead in whatever direction resonates best with our Soul. We are meant to actively pursue our lives rather than coasting along or bouncing like a pinball. This action is the essence of empowerment; it doesn't matter if we make the wrong choices. That is different from bad decisions. Those have consequences. You can't make wrong choices on your path because you will always have Spirit to guide you back to where you need to be.

There is Always Change on the Horizon.

Change of any sort can be very frightening. You may already feel the pangs of change and a sense of excitement. You may not know why this is. But your Soul communicates with you all the time and guides you in the directions that will further your growth and realignment with your true Soul purpose and calling. Listen and watch for the signs. You can't blow this. You can prolong the inevitable, but if you genuinely resist, you will feel at odds with your inner being. This is the essence of fear, anxiety, sadness, and depression. Please note I am not referring to physiological depression, or mental illness, although it may share some roots with Soul dissonance.

When you try too hard to control your destiny, you may feel it is evading you. You are in partnership with God and your Guides, and your spiritual path has a curriculum. When faced with uncomfortable change, try to turn it over to God and your Spirit Guides and ask that you be open to change that will bring new light while helping you be a part of your global family.

Add the prayer that you will serve humanity for your greater good and the greater good of all. Embrace the sense of well-being you will receive when you open to this new energy.

Do you Need to Fight?

Do you feel you have had to fight throughout your life? When comparing yourself with others, does it seem you have had struggles beyond what they have faced? Sometimes we think it is unfair to be challenged with so much, and we may even implore God, "why me?"

Believe it or not, with the help of Spirit, we choose environments that will help us grow our Souls. We have significant challenges because they are the grinding stones that refine us. Without them, we have no real reason to develop and pursue spiritual awakening. Nothing is pushing us. However, you may be under the misperception that you live in a world out to get you. The lesson of Courage suggests that if you step back and reframe your thinking by adding God into the equation, you may not have to fight so hard. You might acknowledge that you are fully grown and no longer subject to the control of others. If you invite God, the Angels, your Spirit Guides, and all the love that has always been around you into your heart, you may be able to experience a life without as much chaos and conflict.

On the other hand, you may face lessons or situations where you will be called out of your place of tranquility to put your energy into something that you would rather avoid. It is much easier for us to live in apathy and think that someone else will take care of things for us. For example, God is calling upon us and our spiritual brothers and sisters to fight for the life of our planet and each other. The lesson of Courage teaches us there are times to fight for the greater good.

Fear and the Lesson of Courage.

Fear is the opposite of faith. There is a healthy fear that motivates us not to take risks that can put us in harm's way. However, fear in this context leads to a sense of hopelessness. Fear is one of the most significant challenges of living as a human being in this time of consciousness change because the balance of darkness is upset when we no longer fear the unknown. When we know that we have a Soul purpose, are on a journey, and that God and our Guides and Spirit are always connected, no obstacle cannot be overcome. There is nothing we can't change. It is a matter of changing our thinking about a situation.

It is to the advantage of negativity for humans to live in fear because we are most powerful when we believe in ourselves and connect with our inner truth. As many people say, Fear means false evidence appearing real. If you are afraid of the dark, you turn on a light. Then you see that the things that were monsters were nothing more than things that could not hurt you. The emotion of fear is not all bad. It is an advantage for us so we can protect ourselves when necessary. Nothing is completely bad or good. We have an internal sensitivity if something is potentially harmful to us. We don't want to be reckless. We have a life, a path, and a body. Maybe a little bit of fear is a good thing. Enough fear to be cautious but not too much to be overwhelming.

Facing fear and not succumbing to it is especially trying during these chaotic times. Spiritual messengers are more critical than ever to break through the illusions that darkness is thrusting upon us. Remember, when people commit acts of domestic terrorism, it is to spark fear and gain attention. The people who perpetrate these acts are vessels for darkness. You, as spiritual messengers, can push through the lesson of courage by standing in your truth and pushing back against messages of hopelessness. That is the lesson of courage at its best.

Courage Requires Speaking and Writing with Clarity.

We are each given an individual voice to express in speaking or through our written words. Part of our Soul's purpose is to find it. Once we find it and know our truth, we can learn to express it in ways that people can receive it. This does not mean harshness or aggression unless the circumstance calls for it. Sometimes we persuade with power—other times with understated purpose.

For most of us, it begins with knowing what we want to say and then saying it with the strength of God behind us. And we need to believe that we are as important as anyone else is. Because on our Spiritual path, we all are the voice of God manifested in this world.

Learn to be honest with yourself and others. You might not know what your authentic truth is. You may not yet have the inner strength to risk another person's disagreement due to potential repercussions. We are the witnesses of the world. There is a time to speak up and a time to hold our tongue. You may not know what you believe. That is also part of the spiritual path. And this does not necessarily mean that you must now become highly verbal and the life of the party. It means that if something needs to be said, say it. And feel strong enough that the universe is with you and will help you.

The Greatest Act of Courage is Following your Heart.

You will know your heart's desire if you look deep within yourself. Try to look at yourself without all the dos and don'ts imposed upon you by everyone you have ever met. You have the programming for a heart's desire to help you find the foundation of your journey. Strip away all the things you believe about yourself that others place there. Remember who you were when you were a little child. Even if you had a less than ideal childhood, the person you were then is the person you are now. What did you like to do? What filled you with wonder? What do you believe? The process of Soul Odyssey can be as simple as getting to the core of what you enjoy. Be who you are. The things that attract you are the things you attract by your inner being. They are clues to where you are headed.

It is more difficult to express your Spirituality by living in a world of people and variables. However, Spirit may be trying to tell you that you might be avoiding finding your true passion, fearing that you will displease others, or placing yourself at risk of being considered strange. The happiest people are right with themselves and God and know they do not need approval from others. If you are ethical, honest, and cause no harm to others, seriously consider pursuing your passion in a way that is reasonable in your life. Use this inner guidance to map your path to greater awareness and authenticity.

The Lesson of Courage Teaches us that our Truth is God's Truth.

It requires a leap of faith to accept that you can be right when everyone around you is saying something else. There is enough to address in the business of daily living without adding a layer of internal conflict. The universe does not want you to live a life of suffering and confusion. Slow down and recognize that your Truth is God's truth. It is the same. You can count on it if it comes from the most authentic place in your being. Stop questioning everything and Trust that God approves of positive, loving thoughts about yourself. You are worth it. Your inner truth is truth. You can create and accept a reality that resonates with your highest ideals. You have a Divine Spark, and you are directly linked with God. It doesn't mean that you now become Godlike and impose your truth on everyone else. See the Tolerance and Ego lessons. This aspect of courage has to do with your ability to connect with your authentic self. You are learning to trust it and to love it.

I can't stress enough that this does not mean you should hang out your God shingle. You can change the world; your light is an entire universe, but you work in connection with God, the greater beings, and your spiritual brothers and sisters. Follow your heart. You have within you the seed of all reality. You have the Source of all the Truth.

Like most people, you may require a so-called day job. However, if you become aware of the signs, symbols, and feelings within you, you will know your heart's desire. You will find your Soul's purpose. If there is something that gives you great passion and pleasure and joy, that is likely a way for you to find the gifts you can contribute to the greater good. If you don't have a sense of your Soul's purpose on a conscious level, meditate, try to find it, and have the strength to follow it. Be who you are because that is your real job, even if what you do during the day to put food on the table is entirely separate from your spiritual identity.

Takeaways for Spiritual Writers.

The call to write is not only a privilege but also a guarantee that you will likely never feel fully participating in a so-called "normal" life. Writers view life differently than others, and spiritual writers view it through added dimensions. Spiritual awareness is good, but it can also be lonely when you perceive that you are different from others.

One of our challenges as spiritual writers is to resist the natural desire to fit in. We often try to do everything we can to deny the intuitive wisdom knocking at our Souls. Because we can be in perpetual conflict with ourselves and the institutions and people in our lives, spiritual writers always go through lessons in courage. While our spirit asks us to serve the greater good through our writing, the loneliness and exposure this brings can be terrifying.

One of the most powerful lessons of courage comes when we realize that what we know and what people we should trust have taught us is not reconcilable. Do you remember when you first began questioning what you then took for spiritual truth? These questions do not mean that our teachers were wrong but rather that we are driven toward a more personal spiritual path. We must experience faith for ourselves to understand it within our Souls; we can't simply adopt another's version of it. If we as spiritual writers are to be teachers, we must first accept our role as students with courage. This often brings us into conflict with loved ones and friends as we take charge of our direction. Human beings are like pack animals. We don't like to do things alone, and the pack has a way of discouraging those who try to go their own way. But as the spiritual writer learns very early to experience spirit personally, you must have the courage to explore. Each path has room for one traveler.

We can be parallel but cannot simultaneously inhabit the same space. We experience lessons in courage at every turn because to write from Spirit; we seek truth, support it, and commit to it by putting it in a concrete form: our writing. Once we write something down, it no longer belongs to us. We send it into the world as we do our children. We cannot control how people receive it, and we must accept any consequences associated with it.

We can write simply to please others, but that does not take courage. The challenge lies in embracing the lessons that will push your Spirit to show its true self, your highest self. And as your Soul progresses, your awareness grows.

TOLERANCE

As one of the Seven Lessons, Tolerance can be as simple as being patient with the person standing in the checkout line in front of you. We share our world with many people and with all kinds of other beings. We also live on a planet that is itself a sentient being. The Tolerance lesson is challenging because we are under the illusion that we are unique separate units. Our instincts are to think of ourselves, our needs, and our inconveniences.

Taking it to a spiritual level, Tolerance also comes to play when we have found what we believe is our truth and our God connection. We may want other people to see the world as we do. We may see our role as to save others' lives through imposing our ideas. The lesson of Tolerance is that everyone is on a path to God; we can guide if asked, but it is their right to be wrong.

If we believe they are wrong or misguided, we can stand in our truth, write about it, and hope they want what we have. However, it is possible that what we believe is only valid for us. As we have experienced lessons to find our path to the Divine Source, we must allow others to do the same. The goal on the spiritual path is to connect to that higher self within that brings us directly to a conversation with the Divine. It is difficult when we feel love and connection to God not to want to share it with others. Shining your light changes everyone's vibration.

There are many paths to the same place. We have seen throughout history many well-meaning people imposing their version of faith on other people.

We have perceived indigenous people as less than us because their methods of prayer did not fit within our ideals. Many people have perpetrated great injustices through this hubris. The Source of God is known to all who are open to it. Whether we name it Akua, Allah, Creator, Goddess, Great Spirit, Hashem, Jehovah, Jesus, The Supreme Being, or the numerous other names for this energy, the lesson of Tolerance teaches us we are not the only people on a path. Perhaps many faith traditions hold only a piece of the puzzle. I hope we compare notes and maybe someday become one people sharing equally in God's love.

The Tolerance Lesson Teaches us About Judgment.

As human beings, we have the disadvantage of being in physical bodies that cause us to feel separate from one another. We also feel disconnected from God. The only natural way we see our physical form is by looking in a mirror. We often look at others as mirrors of ourselves and judge each other harshly. The Tolerance lesson causes us to look at our judgmentalism. We learn not to judge others too harshly because all people have the potential to be Angels. What we see on the outside might not be close to what is on the inside. Even those we perceive as evil will ultimately answer to the creator, not us.

Through the lesson of Tolerance, Spirit gently points out that we waste energy judging others. To feel right about ourselves, we look to other people for comparison. We tell ourselves we are better than them. Or maybe we tell ourselves we are better off than them. This Tolerance lesson sometimes boils down to insecurity as we try to learn about ourselves in others' reflections. There is an illusion that this will give us protection.

When we rise above judging others, we can experience love, especially loving ourselves. We often judge ourselves most harshly than others and then project this onto them. We feel inadequate. If we learn to understand God's nature, we can trust that God does not judge us in the way we judge ourselves or others. God and the universe love us unconditionally. It is an exceedingly tricky concept to grasp. There are consequences to our actions. There are lessons. If we can define them in human terms, our Spirit Guides have compassion and sadness because we do not understand our greatness. We do not experience or internalize how much we are loved.

Tolerance asks that we examine our relationships with other people. Being judgmental does not mean that you are a terrible person. It means that you are looking for ways to connect. Know that God, the Angels, and your Spirit Guides are always with you. Then acknowledge your need for connection and reach out to others without judgment.

The Tolerance Lesson is Relevant to Raising Children.

As parents, it is essential for us to allow our children to experience their lessons and for us to grow with them as they ultimately prepare to leave us. Many of us dedicate too much to protecting our children from learning about the world that we do not continue to progress on our paths. As they grow, we must grow, so when the time comes to separate, both parent and child are ready,

Parenting takes up a lot of time and energy. However, it is an excellent time for spiritual writers to grow their craft. You may not have the time you will have after your children leave the nest, but it is a mistake to believe your path stops during those formative years. That would be a missed opportunity and is not the way nature intends.

Tolerance Asks us to Send Love to Others Consciously.

We have the power to send out the essence of love to people in need. The energy it creates can change the course of events. It can diffuse anger in other people. It can diffuse any negativity. It is the greatest weapon and gift that you have. The ability to send love is using your Divine Spark. Maybe there is someone in your life who may be feeling troubled and lost. You can be a vehicle for light by sending them love.

There is a technique I like to use where I take in white or purple light through my crown chakra. The chakras are the energy centers surrounding our bodies. Think of it as the top of your head. Imagine the purple or white light coming into the top of your head and then pouring out of your heart. Then think of the person you want to send this love to and imagine the purple or white light reaching them in the heart. Try to infuse the vision with the feeling of love. Maybe imagine flowers or beautiful scenery if you need something tangible.

I have seen this technique work with animals. I walked up to a truck with a dog in the back seat growling at me. I am not stupid, so as an animal communicator, I knew not to approach a growling, aggressive dog, but I also knew it was acting on instinct and was afraid. I concentrated on loving thoughts, brought in the light through my crown chakra, and then projected it out to the dog through my heart. The dog stopped growling and turned its head to the side. I still didn't approach the dog or put my hand through the window to pet it. Animals are still animals even when they can communicate with you. But the loving energy did diffuse its fear.

It isn't always easy to send love. We interpret people's actions as having to do with us. We often perceive a slight from someone when they act out of some internal misdirected feeling or may not be aware because they are wrapped up in themselves. Our job is to understand where we begin and end. If we can shift our perception of situations to one that acknowledges the depth of another person's internal reality, we can separate ourselves from becoming part of it. Sending love is a way to remove the fog that clouds the truth of a situation. It is as if you can blow it all away as you might extinguish a flame.

The Lesson of Tolerance Often Requires us to Let Go.

As we experience our path and our journey, we retain experiences and feelings along the way. Letting Go has a great deal to do with finding the ability to love and forgive. While in classroom earth, when we learn a lesson and understand it, unless we don't incorporate it into our way of being, we don't need it in our energy field. However, we often hold onto the experiences as self-definition. Therefore, if we enter a similar situation, we will automatically feel the feelings and return to those facts. We allow ourselves to re-experience lessons that we have learned. Tolerance encourages you to let go of the things that no longer suit you. If you have understood, for example, why you did not receive the unconditional love of your mother, and you can see that your mother is a person on a path who had her pain and inability to give you what she didn't have, it is probably time to let go and to move on. To Let Go and forgive is like cleaning out your closet. When you clean your closet and remove things that no longer fit, you make room for the new. You are lightening it up. You are making room for more prosperity, abundance, and gifts from the universe. You are making room for Love in all its many forms.

Tolerance Includes Forgiveness.

Forgiveness is one of the keys to changing the world we live in. It is also how we learn to experience love fully. No one passes through life without being wounded in some way. We can interpret these scars as evidence of our victimhood or embrace the experiences that allow us to grow into full awareness and consciousness. If there are people who have hurt us, if we think about them as other human beings on the path who are experiencing their difficulties, then we can learn to view them with forgiveness and love. No one can give something to someone they do not possess. People do not always have the tools to meet our expectations or needs, so we can be mired in our circumstances or transcend them to become the people we are meant to be.

Forgiveness releases the burdens of our Souls. What about those who commit heinous crimes? Should we forgive them? The Spiritual path says "yes." We send them into God's loving arms because we do not want to retain the burden of judgment and ultimate penalty. Universal law says there is cause and effect to every choice. Forgiving someone who has wronged us is about us and for us.

The more important aspect of forgiveness is to forgive oneself. We are all on a path. We are all progressing. We are perfect in God's eyes but far from perfect. And we will make mistakes. Consider them miss-takes. Perhaps we didn't understand the situation. Maybe if given a do-over, we would do the same things again. We can't make different choices without the tools. As you progress, ask God to help you forgive yourself so you can move toward your authentic self without the burden of old lessons.

The Lesson of Tolerance Helps us Release Anger.

We have the natural tendency to feel anger and resentment because we don't know how to interpret the facts of our lives. Our emotions are tools to help us progress. Anger is a powerful feeling that is not bad or good. We want to release it because it blocks us. Many people become angry at God because they believe that any problem or tragedy is the fault of God. But that is a misinterpretation of our roles and universal law. God is pure love. God is energy beyond this world. We are aspects of God. We can create and manifest. When things don't happen the way we expect them to, for example, when our families don't give us the love that we hope or we are abused, we become angry, and rightfully so.

If we look around us and see all the pain and injustice in the world, it should anger us and call us into action. We are in charge of our world. Perhaps we should let go of angry feelings to create a higher sense of love and forgiveness. Maybe you no longer need to protect yourself with feelings of anger. Because anger does that, it keeps us from moving ahead into our light and power. Pray for the ability to move ahead. Think about people with whom you may feel angry. Those trigger people will put you into a state of negativity and will remove your balance. Maybe you are not the angry one.

Be aware that the lesson of Tolerance also reminds us to shield ourselves from people so we can maintain our balance. And perhaps you can stand as an example to others.

The Lesson of Tolerance Helps you Find your True Self.

Your Soul Odyssey is the journey toward finding your true self. This is the part of you that holds the Divine spark. You combine it with the other aspects of your personality to become a total you. This is your only real job on earth. Each lesson gives you a greater understanding of your Soul's purpose. Perhaps we can also call it "Sole purpose." There may be only one thing you came here to do, and doing it will unlock the key to reconnecting with your Soul and your connection to the Divine. The key to finding your true self is approaching your path without judgment and controlling the outcome. Be open to the signs and learn to listen with your heart. You have all the mechanisms within you to know what is right and wrong. You know how to hear the wind whispering back to you. It is all a matter of perception and willingness to accept responsibility for your actions and choices. If you know that your thoughts have power, your intentions have life, and your love can move mountains, you will think differently about your role in the scheme of things.

You are on the path. You may try hard to do the right things. Let yourself off the hook to the extent that you are a Soul in progress. You are not expected to know all this stuff. You may want to fit in, but you don't. You can learn not to alienate people who don't feel like you. That is getting along in the world. But for your inner being, the best strategy is to allow the universe to connect you with like-minded people so you can be your true self with others who respect and appreciate you.

The Tolerance Lesson Asks you to Heal Yourself.

We all have the inner resources to change our physical well-being and to learn about the mind/body connection. But if you put it in the Tolerance category, it can also mean that before we can become another's teacher or tell people how to live, be or change, we need to heal ourselves. We are all travelers together. What we know as our truth may not be someone else's truth. We must follow our paths, willing to face our foibles before we can be vessels for God's teachings. We want to share with others, but the place to start is with balance and some awareness of our strengths and weaknesses.

Takeaways for Spiritual Writers.

We can become overly exuberant when we find our truth and courageously write about it. We can be like a recently happily married person who tries to fix up all her friends so they can be "happy" too. We become spiritual matchmakers. The lesson of Tolerance is essential for spiritual writers, as it teaches us to allow people to pursue their truth at their own pace.

Tolerance is not antithetical to our role as spiritual messengers. As messengers, it is essential to avoid the pitfall of trying to force people to believe as we believe. This doesn't work anyway. There is no way to force a person to change his inner truth, and why would you want to? Many different paths lead to the same place. If you pressure people into seeing things your way, this is not being a spiritual messenger. It is bullying.

To deliver a message well and with Tolerance is to make it available to those who want it, can understand it, or are ready to become illuminated.

Another important aspect of Tolerance is that it teaches us that we will never know everything. We are always on a path. If we become too smug, we will be reminded that we have feet of clay like everyone else. We all progress at different rates and have things we need to learn. Tolerance lessons teach us to allow people their struggles. We all want to help each other, but sometimes, too much help will eliminate a person's right to learn a lesson honestly. No one can experience the triumph of self-respect if they do not achieve it on their own.,

So, spiritual writers need to maintain boundaries that give people room to grow. If you have children, then you already know since childrearing is full of lessons of this kind. For example, one of the most challenging tasks is to allow our children to experience pain. We want them to grow as whole human beings, yet we want to share our years of experience with them so that they do not make the same mistakes. In the process, we can suffocate them or disempower them from developing self-sufficiency. We have good intentions but must loosen the reins. As writers, we have a similar role. We serve the greater good if we present our work humbly and with gratitude allowing our readers to accept what they need and disregard what does not resonate. We do not own our words; they come through us as gifts from Spirit.

SELF-PROTECTION

The lesson of Self-Protection has two significant sides. The first is learning who to trust or who not to trust. Those of us on a spiritual path often see people as they could be rather than as who they are. The Soul potential shines through, and that is the aspect that resonates with us. On the surface, this seems like a blessing, but it also creates an illusion that can leave us vulnerable to negativity from those not living up to their Soul's potential.

There is darkness in this world. It exists, and while it should not be feared, it should be respected. It should be questioned to pierce the deception that it uses as its weapon. There are metaphysical dangers for people whose light shines beyond the veil. Spiritual messengers are conduits for God's energy in this physical plane. Classroom earth is constantly struggling between darkness and light and positive and negative. In other words, we are always in a spiritual war. While God and the higher beings provide guidance and protection, this is our world and a place where we learn lessons through our choices.

When our light is shining, we become targets for the lower energies as they want to add us to their cause. As writers, this may seem like the stuff of fantasy fiction. However, it is the energetic essence of our world. The Seven Lessons describe in terms we can understand how each of us experiences the Soul journey. They are vulnerabilities through which the lower energies can test and interfere with us. When my son was very young, he said something that perfectly describes how these lessons work. He said, thoughtfully, "mom, I think the devil works for God." He explained that the devil's job is to test us to see what choices we will make. Thinking back, he was young to have figured that out, but that is why the expression: "out of the mouths of babes."

Although I am not an expert in demonology, I have had personal experience with what can happen if you don't believe in evil. This lesson hit me hard. Thankfully I realized God and my Guides were with me the entire time, but I dealt with a malicious attachment that was deceiving me, taking my energy, and causing me to wither away. It started innocently enough with my experimenting with automatic writing before I knew how to shield myself. At the time, I thought all things other-worldly were good. When I contacted Spirit, I assumed it was a good thing. It definitely was not.

My Self-Protection lesson ended with me prostrate on the floor of a New York hotel room, praying for God to help me. I fully surrendered but still needed the help of people who understood psychic Self-Protection to ensure I was safe. There are different perspectives on how to deal with evil entities, but for me, it was with prayer, ritual, and the help of some shamans.

Not everyone is vulnerable to the Self-Protection lesson. However, please use my experience as a cautionary tale of what can happen if you dabble in things you do not understand. Early in the awakening process, it is exciting to embrace everything. But we are like children seeing the world for the first time. Children are to be protected from the dangers they see as benign. As we grow into spiritual maturation, we defend ourselves by asking God for help and guidance.

On the human side of this lesson, many of us do not see that there are people who act in self-interest. We are typically magnets for narcissists who will flatter their way into our lives. Then when it is too late, we are devalued and possibly made to question ourselves and our sanity.

This lesson is also about making good decisions when it comes to business. Writing seems like a glamorous career. There are too many unscrupulous people who see the population of writers as easy targets for schemes and scams. A significant part of this lesson is always to step back and do your due diligence when things are too good to be true. If you are vulnerable to the Self-Protection lesson, watch out for all the ways people will try to separate you from your money. Some great people can offer products and services that will genuinely benefit you. Just remain cautious, as this is a lesson about discernment. Just as you must discern if something is of God, on the human level, you must determine if someone is telling you the truth or just setting you up as a mark.

A second side to this lesson deals with who to trust and who not to trust. Sometimes we become so self-protective that we do not trust anyone. We close off the possibility of positive relationships and friendships. This may seem like the easy way out, but it will always make things worse. You can't hide in a cave to avoid these lessons. The reward for taking the chance and exercising your powers of discernment is drawing in and maintaining loving relationships with people you can trust.

Takeaways for Spiritual Writers.

The lesson of Self-Protection is a way for you to learn how to live in this world without leaving yourself open to the influences of negativity. Perhaps you leave yourself open on a spiritual level or in everyday life by not being aware that there are people who might want to take advantage of you. Perhaps things are just not what they seem. This may be the lesson you are coming to Earth to learn. Know that your Angels and Guides want you to know that you are precious, that you do not need to shut out the entire world, but you do need to know that there may be people who do not have your best interests at heart. Perhaps they are people who should. You may want to fine-tune and use your special radar to know if someone is trying to influence you away from your path or to get the better of you for their own purposes. Sometimes some people are energetically envious or frightened of your light. Even though they may mean well, they can bring down your energy. You should be aware and avoid being around people who do that to you. Your job on this planet is to find your Soul destiny and purpose. Your Soul Odyssey is a singular one. You must guard your path with your being and call upon God and the Angels at all times to protect you on your way. These challenges are put on your path to help you realize your journey's importance, so you will fight for it with everything you have.

Self-Protection is About Trust.

This is a challenge for all human beings because we trust everything from the time we are born. We don't understand it, but we believe everything we see, feel, smell, and touch is real. We experience these things as neutral. We believe there is no reason to question or to suspect they could harm us. As we grow, we encounter circumstances where we are hurt or our needs are not met. This is when we begin to learn not to trust. It becomes a protective mechanism that is warranted in the right situations. If you put your hand on a hot stove, you learn not to do that again. But in other cases, particularly when neglected or abused by those who should care for us, it can become a maladaptive way of coping with this world. We learn to survive and maintain this high alert long after the threat has passed. As we evolve and become more spiritually awake and conscious, we strive to learn to trust again because trust and love are intertwined.

As we learn who to trust and what to believe, we experience God in contrast. What feels like it is of God, and what does not? This becomes our touchstone. All the lessons are a way for us to connect with our higher selves and the Divine inner spark. Although we do not want to judge others harshly, we can exercise the courage to acknowledge if a person or situation is not trustworthy or good for us. Then we can exercise our right to choose not to engage with them. The Self-Protection lesson is about setting proper boundaries. This is difficult for many people, especially those on a spiritual path. Spiritual messengers are challenged to understand limits on all levels, so our creative energy is available for our work and not usurped by those who will exploit it.

Trust, when experienced with proper boundaries, is not the same as enmeshment. When we know clearly where we begin and end, we can see others for who they are. We can experience love for another because we know them and appreciate them as separate. Two people can create a much brighter flame together when they stand in their light.

The lesson of Self-Protection is not easy on a spiritual or human level. It is complex and, at times, confusing. It is about balance and personhood. You can begin your day with some added habits to help you stay centered and create a conscious shield around your energy. Just as you brush your teeth or drink your morning coffee, you can take a moment to pray for the highest levels of protection. Acknowledge you are not alone in the universe and that there are beings who love you and want what is best. Just as a parent should protect a child from unseen dangers, ask God, the Angels, your Spirit Guides, and Archangel Michael to bathe you in the highest shield of energy because you as an individual Soul are as crucial to the scheme of things as anyone else. You are not bothering anyone. You are protecting the Divine Balance.

There Will Always be Turbulence.

To be a human being is to live in turbulence. We live in a world of constantly battling forces vying for dominance. This is true in the insect world and the animal kingdom, so it is no less true for us. Even the weather is created by warm and cold fronts hitting each other to create the perfect storm.

Although others may disagree, the time we live in now is a perfect example of chaos and turbulence. The lesson of Self-Protection challenges us to see how we will cope with it. Some people jump into the fray, becoming news junkies and social media pundits. Everyone seems to have an opinion and, with complete access to others through the internet, has many options to express them.

A distressing thing about the time we live in is how aggressive people have become from the safety of their computers. People who might otherwise not argue or express rage have no qualms about spreading their venom throughout cyberspace.

As spiritual messengers, we are held to a higher standard. We can choose to jump into the turbulence giving it energy and a life of its own, or we can be more calculating in how we participate. Keep in mind the chaos and conflict in the media and on the internet is a way to keep people from joining together for the common goal of bringing light into the world. It keeps us frightened, skeptical, and on edge. There are so many rabbit holes of conspiracy that it is difficult to find a point of reality you can embrace. Truth has become a moving target forcing people to look outside themselves for answers.

Remember that your center point for all Truth is your connection to the Source. Everything else is a distraction meant to keep you off balance. It doesn't mean we should not be aware of the world and sit back when there are injustices. It means to preserve energy for the things you can do to change things rather than dissipating your light by giving it to the darkness. You can't illuminate a black hole.

On a human level, turbulence is caused by the unpredictability of circumstances. It is an unavoidable part of our experience. If you are in an airplane, turbulence is when you hit pockets of air that shake the plane back and forth and cause you to feel out of control. When you are an object in a much larger machine, all you can do is relax into it to avoid getting sick to your stomach. It would help if you buckled your seatbelt for safety, but resistance will not stop the plane's movement. Often you need to relax and ride the wave of your life without fear.

Turbulence is the storm before the calm. It may be what your life was like during childhood, but as conscious adults, you can rewrite your story to rise above subconscious messages that danger is afoot. You can reboot your fight or flight mechanism with interventions such as therapy and meditation. You can unpack your life by writing, journaling, and connecting to your Divine spark. Those on a spiritual path are often given the most challenging circumstances to push them toward their lessons. Remember this and reach out to God, your Guides, and all the positive forces of the universe to help you heal and move ahead.

Right now, we are in a period of a universal consciousness shift. But returning to our airplane metaphor, you can ride it out until it passes. There is no indication that you will crash, so don't go there in your mind and heart. This is temporary. It is a means through which you will learn to draw upon your inner strengths. It may be the way to push you to complete surrender and connection with the Divine. Bless the turbulence in your life. Do not be afraid. It is simply part of the journey.

The Self-Protection Lesson Requires Scrutiny.

Any new situation requires you to take the time to study the facts and how they will affect you. Spiritual writers or those on a spiritual path often rely on gut feelings for decision-making. Think back to our discussion of how we often see the Soul potential in a person who is not yet living in their light. In any relationship, we may ignore the signs about their character and rush into things. We may feel familiarity and skip over the real-world process of getting to know someone because we embrace the intuitive connection to their future selves.

Many of us also have an internal sense of Divine time which conflicts with linear time. We may see into a future that may never happen. We know that our time here is but a blink, so we rush things without the proper scrutiny. Speaking for myself, I am a person who looks for signs and trusts intuition. However, I have made impulsive decisions about relationships and had to live with the consequences. I know that everything is always for good, and when the lessons are learned, the right shift happens, but constantly having a two-by-four hit you on the head might be best avoided. It can be painful.

I figured out the hard way that God will guide you to the proper path. Patience is a virtue because it allows things to align properly. However, as human beings, we will continue to avoid looking at all the facts. We were given the power of free will and analytical reasoning, but it is much more fun to live by emotions alone. The Self-Protection lesson teaches us to combine emotion and intuition with good common sense. Try to rise above denial when the facts do not align with what you hope to be true. There are times when we can be companions on the journeys of our Soul mates. None of us are expected to be fully actualized before joining together. If that were the case, we would never find a mate. People will always be at different stages of the path.

Through this lesson, we learn to discern the character or intentions of people who want to connect with us. A simple bit of fine-tuning of our Self-Protection radar will help us avoid being the dupes of all whose intentions are not honorable. We would never want to do something to upset the balance of the Divine plan. Therefore, we can make sure others do not use us to do so. We must learn to use our energy and our gifts of intuition to determine if a situation is what it seems.

On the flip side, we may sometimes feel uncomfortable because someone is not warming up to us as quickly as we think they should. Remember, people with intuition can often feel they know people without giving the other person time to catch up. If you think you are being scrutinized, don't worry. Just give people time to learn that what they see is what they get. Give them a chance to trust and love you. It is worth the wait.

Self-Protection Shields us from Negativity.

Negativity is like a virus. All people are made up of energy. We often don't realize that much communication is done through vibration before word one is spoken. Many people on the spiritual path are experiencing a raising in their energy frequencies. They are becoming even greater sponges for other people's energies. It is not enough to dress for the weather. It is now essential for spiritual people who are open, to dress (shield) for the energies they will be exposed to. Energy originates in thought, and thought has power. Unbeknownst to us, our thoughts do not remain within the confines of our brains. We may have internal private conversations, but what we think sends vibrations to others. Make sure you are not creating negativity.

As an animal communicator, I saw this process of thought transfer in action. I was called to a barn to see if I could figure out why a horse was not behaving correctly. This was a trained carriage driving horse from a long line of well-bred champions. But horses are sentient beings and are often underestimated for how much they understand. I find communicating with horses to be easier than with some animals. I don't know if it is just how my brain works or my love of the species, but I hear them as clearly as I speak to someone.

This was an amusing encounter. The owners and drivers of this horse were a husband-and-wife team. It was the wife who had asked me to "read" the horse to find out why he was being stubborn. He was trained not to lift his head while in formation and seemed to resist their instructions.

When I tuned into the horse, he showed me a vision of the wife and said, "she yells at me." I knew this person and could not imagine her ever yelling at a horse, even in frustration. But I have learned to trust what animals share. For example, dogs may want things they shouldn't have, like table scraps, but they will not be deceptive about it. I told the woman what the horse said, and she turned flushed. Then she said, "I never said it out loud, but I was angry, so I cursed him out in my thoughts." Mystery solved. The horse knew she was upset with him, making it worse. She reported that she apologized through her thoughts and gave him positive reinforcement. His behavior improved almost miraculously.

This lesson is that thoughts have energy, especially if combined with emotion. We are all senders and receivers, some more than others. The only thing over which we have any real power is our thoughts. It is impossible not to sometimes slip into negativity, but we can consciously try not to stay there. If we know the power of thoughts and words, we can guide them in a more positive direction. Judaism has a concept of a prohibition against negative speech called *Loshon hora*. One is not supposed to speak ill of another person even if the statements are factual. If negative speech can damage a person in the eyes of another, it is considered wrong. This concept is a very ancient recognition of the power of words which can certainly be extrapolated to the power of thoughts.

If we keep our thoughts positive and loving, we can join with the Divine light of others. If we are around people with negative thoughts, we may feel pulled to join them. Here is another reason to learn how to set boundaries with people. Some people may cause you to feel self-doubt without even meaning to. But this can take you off your path. They may be a vessel for negativity simply because they lack spiritual protection. But ultimately, this is about you. You are the one who can evaluate your feelings without blaming the other person. If someone is toxic to your energy, it is your responsibility to limit your exposure. Also, ensure that you keep your thoughts filled with light and love so you are not the person sending out the negativity.

This is another reason to avoid engaging in the divisiveness you will find in social media or the news. People want to bring you to their side of the argument when perhaps they are operating out of fear. Try to surround yourself with people who see and bring good into the world because that is your strongest protection. Remember that hope and love are the two most important challenges for humanity right now. We will discuss love next, but hope is vital to our survival as a species. It keeps us from giving in to fear which is the opposite of faith. People around the globe are feeling hopeless. As spiritual writers and messengers, we must do everything we can to uplift those experiencing despair. Hopelessness diminishes our ability to find creative solutions to the challenges of life. Our job is to shine light into darkness.

Self-Protection can be Accomplished by Grounding Yourself.

As a person on a spiritual path, you may sometimes have your mind in the ethers. Spirituality and the universe make sense. The world and the choices human beings make often do not. We have conflicting Soul journeys and a constant struggle between darkness and light. It is an essential aspect of Self-Protection to remain connected to the Earth. Your day-to-day life is as significant to your spiritual path as whether you can astral project, have supernatural gifts, or talk to departed Spirits. Spiritual gifts may result from the path, but spirituality is a balance between your Soul and your physical being. Your lessons happen here and give you the best chance to connect with your Divine spark. Spiritual people may find it more interesting to live in other-dimensional ways. Maybe it is just me, but there have been times when I am unaware of my surroundings. As you expand your consciousness and vibration, it can be a challenge to simply be aware of putting one foot in front of another. Again, it may just be me, but I have bumped into doors and walls because I allowed my energy body to be too expansive. I whole heartily accept my weirdness, but I know this is not uncommon as energy is finding its balance.

It is challenging for creative people in general and spiritual people specifically to pay attention to day-to-day life. You are accountable for your actions and path toward becoming a good citizen of the universe. There are realities to living on this planet that you can't ignore, or they will cause you trouble. The Self-Protection lesson teaches us to seek balance in our energy so we can stop fighting against the details that stand in the way of our spiritual mission.

There are many ways to become grounded. Being around horses is very helpful because you must stay present and pay attention. Crystals can help you, such as wearing hematite. Hematite is known to have grounding qualities and is also good for shielding. Soaking or swimming in water is excellent for healing and grounding. Remembering to hydrate also helps you stay centered. Self-Protection reminds you that being present in this world is as important as connecting to Spirit. You are here because you are supposed to be here.

You are Surrounded by Light.

Never be afraid that you are alone. You are always infused with the love and protection of innumerable beings of light and the direct Source of Divine love. If you have the Self-Protection lesson as one of your primary challenges, remember to take charge of your path by experiencing your inner strength. The protection is there, but you need to call upon it. You are on a spiritual path for a reason. You have a Soul commitment you made long before you arrived in classroom Earth. You are here to grow your Soul and contribute to light redistribution in this beautiful world. Know that you are as crucial to the scheme of things as anyone else. You deserve the same Divine protection as all of God's children. Remember to check your shield every morning. Become consciously aware of its presence. It will give you the strength and fortitude to pursue directions that might otherwise stop you in your tracks. Once you know who you are and what you are made of, you can be free to live your destiny.

Takeaways for Spiritual Writers.

Self-Protection lessons remind us that we are spiritual beings in a relatively nonspiritual world. We learn through our Self-Protection lessons that we must be vigilant in guarding our energy against others' negativity.

One of our challenges is we tend to project onto people what we see as the potential of their higher selves or our light. We dismiss reality and can become too trusting and sometimes too helpful. We may allow our valuable spiritual energy to be consumed by people who are essentially energy vampires. Learning to conserve our energy and use it only where it will do the best is essential.

In learning who to trust or who not to trust, we can lose all sense of perspective around certain people and allow them to steer us off our path. Sometimes these people are those who are closest to us. These lessons can be difficult, as they usually lead to disillusionment or loss. We must maintain our balance with those who bring out our vulnerabilities. We can learn to create a shield around ourselves.

We are also given lessons about our lack of faith in ourselves. Just because we open ourselves to Spirit does not make us invulnerable to our internal negativity. We may be filled with doubts, fears, and envy of other writers' accomplishments. If we are not careful, the negativity can contaminate our writer's journey within us. That is why Self-Protection lessons are essential to spiritual writers. Anything that throws us off our path prevents the purity of our message from reaching its intended audience. And one of our jobs is to shield our vulnerable points so that we don't become vessels for imbalance.

On a very practical level for spiritual writers, we may lack boundaries in our business life if we are too trusting. Many working writers use their skills for others through ghostwriting, editing, or collaboration. Our relationships in business may become blurred where they seem like friendships. This can be fraught with problems because of a lack of clarity with expectations.

I think I have had to learn all these lessons in dramatic ways so I could illustrate them. Or maybe, as I have described, I am just hard-headed. Many years ago, when I was first becoming an editor in between the times of writing my material, I took on a project from another editor and should have known it was a dog. It was a direct translation from another language so literal that it was incomprehensible. I agreed to edit it so it would read better for an English audience but had no idea that the book I had seen in a bound copy turned out to be at least 400 pages of Klingon. It looked like English but was going to require a rewrite from top to bottom.

Believe it or not, I did it. I completely rewrote the book, so it made sense. It took hours upon hours. When I handed in the final product, the client said she wanted me to edit the two other follow-up books for the same money. I said no and kind of left in a huff. Not my finest moment.

But in business, we have a definite learning curve. This lesson causes us to learn our value. But what it also teaches us is to protect ourselves with clarity. I should have written out clearly what my deliverables would be. Right before I wrote this book section, ten years later, I was contacted by the former client. She knew I was now a publisher and wanted me to help with the book. She had self-published it and wanted help with marketing.

I was sentimental about it and not happy with how I left things, so I naively had a meeting with her and said I would help. Then she sent me the book she self-published, the original unedited version. She hadn't used any of what I had done. I said I couldn't possibly publish and promote the original book, and she went ballistic. She said she never saw a finished product and paid me for nothing. She demanded I publish and promote the book as is, or she would sue me for the money she paid me with ten years of interest.

The energy she sent was awful. Thank God I remembered which old computer I had used to write the book and found the fully edited 350- page manuscript. I sent it to her and reminded her that I had finished the book as promised. I still don't know if she plans to sue me, but I know she will be the one to look crazy.

But the concern is not how she behaved; it is how I left myself vulnerable without having things clear and in writing. Her reaction was extreme because I was working on assumptions without fully knowing that she had never used my work in the book she wanted me to promote. I should have examined the facts before I promised anything. And I probably should not have entertained working with her again in the first place because of how challenging the project was at that time. I am too busy now to give away my time to something that essentially becomes an abyss. Our time is valuable and is also part of our energy. But my boundaries were too loose ten years ago, and I had to be reminded of this lesson. It is easy to slip back into old patterns. I hope I am much better now at writing clear agreements with expectations. However, we always teach about the things we need to learn.

So, I accept the experience as my reminder to keep expectations clear and to give you an illustration so you can avoid these situations for yourselves.

You have a mission. As spiritual writers, obstacles will be thrown in your path to limit you. But knowing this, you can break through the barriers to fulfill your calling.

SELF-LOVE

Self-Love is one of the most common lessons people come here to learn. It is much easier to look at what we are not than to recognize how wonderful we are. We can see the good in other people and worship God, but we may find it difficult to know that we are worthy. When you are in a situation that makes you feel less than the fantastic person that you are, remind yourself that it is you who feels unworthy. It is not a fact. For this lesson, examine your life and your circumstances, considering where you might be selling yourself short for what is your true potential.

We are often filled with self-loathing because we mistakenly compare ourselves to others and believe we don't measure up. Spiritual writers especially hold themselves up to impossible standards. We are not God, and we don't have to be perfect. I can be very condemning when I fall off my diet wagon. I know I should be at peace with myself, my body, and my age, but I am trying to hold back the sands of time drifting to my stomach. A simple thing like not being able to resist cookies can put me into a tailspin of negative self-talk until I finally realize I am doing it to myself. This is a simple example of the Self-Love lesson because we tend to waste our valuable creative energy being our worst enemies. Unless we are disturbed, most of us wouldn't want to condemn our children the way we beat ourselves up for simple lapses.

The lesson of Self-Love can be a significant block for spiritual writers because we will never think our work is good enough. We are each a purposeful universe. In other words, God made us the way we are for a reason. The big picture is our Soul's growth, understanding the essence of God, and helping others along the way. Our paths are not easy, and the natural inclination is to ask, "why?" Why don't I have a loving family who sees and appreciates me? Why wasn't I born into wealth? Why can't I eat cookies and stop at one? Why can't I resist alcohol and only drink socially? There is a great expression that you should never measure your insides by someone else's outsides. Perhaps this is a symbolic meaning to the commandment of "thou shalt not covet thy neighbor's goods," as this kind of outward projection causes us to devalue who we are. Another good expression to remember is when coveting that another person can eat cookies and stop at one. "Good for them!"

All our challenges and obstacles can be transmuted into ways to connect to Source because we know what it is like to be disconnected. Whenever we judge ourselves harshly and hatefully because we are not what we perceive as the perfection of others, we turn our backs on the Divine Source. It is like pulling out the plug on our laptop. Eventually, the battery will wear down. It is not the electricity in the wall that has pulled away from it; it is a constant. That is what God is. And our negativity and self-judgment are what unplugs us from the Source. The Self-Love lesson teaches us to know that we can always reconnect.

The Need for Validation is Part of the Self-Love Lesson.

Being a writer is a path filled with rejection. If we constantly need validation, we will never achieve our goals. None of us will appeal to everyone. That is why in the last section of this book, I give you tips for finding your tribe. It is a better use of energy to appeal to those who resonate with you. And there will be people who do. If you are tapping into Source, there are readers who want what you have.

You only need validation from yourself and God. If you are true to yourself and accept that you are a work in progress, you will have God's approval. It is not conditioned on perfection.

Self-Love Begins with Gratitude.

Another aspect of the Self-Love lesson is the "I can do it myself" syndrome. We see ourselves as burdens to other people and don't want to ask for help when we need it. But we are depriving others of doing good deeds for us. Receiving gratefully is often as important as giving.

If we take this a step further, our perception that we should not ask for or expect help or caring from others feeds our sense of unworthiness. We can become martyrs or "Debbie do-it-alls," a nickname I picked up as early as elementary school. God-Love my parents, may they rest in peace, but they were young, passionate, volatile, and very chaotic. One of our neighbors, still a friend, remembers when my mother threw my father's suitcases out of the house. Knowing them, he never left because it was part of the dance.

I was a sensitive and empathic child who internalized a desire to make people happy. I turned to school, activities, and doing it all, to be acknowledged and validated. I am grateful that later, as a young woman, I learned a different way to perceive the world, but Self-Love had never come easily to me. One thing I learned is Gratitude is an antidote to self-doubt.

If you begin thinking about all the things you can be grateful for every day, it will remove negativity as if you were blowing away steam with your breath. Even if you are feeling hopeless, aggravated, or sad, Gratitude connects you with God and is a way to change your thinking. It is normal to occasionally feel frightened, sorry for yourself, and confused about your path. Listing the things that are good in your life helps bring clarity. Then your Guides and higher self can help you find the answers you need.

Takeaways for Spiritual Writers.

The lessons of Self-Love involve being worthy of love not only from other people but also from God. This is a lesson spiritual writers must learn if we are to support our inner voice. If we require approval from everyone, we will write to please others rather than reflect the Spirit inside us. We can't be a messenger if we do not have faith enough in ourselves to carry out the job. Aside from causing us to write inauthentically, a constant desire for outside validation can lead to massive writer's block when we realize we can never be perfect and can never be all things to all people.

We all have differing degrees of Self-Love and are given daily lessons to see how wonderful we are. We all have unique qualities and limitations, essential elements in our lives. We, ourselves, are the purveyors of our most challenging Self-Love lessons. When we write, we want to know that our work is good. We want to be noticed, and we want accolades.

Self-Love lessons teach spiritual writers that it isn't necessary to be liked by everyone. You may only resonate with a small audience, but it is enough if your message is important to them. No one's work is suitable for everyone. Even bestselling authors get bad reviews. If you receive positive feedback from ten people, but the eleventh doesn't like you, is that the one you will remember? Will it derail you from feeling good about yourself? These are your Self-Love lessons teaching you to focus on the good things rather than embracing the negative.

Remember that while we may be called to a spiritual mission through writing, we are not being asked to change the world all at once. The lesson of Self-Love encourages us to accept our role in a much bigger picture. We don't even need to be published to have gained love and acceptance from the universe. We will never let the universe down if we do not find a publisher for our book. Of course, if that is your goal, there are many ways to accomplish it, as you will see in the rest of this book. However, these lessons teach us that our path is for us and a higher purpose.

We follow our desire to write books because books are the vehicle through which we give our Spirit to others. This exchange of Spirit elevates all Souls. Even if we never write an opus or never do anything that we feel other people will notice, the lesson of Self-Love teaches us that our living Spirit is enough.

EGO

Ego lessons can be some of the most difficult to learn. Staying humble can be particularly difficult for spiritual writers, who sometimes struggle to separate themselves from their message. When I was an agent, and now as an Indie publisher, I have seen spiritual Ego deadlock some potentially important careers. People turn down offers or have unrealistic expectations of their role in their success because they believe the world is waiting for them. Spiritual writers mustn't succumb to the pull of Ego. Some spiritual mentors have given me a new definition of Ego as Edging God Out. This is very fitting. It is also when you do not fully see and honor God in other people. You may have gifts and important messages but so do other lightworkers and people of Faith. God loves each person, and each person has their Spirit Guides and Angels. We are limited while on our human/spiritual journey. One of our weaknesses is we may perceive God as a limited resource. When we were children, we could not fathom that a parent could have enough love for more than one child. Anyone with siblings knows the pull of jealousy when it seems another child is getting more of whatever it may be.

We live in an abundant universe with many people contributing to the planet's energy. Over the years, I have seen some of the most gifted people given messages and essential information from Spirit, which is meant to help them, and they cannot hear it or see it because they are caught up in the sense of superiority.

On the other hand, you are as special and extraordinary as anyone else because God's love is unconditional. When you want it all for yourself, you forget why you are here in the first place. The same Divine spark connects all human beings. Wars are futile because we are essentially fighting against ourselves. It is the height of irony.

This lesson is problematic because when we feel the link to Spirit, it is natural and easy to become full of ourselves. We believe we are more special and more connected to Source and the lower energies are only all too happy to reinforce this illusion. In the Christian New Testament, there is a story of Jesus in the Garden of Gethsemane. Although this is a very simplistic paraphrase of when Jesus was in the garden, the serpent tried to convince him that instead of serving God, he could be and have everything he surveyed. That is the deception that is the basis of the Ego lesson.

Fortunately, Ego lessons tend to burst the bubble of spiritual superiority, even before it reaches maximum inflation. The reason is apparent: If you put yourself above others, you essentially put yourself above God. You become the message rather than the messenger. If you genuinely want to serve and fulfill your spiritual mission, the universe of Guides and Angels will ensure you pass this test and will keep reminding you until you do.

As an author, I have become a cult expert of sorts. My work on the Manson Family memoir for Dianne Lake showed me how something like that could happen. And although it seems unlikely, following the story of how Charles Manson descended into messianic madness, he may be an extreme example of the Ego lesson gone awry. People have differing opinions about this, but many people who could have done good things with charisma and insight succumb to this lesson and take people off their paths with horrifying results. The people who first followed him were not stupid or throwaways; some were flower children and seekers of something that could make a better world.

I have also been working with survivors of the 1978 Jonestown massacre and researching how that cult happened. While people can say Jim Jones might have started as an evil manipulator, the facts show otherwise. From the perspective of his followers, he offered an expansion of the Christian ideals of making the world better for those who were disenfranchised. He fed the poor and got people off drugs. He had a vision of a utopia. His followers wanted a better life, and some wanted to be more Christlike by doing good works.

Knowing the Ego lesson, I can't dismiss that people like Jim Jones might have used their charisma and vision for good. But they were corrupted by their Egos; in Jones's case, he led his followers to a tragic death.

The Ego lesson is meant to weed out people and, in our case, writers, who would bring in corrupted messages. Negative spiritual Ego is hollow worship of self, which eliminates the possibility of any real love or connection to our higher Spirit. We can lead people off their paths. Our role as spiritual writers is to guide people to their spiritual awakening, not our version of it. We are mentors and want our students to eventually outgrow all we could ever teach them and trust their inner voice. We can also become the focal point for the seeker. We may mistakenly think that having people become dependent on us fulfills our role as spiritual teachers. We can be easily diverted away from our path. The spiritual Ego cannot coexist with faith. We must keep the proper balance between service and wanting to be served.

The lessons of Ego are presented to every spiritual traveler so that we can learn how important it is to be strong in faith. We are here to help ourselves and each other progress in the growth of our Souls and our awareness of Spirit, and we can't assist others on their path if we believe the path leads to us.

I learned this lesson firsthand. When I was coming into awareness, I taught classes for many years that included the Seven Lessons. I would also bring in information from Spirit and answer questions for my students. This was a wonderful experience, and it allowed me to learn what I needed to know while sharing the energy with a close-knit group. However, there were a few students who became dependent on me. It is a sacred trust to be a teacher and mentor. While a few students took the information into the world and their lives, a few looked to me for answers to mundane situations. They also looked to me for perfection, which I certainly was not. I am no one's guru. At that time, I received a message from Spirit: "physician, heal yourself." It was time for me to move on with my path and to learn more of my lessons. I am grateful that although I have other issues, one of them did not seem to be that I was a psychopathic megalomaniac. I didn't want to have a cult of personality nor to be responsible for other people's lives in such an intimate way. So, I disbanded the class, and everyone moved on.

The experience showed me how cults could be formed without the leader's conscious knowledge. And there is a fine line between serving and enjoying being served. I felt special with people listening to me. They treated me well, fulfilling my need to be loved and validated. But I am grateful to God that I was shown a direction that could fulfill my mission in other ways. I still do healing work, but I hope my words and whatever I know can be shared through writing so I can encourage others to reach their Soul destiny.

The Lesson of Spiritual Ego doesn't Mean you can't Promote Yourself.

I have worked with spiritual writers who are confused about how to market their books. They are so concerned about their Egos that they don't want to be visible in any way. Promoting yourself as an author is not the same as being consumed with Ego. It can lead to a hard Ego lesson but does not mean you are doing anything wrong.

If you have been called to write and accept the assignment, you must also help people find your work. You may even be asked to be visible through social media, public speaking, or traditional media. This is all positive if you never forget that you work for the universe. If you always remember to serve the greater good, you are expected to take your place as a representative of the Divine.

This lesson is tricky because it is tempting to buy into your publicity. Just like I enjoyed my students' attention and special treatment, if you are asked to sign books or do interviews, it can be exhilarating. The first time I saw my name on the front of a book, I thought I would burst with pride. Nothing is wrong with feeling good about accomplishments if you do not step into the world of the spiritual diva. Don't go Hollywood. Remember that your readers are essential, and you are a conduit to elevate their Soul paths. Enough said.

The Ego lesson is the flipside of Self-Protection. Too much humility can open you to exploitation; all lessons work in balance with each other.

LOVE OF HUMANITY

Spiritual writers often see the potential in all humans to connect in Spirit. We know that we all have a link to the main generator. We draw from the same intelligence base, have the same choices, needs, and feelings, and learn the same lessons.

That said, it still isn't easy to look at the world without judgment. While we can't write to please everyone, we must take care not to write in a way that excludes those whose spiritual path differs from ours, assuming they are incapable of spiritual growth. That is spiritual snobbery. During the late 1980s, with the burgeoning new age, many people left their spouses because they didn't think they were evolving fast enough. Or they would say things like, "I don't want to be here" because they thought the earth was beneath them. Of course, the earth is beneath you. And if you are here, there is a purpose. These people were not suicidal; they were trying to say they were better Spirits than others. One woman who ran an esoteric bookstore once told me, "I only speak to the ascended masters." I couldn't help myself. I looked at her seriously and said, "I am one." The greatest of us and the least of us are the same. We may have different challenges, but we are heading to the same place. Ultimately, we are on a path to reuniting with Source. This is the essence of the lesson of the Love of Humanity. And, yes, it is very tied into the others.

Another aspect of this lesson is assuming you know more than someone else. I know I can be intellectually judgmental if I am being completely objective. I have learned not to do things for people they can do for themselves. I don't always do this out of kindness; being a problem-solver makes me feel good about myself. I may not see the other person's potential. Love of Humanity teaches us to honor the lives and abilities of others.

Although I have never understood the full implications of this lesson, it seems it encompasses all of them. We live in a dualistic world with conflict and challenges. These things do not exist similarly when we are on the other side. From my experiences communicating with people across the veil, I know they still learn lessons. I have asked Spirits what it is like, and they can't explain it. Maybe others have gotten better answers, but my descriptions have been vague and fraught with "you won't understand it until you are here." They say it is not the same as physicality, yet they exist and do things we can relate to. I have my imagination of what it must be like there. Maybe they move by the speed of thought. I imagine they can access any information they wish. That would be my heaven. A massive library with every book ever written would be something I could enjoy.

My favorite movie is *Defending Your Life.* (1991). It was written by and starred Albert Brooks as a somewhat bumbling human who dies unexpectedly through his own negligence. He goes to a type of way station where it will be determined through a hearing whether he will move on to a better place or be returned to earth. He is very defensive during what he thinks is a trial. But as described, it is a life review that happens when people first pass over. Although he is unaware of this, and while there are facilitators, he judges himself. They show him scenes from his life, so he will understand that he held himself back through fear. It wasn't God who was judging him; in my interpretation, he was learning the same lessons over and over.

Of course, my favorite part of the movie was a montage of all the stupid things he did. I could certainly see myself in these scenes. They called them misjudgments like drinking shampoo thinking it was mouthwash. We all do things like these, but part of his lesson was to accept himself, screw-ups and all. Meryl Streep is wonderful as the perceived perfect person defending her remarkable life. He loves her but feels inadequate. I won't give away the end, but this movie is uncanny in depicting what I think happens in classroom earth and beyond.

When we all get to the next destination, I often wonder if we will realize the biggest joke is what will happen when we shed our bodies and become nothing but energy. There will be no races or cultural differences. There is only love. We are the same. And all our lessons push us toward knowing and connecting to all God's creations. Imagine.

Takeaways for Spiritual Writers.

If you write for a particular market, such as Christian or New Age, it is possible to identify yourself with that genre without denigrating other paths. Don't waste energy proving people wrong; give energy to what you believe is right. As writers, we never really know who will read our books or whose lives will be influenced by what we write. When we learn the lesson of Love of Humanity, we become willing to let go of our words so that they will reach whoever needs them. Even though we do not have physical control over our books, we have spiritual control over how willing we are to give them a life separate from us.

When called to a mission as a spiritual writer, you will constantly expand your understanding of the seen and unseen. Trust your inner voice to guide you. While you should not try to be all things to all people when you sit down to write, pray that what you create will serve the greater good of all. Pray to be in service to humanity and then follow the signs.

GOD-LOVE.

When you learn the first six lessons, you remove some of the doubts about your own higher truth. God-Love is achieved for a spiritual writer when you surrender to your Divine inner voice and allow it to work through you.

God-Love is the most personal of the Seven Lessons, providing you with a knowledge of the Spirit that extends beyond belief. Many of you who are called to write about your spiritual journey know that there came a point at which no one could persuade you away from your faith. The lessons of God-Love feed this internal link between mind and Spirit.

I have met many spiritual people who do not want to admit having many moments of questioning. It is not automatic that we embrace a sense of God with all our being. Many of us have been turned off to God because we were spoon-fed other people's definitions of who and what God is. The only truth of God comes from personal experience. You may follow any religion you like, but until you find a direct connection, you will have a watered-down version of your direct link to Source.

We have misconceptions about God and his/her role in our path. Some of us think of God as a stern parent who will be either pleased or disappointed in us. We fear retribution if we do something wrong.

Some of us view God as a glorified Santa Claus here to fulfill our desires. Sometimes we do not know what is best for us. So, asking for specific things and being angry when we don't get them may be an expectation sure to lead to disappointment.

We often blame God for the bad things that happen in the world, entirely forgetting our role in free will and choices. Some horrible people embody evil. If God were to prevent all these things from happening, would there be any motivation for us to take a stand and choose to help others? This is our world, and we are responsible for what happens here.

We are not in a completely random world. When we fully surrender to God and the Divine Source, we tend to receive answers and guidance that improve our lives. There are also spiritual teachers and helpers put in our path to help us find our way to the Source. But these teachers and helpers are meant to guide us, so we learn to rely on our internal knowledge of Truth and God.

The lessons of God-Love eventually push us out of the nest so that we can become true messengers. Then we can add our voices to the spiritual chorus. Don't ever be ashamed if you are angry at God. It is expected that you will experience this at one point or another. The world is not the place as God intended for us. This is a place we can create for God. By doing all the good we can in the world, we improve the energy and help light the way for other spiritual Souls.

The spiritual path and the human condition are often ones of profound loneliness. We live in a dimension where we perceive we are hidden from God. Most of us feel disconnected from God and other human beings. We have an empty hole inside us that we try to fill with things, activities, addictions, materialism, and unhealthy relationships.

When we learn the lessons of God-Love, we can feel undeniably that we are never alone. We are always part of something that guides us through our lives. We have a sense of purpose and, as spiritual writers, often seek to help fellow travelers.

Lessons of God-Love Help us Overcome Fear.

When we have a God-Love lesson, we often experience God's energy in a way that proves to us it is real and not the stuff of imagination. Many of us only get this feeling by reaching a rock bottom point where there is nowhere else to go but up. Although addictions are tragic, they can sometimes lead to some of the most extraordinary surrender experiences possible. Many people in recovery bless their experience as a way they discover there is something greater than themselves. They may refer to it as a higher power, but eventually, many refer to it as God.

Classroom Earth is filled with paths toward surrender that don't require vast suffering. Unfortunately, I have found some of the most spiritually awake people have had to survive horrific challenges. Maybe it is to assure we will never question the power of the universe and how much good there is despite the bad. I have no answers for this.

I know that we have unconditional love from God and the universe, but while there are beautiful oceans, they are filled with sharks. Sharks are predators and have a reason to exist, but they are dangerous to baby seals and us. Nature is neutral, but we might not want to swim in waters where there are baby seals and sharks.

The Lessons of God-Love Help us Rise Above Worry.

When we fully surrender to God with connection to our Divine inner voice, we can transcend worry. This is not to say we suddenly no longer benefit from anti-depressants and anxiety medicines. There is so much crazy vibration and toxicity in this world that many take medications to keep our physiology balanced. No judgment here.

But on a spiritual level, we have been conditioned to believe that worry is a natural part of life. On the contrary, when we allow the noise of worry to dominate our thoughts, we can't live in the true present. We cannot access the creative resources we can innately tap to resolve any problem we encounter. When we worry, we tell ourselves that we do not believe we are capable or that the universe will provide for us. A quiet mind can find solutions because it is open to answers. Worry wastes precious energy. When you are harmonious inside, you will find your surroundings will follow suit.

Takeaways for Spiritual Writers.

We are living in a world with lots of chaotic energy. You, as spiritual writers, can do your best to rise above the illusions that everything is terrible and the world is going to hell. I am not well-versed in the law of attraction, so I will not refer to it here. But it makes sense that the universe will allow us to create a picture of what our world is through our thoughts. Try to reframe your perspective to everything is for good. Even the things that look bad at the moment are likely temporary. Perhaps you may think I am living in a world of denial. However, when I reframed my thoughts to an underlying awareness that positive energy is given reinforcement by God and all the Guides surrounding us, I stopped worrying.

Anyone who knows me has seen me struggle with self-esteem, hurt feelings, writer's block, self-consciousness, and the occasional bout of terror. However, when I step back and do a spiritual reset, I feel blessed to have a way to understand the situations in my life. Therefore, I want this for you.

I had a major spiritual initiation when I was in my mid-twenties. I may someday write the whole story as even I can't believe the details of how it happened. I went on a type of vision quest which resulted in me laying prone on the floor of a hotel room, asking that God become the center of my existence. That is all I wanted. I was confused and was first learning about life beyond the five senses and was scared. I also believe Spirit was testing my ego. Everything was happening very fast, and I knew if I was on my own, there was no telling where it would lead. The surrender was a mystical experience, and I know it was real. It changed me forever. I am still a bumbling human far from perfect, but there is no doubt in my mind there is a much bigger plan for all of us. We are privileged to bring light into the world through our words, but I know, perhaps more than some, the sacredness of the responsibility.

Your journeys are unique. One day, you may pray for God to be at the center of your life and stop the chaos. Or you may not have an experience like that. It doesn't matter. I feel blessed because, in the years that followed, as I taught spirituality classes, I learned the Seven Lessons through teaching them. I am still learning what they mean and how they play out in our lives. That is why I have left room for you to interpret them and how they fit into your world if indeed they do. I believe when the phrase Soul Odyssey popped into my mind while I was in the shower many years after I began teaching about the Seven Lessons, I received an answer. Like any system, study helps. You will see new things as you let the thoughts germinate.

As part of your God-Love lesson, allow your Spirit Guides to connect you with various books and teachers to help you understand things that cannot be learned linearly. Sometimes a Spirit Guide is a voice or feeling. Sometimes it is straightforward, like a book falling on your head. Pay attention to the signs. We are all initiates on this spiritual mystery path. The universe finds a way to teach us what we need to know. We will learn what we need at the right pace if we are open and do not expect immediate results.

If you try to read a book that everyone else recommends and don't feel it resonates with you, it may not be what will guide you to a greater connection with your Soul and God. You are on an individual curriculum. Explore many avenues, but ultimately allow Spirit to bring you your education. You don't have to know everything, and you will never stop learning even when you pass to the next place.

The God-Love lesson teaches us to Harness our Energy and Be Accountable.

Your thoughts can influence your health in both a positive and negative manner. The unconscious messages are constantly telling your body how to respond. If you harness the energy of your mind and your body, you can optimize your health and maintain greater physical harmony. Be mindful of other people's energy as it can be absorbed into yours, particularly in the early stages of spiritual development. The conscious harnessing of energy can help you determine what is yours and what belongs to someone else. It enables you to connect to your Divine Spark.,

We often blame God for injustice. But this is our world, and we have the power to change it. We have all that we need. Here is an interesting quote from the renowned guru Paramahansa Yogananda.

"When you begin to see clearly the imperfection of the world, you will begin to see the perfection of God. The truth is that God is using evil, not to destroy us, but to make us disillusioned with his toys, with the playthings of this world, so that we might seek him. This is why the Lord himself permits injustices and evil. But I have said to him, "Lord, you have never suffered. You have always been perfect. How do you know what suffering is?

The Lord answered, "You don't have to go on suffering; I have given everyone the free will to choose good instead of evil, and thus come back to me," So evil is the test of God to see if we will choose him or his gifts. He created us in His image and gave us the power to free ourselves, but we don't use that power."

Paramahansa Yogananda's "Why God Permits Evil and How to Rise Above it."

The most troubling question will always remain why God doesn't intervene and protect innocent people from horrible events. Perhaps it is the same as the Star Trek Prime Directive. Yes, I am that kind of a nerd, and I hope some of you are too. The prime directive prohibits Starfleet officers from interfering with the natural development of "alien" civilizations.

According to the fictional world of Star Trek, this protects civilizations that may be unprepared from crew members who may have good intentions, from introducing technology or knowledge before they are ready to receive it. Many people believe Star Trek creator Gene Roddenberry was ahead of his time or tuned in to a higher Truth. This is as good an explanation as any of why God would allow us, if we are the "alien" civilization, to take our time learning and to advance at a pace suitable to our planet.

As spiritual writers, you are tasked with sharing what you know, but as we learn through the other lessons, making it available to those ready for it. We don't impose it, and we don't assume we have the big picture of all there is to learn. We are blessed to do for our planet what God and the Angels will only do in absentia. While God is in everything and is everywhere, the Creative Source works through us with guidance so we can fulfill the promise of making this a heaven on earth.

THE SEVEN LESSONS SUMMARY

There is a long way to go from opening the path to being ready to teach it. We are all each other's teachers no matter where we are along the way, but it is Spirit guiding the lesson plan. Many of us are being called to do healing work for humanity. If you are a teacher or healer, check yourself against the lessons to see if you have any vulnerabilities that could open you to negativity. As the light shines, the darkness wants to drain it and misdirect it. As well-intentioned as we are, we want to examine ourselves objectively and pray for guidance to be a pure vessel for Divine love. We must check that our Egos are balanced and call upon our Self-Love to keep appropriate boundaries. Ask God for Guidance if you have any doubts.

Here is a quick key to the lessons:

Courage: Moving beyond what others believe to your inner truth.

Tolerance: Allowing others to follow their Soul paths while standing as an example.

Self-Protection: Knowing who to trust and not to trust. General discernment.

Self-Love: Knowing you are worthy of love and allowing others into your life.

Ego: Choosing to be the messenger rather than the message.

Love of Humanity: Recognizing that we are all from the same Source.

God-Love: Surrendering to a direct relationship with God.

3

THE SEVEN LESSONS OF
SOUL ODYSSEY JOURNAL

Before we get into the nitty-gritty of writing and publishing, I recommend you review the Seven Lessons and spend time journaling about them. You can return to these journal exercises at any time and skip ahead to the meat of the book. These are here to help you gain self-awareness to find your authentic voice. The journal exercises are tools to help you go inward and prepare yourself to write from your highest level of purpose.

Your best writing happens when you are in tune with your Divine inner voice. When you look at your life and your writer's journey through these Seven Lessons, you can see how you may have repeated some experiences over and over. These lessons lead to awakening. As you proceed with your journaling, you may get to the point where you can feel a lesson take shape. You may not know what to do about it because you aren't sure what you are to learn, but when you experience a lesson, you will be aware that you have changed.

- Use these lessons as catalysts to begin a dialogue with yourself.
- Use them to forge a connection to Spirit, your inner teacher.
- Your journal can be a form of meditation, a blessing—whether or not you publish— because it helps you grow.

Consider this process spiritual therapy. You may be surprised at the words that come forth as you start addressing the journal questions. You may want to start journaling by directly addressing your Angels and Guides. You can write in the form of a question: Dear Angels and Guides, what am I to learn from this exercise? Then start writing as if your Angels and Guides have answered you.

Dear one, we are your Angels and Guides, and we want you to pay attention to…. and see what words flow. Try not to edit what comes into your mind. Make sure to pray before you do an exercise like this to enable your shield. Before any meditative session, ask that you be surrounded with the light of love and protection and that what you receive is from God, from the highest of the high, to help you serve humanity. That is one of the best ways to set the right mood for your writing and journaling sessions.

Be aware that it is not always easy to learn about yourself. It can be as difficult as trying to edit your own manuscript. Spiritual journaling requires objectivity to avoid dismissing what changes you might want to make. On the other hand, it is equally difficult to look at oneself kindly if we are measuring ourselves against perceived spiritual ideals.

Your work as a spiritual writer is mainly meant for popular consumption. But for many spiritual writers, our first books are typically about our inner journey. In all honesty, these books mean the most to us but are the least likely to be published unless we have a significant following or are extraordinary writers. I have a first book sealed in shrink wrap, which is so personal that I will likely never show it to anyone—not even myself!

Not all first manuscripts should be shrink-wrapped. If you think yours should be shared with the world, the rest of this book will show you how to submit it for publication. However, if you write in your journal using the Seven Lessons as guidelines as you experience a process of spiritual self-discovery, you may get some things out of your system so you can work on a first book that may be more commercially viable., These lessons will also help keep you grounded in how to live spiritually in this world. We are not here to learn how to be Spirit. We already are. Your journal writing will help you learn how to integrate your Spirit with your daily life so you can contribute to the growth of your Soul and the process of Soul evolution for everyone.

Before writing in your journal, create a sacred space for yourself. If you are most comfortable with a computer, there is no reason this cannot represent your sacred space and if you are a pen-and-paper person, set aside several notebooks for journaling. I like composition books, but there are many other beautiful ways to create a special journal to hold your thoughts and feelings. The main thing is to set the time aside to dialogue, to open a portal between you and Spirit.

When you begin your journal, list the Seven Lessons on the first page, using your intuition to determine which have influenced your life most. If you believe you have passed through or beyond a particular lesson, indicate this by writing yes next to it. Write no if you think you have yet to learn or complete a specific lesson. Write your first response, as intellectualizing can prevent us from being honest with ourselves. You might be surprised with your intuitive answers, which will give you some material to discuss in your journal.

Sometimes opening an inspirational book will yield answers that can help you decide if you have learned a lesson from a subconscious level. Don't be nervous if you feel that you have not yet learned anything.

The lessons are simply a guide for your path. There is no time limit, and you can't be expelled from the school of Spirit. You may have to repeat a grade—as I have done many times—but you will always be measured against your awareness of Self. You are not in competition. You are looking for illumination, balance, and spiritual connection.

And you will find answers. You can be honest in your journals because there is no judgment in the world of Spirit, only unconditional love and guidance. Spirit knows what is in your heart, even with the limitations of language. What you write is for you. You are safe. You are loved. You are free to be your true self.

Allow yourself plenty of time. Your journals are not a luxury. Your spiritual path and your writer's journey are the basis for your existence.

While you attend to the responsibilities of your daily life, you must not forget to nourish your Spirit. Don't feel guilty about journaling because you think you should be writing your book or proposal or doing something more worthwhile. As you may have already discovered, with the awareness that journal-writing brings and the way it exercises your voice, your writing will be easier and better with the journal than without.

And when you take care of your daily responsibilities, don't feel guilty that you are not writing in your journal. You have a lifetime to explore and grow in Spirit and writing. You can keep this journal until your final moments on earth, and you will always learn something new. I would never want to give a fellow writer a reason to be more neurotic and anxious than we already tend to be! Writing in the first place takes a certain amount of anxiety and adrenaline, so don't waste it worrying about your journal.

It can be productive to begin journal-writing sessions with a prayer, a special thought, some affirmation, or even petting your cat—anything that makes you feel calm and focused.

But there can also be benefits to writing when you are the least centered. Sometimes it is helpful to write while you are agitated. Anger at life and God or others is undoubtedly part of the rhythm of life and has a place in your journal. Throw some pots if you want to. Scream! The spiritual path is not all rainbows, ethereal music, or fellowship.

Follow along with your lessons as if they are a translation of the language of your life. Your willingness to accept your challenges and to learn from them will directly influence your path. This is not all hindsight.

Why repeat lessons if you can learn them? Awareness allows you to make different decisions the next time.

Before you begin this part of your writer's journey, I would like to leave you with this prayer:

May the beloved creator of your understanding be with you on your spiritual and writer's journey.

And may these lessons and exercises give you the insights and confidence you need to sustain you on your path.

Exercises.

Each time you write in your journal, which for some of you can certainly be done through a keyboard, choose one of the Seven Lessons and then ask yourself a question, such as those below. Of course, you don't have to start with a question. Sometimes contemplation or anger can reveal things that you had not considered. As with everything spiritual, get out of the way. Let your Spirit be free. Find your authentic voice and connection with the divine.

Have there been examples of this lesson in my life?

Have I learned this lesson?

Do I have more to learn?

What were the circumstances around this lesson?

Have I experienced this lesson before?

Why do I keep repeating this lesson?

What does this lesson mean to me?

How do the qualities implied by this lesson influence my writer's journey?

What do I see as my vulnerabilities?

What can I learn from this lesson?

How can this lesson change how I live my life?

When did I first believe in my ideas over others?

Have I had to defend my beliefs?

What is my mission, and what obstacles do I face in carrying it out?

Have I ever felt resistance from a person but persisted only to get nowhere?

How has God been present in my life today?

Can I see a pattern in my circumstances?

Am I being aware of others around me and setting firm boundaries?

Am I reinforcing my worthiness to be loved?

Am I taking care of myself in a loving way?

Am I keeping my ego in balance?

Am I reminding myself that I am a messenger and not the message?

Do I see the light of God in other people?

Do I have empathy?

Do I believe my life is not random but part of an interconnected web of God's light?

Can people hurt me with their words?

What words hurt me the most?

When am I the most vulnerable?

What situations cause me not to believe in myself?

How do I move past them?

How long does it take to feel whole?

Do I ever feel whole?

You might want to add some questions to help you focus on the book you want to write or the message you want to convey.

What am I most passionate about?

What do I know the most about that might benefit someone else?

Why do I want to write?

How will writing change me?

How can I describe my mission in as few sentences as possible?

This last one is a bit of a trick. When writing anything, you want to be focused like a laser on what you are trying to say, why you are saying and who will listen.

And lastly, picture your ideal reader. Do you have a sense of your tribe? Where do you feel you belong?

4

WHY SPIRITUAL WRITERS WRITE AND OTHER UNIQUE CHALLENGES

I first wrote this book in the early 2000s to respond to the submissions we received at the agency where well-meaning writers claimed things like "God told me to write this." Or "my psychic told me I will have a bestseller." We also received channeled work that was unedited with claims that the work had to be published right away precisely as presented. Many agents and editors dismissed this work out of hand, but I was straddling the publishing business world and a somewhat unconventional spiritual path. Who was I to judge or say that God didn't tell someone to write a book or that a psychic was wrong? What I did feel qualified to address was that many people felt called to a spiritual mission with no idea how to approach publishing protocols. I didn't want to relegate these writers to the "woo woo" pile like many other agents were doing, so I first started teaching "writing as a spiritual journey" and eventually wrote this book.

Here are some facts for spiritual writers:

1. Don't say God told you to write the book even if it is true.
2. Understand that God's time and linear time are different things.
3. Conventional publishing is on a one to two-year timeframe, so no book will come out when you want it to.
4. All writing needs a good editor, even if it is directly from the Source.
5. Your work is not so urgent that the world will end if it is not published.
6. You will need to invest in your book to make it successful either

monetarily or with a lot of hard work.

7. You have as much of a chance as anyone else if you learn about the business of publishing and take it seriously.

As we saw in the discussion about the Seven Lessons and how they relate to spiritual writing, while you are sharing your insight and wisdom with others through the act of writing, your wisdom increases many times over, almost as though you are being taught by your own hand. If you have a calling to write, if there is an inner voice begging to be heard, you are already blessed. There are no better means through which to grow and become enriched. You may not believe it now, but no matter how hard you try, even with all the information and tips you will read in the following chapters, you might not reach your goal of a traditionally published book. Not everyone needs to be published by (name the publishing house of choice or your imagination) to be successful.

You may pursue the non-traditional route of publishing or choose to self-publish and reach only ten people. That is a real statistic. Or maybe it is folklore that self-published books typically sell only ten copies. But I think it is true.

You can fulfill your mission and dream in many ways. Your goal of being published may not be your true destiny. Just because someone tells you to write a book doesn't mean you ought to. I have often heard that someone had such an exciting life that their friends told them they needed to write a book. I hope you have an exciting life because that is the essence of the spiritual journey. However, a book can only succeed if there is a reader who wants it. If someone insists you need to write a book or your psychic says, "I see you writing a book," tell them to sit in front of a computer screen for hours while turning their Soul inside out. You can journal, write for enjoyment, and connect to Spirit in amazing ways. No one need ever read that for it to be worthwhile.

But if you are significantly motivated and want to be published, remember the spiritual path has many mysteries. As you may have discovered, sometimes it's best to go along for the ride and to have faith in what unfolds.

A common thread in the submissions we received when I was curating for our literary agency in this genre is the sense that the writer has figured out some profound truth. This discovery is the essence of "Aha!"—the moment when the Spirit and intellect collide and form a union of consciousness. Understandably, when a person decodes some of the hidden languages of reality, she feels compelled to share it with others. We are all teachers by nature. When your pilot is lit, and your flame bursts forth, you can become engulfed—so caught up in the ecstatic experience of awakening that you can lose your grounding.

This can be a vulnerable time for those on the spiritual path because it is when we can be too anxious to share what we have learned. We run the risk of distracting ourselves and losing our discernment.

We can also forget that we are not only teachers; we will always be students. We never teach anything that we have not needed to learn or are not still learning ourselves. Sometimes we want to share our understanding before it is fully developed and rush into trying to get it published.

Some say that each of us writes the book we need to read! You will see more clearly what this need for discernment means as you read through the chapters of this book. For example, while you want to present yourself as a person qualified to write on a spiritual subject, if you proclaim yourself the only and final authority about it, you will probably ruin your chances of being published. You will put a tremendous burden on yourself to prove this. A humble attitude combined with healthy self-promotion is always the best policy. This way, you will not do a disservice to your truth and the essence of your message. You will learn to write with authority but not from a place of infallibility. As you pursue your spiritual path, you will find that all truth comes from the same Source, and no one human being has a corner on it.

It isn't easy to imagine that at the first writing of this book, there were only the earliest signs of the burgeoning opportunity of self-publishing and easy access to direct upload. Amazon publishing and all the other platforms were in their infancy, as was E-book publishing. Think about that. Websites were happening but not with the ease of drag and drop platforms, and blogging was not a thing. This was even before Myspace became a place for teenagers to connect with friends and Facebook wasn't yet a twinkle in Mark Zuckerberg's mind, although we don't know that for sure. He may have been born with the idea.

The focus of the first version of this book was to help the misunderstood spiritual writer navigate the waters of the publishing industry. I remember when agents and editors didn't know what to do with this material. They believed people claiming to have mystical experiences were too fringe to make it in the mainstream of publishing. I was motivated to write the book because I was an agent, spiritual writer, and intuitive teacher and understood these writers' challenges. Even if a writer was in a "traditional" religious genre, there were still unknown challenges and protocols. For example, a layperson who wanted to write a new interpretation of the *Bible* would not get very far. Most submissions we received from Christian writers wanted to do just that. I saw them fitting in with the same challenges as more general spiritual writers who felt a Divine calling and connection to Spirit but with no guidance on what to do about it.

The ease of self-publishing made it easier for people with "fringe" ideas to upload books to places like Amazon.com, lulu, Smashwords, book baby, and on and on. Today there are numerous platforms. The problem became the ease of access flooded the book market with marginal projects and many disappointed writers.

I found this firsthand when in 2013, I was offered the chance to take over a self-publishing website. The person who started it no longer had the time to run it. I completed my MBA certifications with the Rutgers mini-MBA program in digital marketing and social media strategy, which gave me a different perspective. After being in the business for so long, it seemed like a great match. I discovered that many writers were uploading books to the system and having the books distributed online with minimal results. The idea was great, but after curating titles for the literary agency for so long, I could see why the authors were unsuccessful. The books were not well-edited, the covers were not customized, and there was no marketing strategy.

For me, the biggest concern was the poorly edited books. It went against my sensibility as an author, editor, and literary agent who spent so long helping authors perfect their book proposals. My husband Jeff Herman and I had written the book *Write the Perfect Book Proposal: Ten Proposals that Worked and Why*, and it went against my conscience to know why these books were not competitive with the traditionally published offerings and not do something about it. My only natural choice was to close that website and rebrand and restructure as my indie publishing company Micro Publishing Media, Inc. No matter where you choose, authors should try to recreate the advantages of traditional publishing houses. It is difficult to do this independently without a huge learning curve, but not impossible.

We created an alternative to simple upload or traditional publishing by offering the services needed to bring a book from curation to success. Many high-quality hybrid publishing companies provide the same support. Books need the following:

1. Curation: someone with professional experience must determine if a book is viable and if there is a market for it.
2. Developmental Editing: Very few books arrive at a publisher's desk ready to go. If you go the nontraditional publishing route, you still need to give it the benefit it would receive with a professional publisher.
3. Copy Editing: This is very different from developmental editing. This type of editing is essentially proofreading to prepare the book for design.
4. You should never rely solely on yourself to do this critical task.
5. Professional design: If you are familiar with design software, give it a shot. The platforms with easy upload can provide this for you, but it will most likely look self-published.
6. A professional book cover: The self-publishing platforms provide free cover generators, but you need to know what works. Very few of these covers look like anything but what they are.

We will discuss these alternatives further in the nuts-and-bolts section of the book. I want to clarify from the outset that ease of access will not be an answer for you if you are looking for publishing success. It becomes a form of arrogance when writers think they know better than publishing professionals. We make it look too easy. Be patient and learn your craft. This includes how to be professionally published. You can become a self-publisher, choose to work with an author services company or a hybrid publisher (there is a distinction between them) or seek and succeed with a traditional publishing route. There have never been as many opportunities for spiritual writers as now to fulfill your mission. You just need to be willing to learn the protocols.

Many spiritual writers choose to self-publish for what I consider to be questionable reasons. They may simply be impatient with the process and want to jump to the experience of seeing their words in print with their name on the cover. You can do this easily in today's world. But maybe your book, if given time and the proper education and input, may be suitable for the traditional publishing route. Or, if you find the right hybrid publisher to shepherd you through creating a good book, you will find more professional success. Or, if you gestate the idea and learn the craft, you can succeed on your own.

If you lack patience, you may push it out before it is ready. The first consideration is whether your book is professionally written. You want your self-published book to be able to stand tall next to books that are traditionally published. There is a reason that publishing companies are willing to pay for the books they choose to publish. These books are vetted and edited to represent that house's quality. They also need to develop a good "word of mouth" audience because they are of high enough quality to warrant such great reviews. If you want to self-publish, you must still learn how to compete in the big leagues. Give your work the best chance you can so it can succeed in the general marketplace. Self-publishing/micro-publishing is gaining credibility. You must then learn how to promote your traditionally or self-published books.

The priority should be learning your craft to reflect the quality of the message. You may also want to hire a professional editor who has worked in traditional publishing to enhance the readiness of your work before you invest in the self-publishing route. Some companies, including my own, offer hybrid publishing, conversion to E-books, and distribution channels at affordable prices. Then others charge a great deal of money with empty promises. This is the time for your Self-Protection due diligence lesson to kick in. Make sure what you are getting is worth what you spend. It is very tempting to jump ahead. Take the time to ensure your book is as good as it can be. Research and compare companies if you plan to work with author service companies and publishing professionals. You are investing in yourself and your work. Who knows, you may become the next breakthrough book that receives a substantial licensing deal from a major publisher. The sky is the limit if you take the time to learn the craft and the tools.

I am explaining alternative publishing routes and the way to be professional, even if relatively on your own, because there are fewer opportunities out there than there used to be. For example, I happened to run into an executive from one of the largest publishing companies visiting near where I live. I had no idea who he was until we started discussing books. I was genuinely shocked when he said they look for people with social media followings in the millions. I doubt that is true for every house, but I believe they see those numbers as a sign of success. As a digital marketing strategist, I know those numbers do not necessarily reflect an author's reach, but that is a number they see and can use to base their decisions. It used to be recommendations from talk shows.

I don't' want you to be discouraged by this. You are not necessarily looking for this route to publishing. You can improve your following and prove your market but writing from your assigned mission is more critical. My goal with this new edition is to give you every avenue to reach your readers. You may gain a following that impresses editors who have been on the job even before the internet became a factor. They have always looked at the authors at the highest echelon of reach. It is always about what the author brings to the table that will sell books. But you have a more expansive role. You are trying to reach your intended audience. Whether you find a traditional publisher or do it independently, you can do that. There are also publishing houses along the spectrum, from hybrid to the top five, now the top four. I mention the top four because the conglomerates are changing every day. Even industry insiders can't keep up with it. The conglomerates are like the classic sci-fi movie *The Blob*. Without consciousness, they keep absorbing each other into one big piece of gelatinous goo. That is a cynical overstatement. I long for the days when the publishing houses had smaller imprints with defined personalities. The acquisition editors at that time had a certain number of smaller books they could take on without having such a high expectation of return. That meant more opportunities to discover new voices that were yet untried. But everything always looks better in retrospect, and as spiritual beings, we hope to live in the True Present. The true present for spiritual writers has many more challenges but many more ways to get where you need to go.

Some good news is that all spiritual disciplines are experiencing a renaissance, making this an excellent time to be a writer in this genre. Once dismissive of New Age or religious work, the publishing industry is now recognizing spiritual awakening as something more than a fad. If you can develop your craft, voice, and credibility, you could have a great career ahead of you! More importantly, the readers are ready for this material and have shown this repeatedly to the traditional publishing world.

Significantly, entire independent houses are devoted to spiritual and transformational material. This also spells excellent news for those who choose to go the non-traditional route or to self-publish. The pioneers of this genre have paved the way for you. They have proven a market, and if you examine the types of books that sell, you can keep your finger on the pulse of what people want to read. Remember to tap into your authentic voice and message. Just because someone is thriving in a specific type of niche does not mean you will be. Spiritual writers are called to their individual messages and missions. Make sure you are not imitating someone because you think that is the way to success. Learn from what people are doing right but apply it to your unique message.

There is constant flux in the traditional and conglomerate publishing world, but over the years since the first edition of this book, spiritual and transformational material crossed over into the mainstream. Even if there are fewer opportunities because the bigger fish have swallowed up the imprints and indie publishers, you can count on the fact there are readers out there who want what you have.

No longer do we need to apologize for our "fringe" beliefs. By utilizing digital marketing and making yourself "searchable" online, you can ring your audience to you. Make it your mantra that writers write and readers read. And there is a much bigger audience for spiritual work and transformational books than publishers and agents realized at the turn of the millennium.

You are a Conduit and an Important Participant.

When you are in the flow of writing, have you ever sensed that you do not know where this energy comes from? Do you feel the words are channeled from some source outside of you? This Source is both within and without. You are linking yourself with the Source of all creation.

But you are not a simple conduit—you are essential to the process. This writing comes from you and your connection to God working hand in hand. You choose to be a vessel for this information. Commend yourself. God and the Angels will. You bring the Divine into the Earth by your willingness to do the hard work and to take the time to make it manifest.

You may have reached the point on your path where your writing seems effortless. For those of you who aren't there yet, take heart. You may not believe it now, but spiritual writing can be effortless if you continue to develop spiritually, follow your path, and surrender to faith. The less resistance you have, the more empowered you become because you can draw on the resources of the universe around you. You can learn to let go. You can reach inside for this link and let its inspiration spill out. It doesn't mean you won't have to go back and edit, but the initial process can be filled with joy.

The seven spiritual lessons highlighted in chapter Two and your Soul's progress on your spiritual path form the foundation of the message you ultimately present for publication. As you develop in your lessons, you grow in your writing. You are moving forward as your writing advances, and your link to God strengthens. When you feel clear about what you are writing and why skip to part two to learn the publishing protocols.

When ready to send your message to the world, have confidence in your work. Although the spiritual path is never-ending, there is a point when you will choose to move your writing to the next step. Keep in mind that you may not succeed right away. I can't stress enough that you, the reader of this updated edition of this book, have far more opportunities to see your book in print or digital form than existed when this book was first created in the ethers. In 2002, few agents or editors knew what to do with spiritually oriented books. Now we live in the age of communication when you all can spread your messages. Remember the responsibility in what you present as you take advantage of the accessibility. Reread chapter two if you forget.

Even if you ultimately decide to self-publish or find a hybrid publisher, many of whom will publish your book with little discernment as to its merits, make sure you have something that passes the test of being a high-quality spiritual messenger. You will know if you approach it from the right place and for the right reasons.

Always ask Spirit to guide you in your writing; then, you can't go wrong. Becoming a luminary in the new thought, spiritual publishing world seems glamourous. Stop here if your only goal is to be a household word and a rich and famous author. That may be the result, and you may manifest all that for yourself. But if that is the goal and you do not feel called to a particular message, it will not bring light into the world other than illuminating your ego and bank account. As we discussed in the Ego lesson section, there is nothing wrong with promotion and book sales. But the center point has got to be passion and an authentic message. Then learn all the tools you need to bring the message to as many people as possible, and Spirit will do the rest.

We all work for the same universe. What you do affects everyone else. Blessings are sent your way for a glorious experience as a spiritual writer, and I am sharing tools for a successful career at it. I will do my best to get you there with everything I have learned in my twenty-five-plus years as a writer, mystic, spiritual teacher, and literary agent. After you have written your book, review the advice on these pages, look objectively at your work, show it to others, and keep writing! Then you can launch it into the world. Learn to be Patient. You can't blow your mission.

One thing to remember is God's time and our time are two entirely different things. You may feel an urgency about your work, but you cannot control the realities of the publishing world. The best you can do is to learn all you can to maximize your chances of breaking through the common obstacles that await you on the road to publication. Your book does not need to be published by a specific date to fulfill your mission. Too many spiritual writers are concerned that they could mess up some Divine plan if their work is not published immediately.

You aren't the one in control of the Divine plan. Be sure you aren't confusing the urgency to publish with your Soul's desire to move ahead on your path. Have faith. We are beacons, and our power and contribution are to bring more love, light, and hope into the world. For this task, timing is infinite.

The universe is abundant, but we must be realistic and responsible. In the world of Spirit, anything is possible. In the physical world, we achieve nothing without roll-up-the-sleeves hard work. You will face many challenges through the writer's journey toward a sale. But you have the same chances as anyone.

Follow the advice in this book and be clear with your vision. Be objective and take the time to organize your project in the most professional manner possible. If you balance your sense of mission with your knowledge of the publishing industry, you will significantly increase your chances of success. Finally, be flexible with how you will reach your goal. Control what you can and see where the path takes you.

What are the Obstacles for Spiritual Writers?

The journey can be challenging. Most writers will encounter significant barriers on the road to finding their most natural and comfortable writing style. And there is more to a spiritual style than the words on paper. The life of a spiritual writer does not begin or end with the book you publish.

Spiritual Writer's Block.

I once had a conversation with one of my favorite Chassidic rabbis. Chassidic rabbis are strictly orthodox with long beards and a belief in the more mystical aspects of Judaism. Rabbis are respected in my home because we are not strict observers and feel humbled by their faith. When my children, who were Bar and Bat Mitzvah age, found out the rabbi was on his way, they ran around the house, cleaning—a miracle in itself—and saying, "The rabbi is coming, the rabbi is coming!"

The rabbi knew I was a writer, and during our conversation about my son's Bar Mitzvah, he asked me for advice: "I am having trouble with an article I am writing. It is for the Jewish newspaper. Writing two paragraphs takes me hours, and then I hate them anyway."

I was surprised that this knowledgeable and respected teacher was stumped over the same issue that I face every time I sit down to write. However, considering how many ways I have learned to procrastinate, even choosing to learn website construction over working on my book, I could understand his angst. At least he was asking me something in my territory. I said, "Rabbi, I think I know the problem."

He looked at me expectantly with those all-knowing rabbi eyes as I continued: "You have so much faith in God and believe so strongly that anything you teach is as an emissary of God that you feel unable to write well enough to do it justice. In other words, you try too hard."

He paused for a few minutes and pondered my words, pulling on the untrimmed ends of his beard in a gesture characteristic of great thinkers. "I believe you are right, Deborah," he replied.

"Phew," I thought. I figured I was on a roll, so I continued: "Any spiritual writer is going to feel this way. We are our own worst critics because we have so much respect for God's authority. But language is by its nature a limited medium. God has no limitations, but we must work with what we have. If we examine every word as we write it, we will never complete anything. All we will have is a string of perfect words with no heart."

"So maybe I should write from the heart first and go back and fix it later," he said. I should have known he would catch on quickly.

"Exactly," I replied. "You are a wonderful speaker because you are confident when you have an immediate connection with your students. You can correct yourself if you believe you have spoken unclearly. You have an element of control. When you write, you are sending your words off into the world and have to trust that they will reach the right people and be understood. There is no immediate connection with your audience. You don't see their response and can only wonder about it."

"Or worry about it," he laughed. " I can hardly watch anyone reading something I have written. I feel like they are scrutinizing every word."

"If you write from your heart, you don't have to worry about how it will be read. You can fix it mechanically, as any good editor can, but you will know that you have captured the essence of what you have to say the best you can. When writing spiritually, it is the Spirit that is important."

"Then I can get something written instead of taking hours to write two paragraphs that will wind up in the wastebasket anyway."

"You have a lot of important things to say that inspire people," I said. "You just need to relax about it a little."

I can't imagine this rabbi relaxing, but the lesson is true, nonetheless. Trying too hard to reflect what we believe is the awesome nature of what we write about can paralyze us and make us unable to write at all. As messengers, it is good to have a healthy respect for what we are writing, but we need to understand the limitations of communication. Spiritual writing must be set free, or its energy will stagnate. It is meant to be shared. This often means it is intended to be shared in its imperfection. This does not mean it is acceptable to write badly. It means that sometimes good enough is good enough in the energy transmission scheme. Learn what you can, edit your work, have others read it who are not related to you or owe you money, and you are on your way.

As we learned with the Self-Love lesson, many writers hesitate because they are afraid of not being good enough. In the next chapter, I will explain how to structure your thoughts into a book. You can learn how to write a book if you have a message and a passion. Focus on the fact that you have a unique perspective. If you feel compelled to write, assume that you have the ability.

If you can get your fears out of the way and tap into the Divine, you will have no reason to think otherwise. I had the advantage of an education in both Law and Journalism. I knew I wanted to write before realizing I was on a Spiritual Path. This education helped me later when I was learning about book proposals and writing books, but in some ways, my early spiritual journey hindered me from writing from my passion. I was confident in writing but lacked clarity and confidence in the messages. I didn't understand the importance of finding my voice and that there would be people who wanted to hear what I had to say. The positive response to the first edition of this book helped me rise above these limiting thoughts. But who am I kidding? My Self-Love lesson has haunted me throughout this revision as I reveal more of my story and truth. I want to help you, but I want you to like me. And I am sure as many of you write your "important" books, you may feel the same.

And as I have been revisiting the Seven Lessons in this updated book, I realize how much easier it is to live in the esoteric and spiritual world. Writing is like being free and floating in the air. It is when we are in the world that things get hinky. That is why spiritual writers and other creatives like to hang around each other and speak the same language. My sister is a gifted medium, and sometimes, when we call each other, we joke, "so how am I doing today?" We like to gossip about our family members, but it is even more fun to tap into the other realms to see what comes through. Don't worry, we are careful. She is still scared from her first séance. And my sister let me be the one to pave the way in our community, where I was practically vilified. Then a few years later, she accepted her gifts and hung her shingle as a spiritual counselor. We have a very interesting family.

When you spend time with people not interested in spirituality, you can feel like you have something to hide. Thank God there are ways to find our people. There is also much more tolerance and acceptance of these subjects than in 2002. I am excited to be reintroducing this book because I believe so many of us are being awakened to your paths on a higher level. There have been so many shifts in energy that they are palpable.

The energy was very different when I had my first spiritual group in Ohio in the late 80s to mid-1990s. We explored spirituality on a much more elementary level, and much of the information came through for the first time. I was teaching about the "Seven Lessons of Soul Odyssey "and learning simultaneously." The people I meet now seem to have a greater knowledge and acceptance. However, I also see people succumbing to negativity and forgetting the power of high vibration. On a positive note, I see a measurable shift from "I" to "we," as people realize that many of us are receiving similar messages. The advent of social media has helped us find each other so we can compare notes. It helps us know that we are not entirely bonkers and can find the pieces of our Soul puzzles by comparing notes. I also see a positive change in comparing various religious structures to one another.

Except for fanatical people who want others to see the world only the way they see it, I am experiencing a joining of faiths into a spiritual recognition of the creator as the same guide for all of us. I hope many of you who find your message and voice will continue encouraging this with your work. The more unified we are in love and light, the better we are. This is the true sustainability of our planet.

We are also being asked to "up our game" in helping bring positive change to this world. Therefore, I wanted to ensure that you, the spiritual writers and messengers of today, can navigate the changing world of publishing. The first edition of this book was entirely focused on how to obtain a traditional publishing contract. It did not anticipate print-on-demand possibilities or E-books because they did not exist as they do now. It did not predict how you can build a platform to rival those who have been pounding the pavement for years with some digital know-how. Your voices can be heard whether you become the next bestselling household name, which may be the best reason to do this.

You may only need to reach a certain number of people in your so-called "Soul circle." Your mission might be to connect with those people who will help you on your path as you teach them what they need for their own. Once again, I want to stress that writing is a worthwhile endeavor. If you want to make money doing it, you must be clever and utilize the left brain you have been given. Activate those business aspects of your DNA. It can be fun. In law school, I wanted nothing to do with corporate law or business. Now I am itching to learn all I can. It is a good balance.

I am returning to my healing work and Spiritual writing because I felt called. It felt like it was the right time. I never share anything that I haven't had to learn myself. I have a great deal of experience in writing non-fiction books and in knowing the ins and outs of the industry, but you have the advantage of living and writing in a time when this kind of material is welcomed. You can write your authentic spiritual message from the outset, not build it into more mainstream books until you can find a way to bring your notes into the world. You don't have to straddle the fence of two worlds, one of Spirit and one of writing.

What Should you Write?

Writing nonfiction is as creative a process as fiction-writing, but it depends on factual information. Because we affect how people feel and influence what they know, we must be vigilant about the accuracy of what we convey. Spiritual writing is not science, however. We do not typically have statistical data to back up our anecdotal evidence that something does or does not exist. We often rely on observation or opinion, writing from faith and belief. Religious writers can refer to scriptural references for examples and support. Spiritual writers may not even have this kind of tangible information to bolster their messages.

Many publishers are looking for applied Spirituality, which may have more tangible subject matter. They like books on quantum physics and things readers can take into their own lives. Don't let that stop you from writing what is in your heart. Remember the difference between what the traditional commercial market may want and what you need to write. Then go about approaching them accordingly.

You have an advantage if you have built a following of people who believe and admire what you say. You need to focus on a specific message. There is a vast universe out there. Before you set out to write a book, search within for your greatest passion and how you feel you can best approach an audience. This is the groundwork that you must do before you begin. It is great to take courses and learn your craft, but everything in your life is part of this journey. Don't spend a lot of money for things you think you need to know or to add a gazillion fans to your Facebook page before you truly understand what you want to say and why you want to say it. You may be called to write fiction. If that is so and you have a story brewing, commit to it and help give it life. The way to begin writing is from the inside out. Find your Divine connection and inner voice, and then build from there.

You can learn how to put those thoughts into a commercial context. If you have a book in you, you can work with professionals to help you draw it out and refine it, but the message's depth must come from you.

Make Sure you Stay Grounded.

As spiritual people, some of us risk becoming ungrounded, like hot-air balloons without a rope. When we taste the Divine, it can be beyond description. Of course, we then set out to describe and share our experiences. But once we become aware of our spiritual mission, we must realize that we are not the only ones with an assignment. Naturally, the spiritual experience is different for everyone. But I have seen writers, including myself, become so caught up in our own experience that we write about it in the form of spirit-babble. If we want to share our experiences with others, we must make them relevant and understandable to the reader.

Much of what we do here on earth is to learn to relate, not to Spirit, but our physical reality. When we place too much importance on our spirituality, we forget that we must set real-world priorities. If we can ground ourselves, we can write in a way that can resonate with people who are not necessarily on our spiritual frequency. One strategy for accomplishing this is learning to tether yourself to the real world and recognize the importance of day-to-day activities as a means of grounding. Here are a few tips for staying grounded:

Stay Financially Solvent.

Many of us would rather not deal with budgets and other annoying details of life. Even if your spiritual advisor has said you will write a book and be successful at it, remember that Spirit is not operating with the laws in this dimension. It is up to you to keep things real. Don't give up your day job to write unless you have Savings.

Plan for your Goals Without Waiting for Fate to Take Over.

We want to flow with spirit, but we do not want to float without direction. Learn how others do it. I have co-founded a social network for writers to help you do this: Writers Networking: www.writersnetworking. com. Find like-minded people and compare notes. Be willing to be open to advice from others without feeling ashamed that you may not always have the adulting skills. Creative people often skip steps in development. To be honest, a disproportionate number of us are not neurotypical. This makes doing life harder than it seems for other people. But we can learn. Just don't beat yourself up over it. And remember, the Self-Love lesson encourages us to ask for help when needed. We are not designed to be perfect and excellent at everything.

Engage in Activities that Require Focus and Concentration.

The simple act of washing dishes helps with focus. I am not insinuating that spiritual people are messy, but I know I can spend days lost in creative thought without realizing that I am wading in a sea of dust and clutter.

Engage in Physical Activities, Such as Gardening.

You and everyone else know that exercise is good for your health, but I, for one, find every excuse not to do it. Don't add guilt to your agenda. It doesn't matter what you do. Doing something physical will help you avoid living only in your mind.

Care for Animals.

Dogs and cats are loving and healing companions, but they also require that you take care of them. They do not grow out of the need to be fed and walked. I bought myself a sweet trail horse who, in 2013, galloped off into the heavenly sunset at 30 or so. My relationship with him was one of the most significant. We came together at a particularly challenging time in my life, and I learned many lessons from him. One of the things I learned was to stay focused on physical reality. If I lost concentration, I could get hurt or stepped on. It wouldn't have been the horse's fault; it would have been mine. I have another lovely horse who is like a large dog. He has a sense of humor and keeps me on my toes.

Involve Yourself in Relationships with Real People.

You can live a monastic life if you believe it will bring you closer to God. However, it doesn't make sense that God would put us here with all these people if we weren't somehow supposed to learn to relate to them. Don't use your spirituality as a means of isolation. Instead, allow yourself to share the love to bring balance into your relationships. Again, writersnetworking.com is a good source for you if you can't get out to meet people. We plan future meetups and have a group just for Spiritual Writing and Publishing.

Refocus your Attention.

Stop everything, breathe, and take notice of the here and now. Learn to work with Crystals. Even though I can never remember the different stones, I like to hold them in my hand. They are comforting and energizing.

These are just a few of so many possible ways to stay balanced. So, naturally, you will want to look at your life and find what works best.

Another Form of Grounding is to Stay Accessible:

Another strategy for staying accessible to readers in the "real" world is to develop the mental discipline to write in a focused manner that can be understood by the uninitiated. As writers, you can do the following to make sure your message is clear:

Outline.

When you write, strive for clarity and connection. As spiritual writers, we may think we can write without any boundaries. Letting words flow is a great start, but the structure is imperative.

Outlines are your friends. They are necessary and are the best way to establish mental discipline for your writing.

Edit.

I don't recommend editing while writing if it will interrupt your flow. As you read over your work, try to ensure you are not writing so far above the average reader's head that you only understand what you are talking about. As you edit, remember that someone will be reading what you have written. People are at all levels of spiritual awareness. If you trust Spirit, there will be enough in your work to meet the needs of all kinds of seekers. Keep the language clear and well organized. Make it user-friendly. Don't try too hard to impress or educate. In many ways, try to keep yourself out of it. Even if you are writing a memoir, look at yourself as if you were a different person and observe how you appear in the pages of your manuscript. Create distance, and then imbue your "character" with the feelings and characteristics that breathe life into it. Too personal and egocentric writing will prevent a reader from becoming involved. Leave room for your reader to have thoughts, feelings, and interpretations.

To summarize, remember your audience, the world around you, and how you fit into the mainstream. If your message is too far away from everyone, you can be sure that few people will be "ready" for it. I have heard many editors lament that the spiritual material they receive is unfocused, esoteric, or too "out there,"—and these comments come from spirit-friendly editors who want to find quality spiritual manuscripts.

They would like nothing more than for you to write in a focused way so they can acquire your manuscript and fulfill the growing need for quality spiritual material. It bears repeating that even if you self-publish, you must ensure your manuscript meets the level of clarity of a traditionally published book. Hire an editor to do what I call a "first read." When I do it, I read the book from beginning to end as if I had just bought it at a store. I do not want to know much about it as I want to have a stream-of-consciousness reaction. I write in the margins and then tell the writer its strengths and weaknesses. If I feel like putting it aside after 25 pages, that is certainly something to consider. A professional first reader can also determine if the book needs more anecdotes in the case of nonfiction and where they should go. In the case of a novel, a professional reader can decide if the story flows and maintains the characterization and pacing to make for a good book. It is worth the investment because traditionally published books have this extra set of professional eyes.

The case against self-publishing from the outside world has always been that they are amateurish. This perception is no longer the case for those authors who treat this as a serious business and are willing to learn the craft or go the next step in hiring the kind of editor they would have at a traditional house. Engaging professionals is a worthwhile investment if comparing all the ways you can spend money. Do not release books prematurely. It is easy today to do so. Respect your work and give it the chance to thrive. As more and more people Self-publish and build the credibility of the books in the marketplace, there will undoubtedly be more opportunities for distribution channels.

Be Clear About your Purpose.

You are getting ready to write your book. You have thought about your passion and message. Now take one more look at why you want to be a writer. Be clear about what it is you want from your writing. Then, it will respond to you.

- Do you want it to help you reflect and deepen your understanding of life and its happenings?
- Do you want to publish your words so they are out there for whoever can find value in them?
- Or do you want nothing less than a blockbuster?

Being clear about this within yourself is important because you are setting expectations. You are putting things in motion but may also create a self-fulfilling prophecy if your goals do not match your path. Examine your motives and be honest with yourself.

Worry and self-doubt can quickly get in the way of the spiritual writer achieving the desired results. If these become your focus, you may cancel out your original intent. The result? Your fears, not your goals, will be realized.

So be clear about your objectives. You're a writer, so write down your plan—and be specific. For example, "I will be published by an independent publisher and hold two monthly seminars to enhance my book sales. I will build a social media platform and blog consistently." Write your goal daily if that's what it takes to keep it in the forefront of your mind.

The preceding example reflects an end goal. How about the many steps it takes to get there? They won't just happen without your conscious commitment. That's where this book comes in. After you read it and learn what it takes to get published, make a monthly plan of actions leading to your final desired result. Work with devoted determination to your goal of the month. Then let go. Let the universe and its helpers arrange the details. Get out of the way!

I know I am making this sound too easy. I am someone who wants to make changes but often will start and then stop. I imagine I am not the only person who does this. However, I have found through experience that writing down these notes and goals works as well as keeping track of your food intake if you want to lose weight. I resist limits and rules at every turn, but consciously taking control helps prevent the embedded subconscious thoughts from ruling your life.

I mean this. I decided to do a bit more self-revelation in this new edition of this book so it didn't sound like I was giving you a ton of advice that I didn't have to learn or implement in my life. Twenty years after the first edition of this book, I find myself well into middle age, some would say early senior, but I will never relate to that even though my grown children are a giveaway. I thought I could not lose the extra pounds from a sedentary lifestyle, the COVID ten, and my aging metabolism. I didn't want to acknowledge that I was contributing to my steady weight plateau until I started using an app where I had to look at what I ate each day. I had been looking at all kinds of deep-seated reasons for the weight gain. Sure, some self-examination helped me see how much I genuinely hate external control of my decisions. Finally, I decided to look straight at what I was consuming daily, and when I stick with it, I can lose weight because I am being honest with myself and making lifestyle changes. Of course, I still face the often-losing battle with cookies, but I accept I am a work in progress.

It is the same with anything we think we "should" do but resist. Of course, there may be many reasons why we avoid the things we know will help us reach our desired results. But, that is what therapy is for, or use your Seven Lessons journal, as you will see in Chapter Three. However, whatever help you need in setting goals and following through with your dreams is as simple as writing down notes to yourself.

Remember to allow the universe to give you possibilities you may not have thought about.

Leave the door open for ideas to float into your consciousness from your Soul. Write your goals, make your plans, and stay present to see the signs.

Educating Yourself About the Publishing Experience.

It is helpful to create a vision for what you are planning. There is strong evidence that our thoughts lead us to ultimate attainment. As an aspiring published writer, you must also educate yourself to ensure that this is what you want it to do. For example, you may want to be published by a prominent New York publishing house because you believe that is the only way to reach the largest audience possible. That's a great goal, but do you know what it entails for you? You may have expectations that are based on the past. While publishing is alive and still kicking, the game has changed from when we started over twenty-five years ago. The Jeff Herman Agency, where I have worked, specializes in non-fiction. We have been known for some huge titles, but mostly we have been a mid-list literary agency.

This does not mean we have been mediocre with mediocre writers.

On the contrary, it simply means that the books we represent are more mainstream titles. The midlist was and to a lesser extent still is the bread and butter of the publishing world other than Romance and top-tier fiction. A house typically acquires a midlist book, expecting it to stay in print for a long time. After the initial introduction, they move the title to the backlist, where it can remain for many years. That becomes an asset of the publishing house that generates revenue for them. Print-on-demand technology has allowed many publishing houses to keep books on their backlist for a long time. They don't' invest much energy in promoting the books but look to them as a form of passive income without much effort.

The front list books are those that may have a celebrity attachment. A front list book can offer the enormous advances that authors think are common in the publishing world. The large advances are given to authors for books that the publishing houses believe will be blockbusters. It is the same idea that we see in the movie industry today. Blockbuster films, like those associated with superheroes, are called tentpole films. They have huge budgets, and studios expect them to bring box office returns to justify the investment. Most of them fulfill the expectations, with only a few independent films rising above the enormity of their revenue.

Publishing used to have more room for the smaller non-tentpole books with modest advances, but now the new authors are relegated to an ever-shrinking midlist. As with indie films, these books are given smaller advances and less effort on the part of the publishing house to promote them. The mid-list books are the ones that come out every season to fill out the catalog for the publishing houses. The difference is there are fewer publishing houses to which literary agents can submit books, and fewer books are acquired. The advances for mid-list books are also lower than in the past.

I do not intend to discourage you. The publishing world is in flux, as is the entire economy. Delivery systems change as many people read with E-readers, but they are still reading.

As you determine the direction you want to go with your publishing goals, I recommend you keep an open mind. If you say, "A New York conglomerate publishing house will publish me," you may fulfill your dream, and I can only hope the advice in this book will help you get there. But don't rule out other opportunities that a shift in understanding could open for you.

You certainly increase your chances of a traditional publishing contract if you bring savvy and marketing to the table. So many of us glaze over at the thought of marketing. We want to write and may just be getting used to the challenges of the mundane world. I still don't like bill paying, house cleaning, and other things that take me away from my bliss. But I am getting to like the challenges of marketing and promotion. I promise you; they can be fun once you get the hang of it.

If you want to go the major publisher route and are fortunate to have that opportunity, you can learn more about what that is like in Chapter Seven. If you want to learn more about publishing beyond what I can cover in this book, get out there and talk to other writers keeping in mind the caveat of professional competitiveness and that many people will take you down many rabbit holes. Take advice and information, discern what feels true to you, and always rely on optimistic and helpful sources. You don't need people projecting negativity on you and your chances of success.

You can connect with writers and some industry insiders through our social network: writersnetworking.com. A social network is only as active as its participants. Ours can go into stasis and then becomes activated depending on the users. You can make of it what you wish. It is a fun platform with some interesting and accomplished people who have signed up.

There are many writer communities on the internet. There are also writer's conferences you can attend. Although some moved to virtual meetings during the height of the pandemic, some are cautiously optimistic and meet in person. In addition, you can go to book signings and talk to the authors. Ask them about their publishing experience: Are they happy with the process? You may develop a connection if you meet authors who write on topics or in genres similar to yours. Networking is how people find authors to write forewords and endorsements for their books. My father, may he rest in peace, had a saying I loved. "If you don't ask, you don't get." While you shouldn't stalk anyone, most celebrities and writers always appreciate a professional and respectful meeting. Of course, there are some exceptions and many divas, but you don't need them anyway.

There are writer's groups on all social media. Check out the writer's communities on Linked In and Facebook. Be mindful of the time you spend in Cyberspace. We made our social network dedicated to writing, publishing, and insider education so you can take a break but still pursue your goals. I can't tell you how many hours I have swiped through TikTok videos and played mindless games on my smartphone. I value my time zoning out and also like to watch reruns of *Frasier*. I thought I was the only one, but I learned other people also find his voice soothing. I also learned through social media posts that people rewatch some shows repeatedly to alleviate anxiety. There is comfort in knowing what is going to happen. While I allow myself time for these indulgences, I can let time slip away if I am not careful. Creative energy is precious. It is essential to harness it.

Social media marketing is valuable to your success as a published writer. However, without a strategy, it can become a time suck. We will discuss ways to make it efficient for you and beneficial to ultimately monetizing a writing or speaking career. Time management is a challenge for everyone juggling a creative endeavor and daily life. Your priority is writing a good book. You can brand yourself and build a platform on your topic while writing your book but try not to give in to the temptation to jump into the publishing side of things until you are ready.

5

WRITING A SALEABLE BOOK

*A*ll the marketing in the world can't make up for a poorly written book. The chances of a traditional publisher taking on your book if you are a first-time author are not great. But we like to think positively and manifest excellent outcomes, so let's refocus on how to beat the odds. Unfortunately, even those spiritual writers with publishing histories can expect to have to jump through the publishing hoops each time they submit a new book. However, you can do so many things to make your book and submission package the best they can be.

I know an editor at a small imprint of a large company that receives ten thousand submissions each year. Between the four editors acquiring material, they publish sixty titles each year, and of these, maybe one or two are by first-time authors. Another small spirit-friendly publishing house receives approximately three thousand unsolicited submissions each year. They have only two acquisitions editors reviewing all the submissions. They publish perhaps twenty titles each year, of which only four or five are by first-time authors.

The Jeff Herman Agency receives from fifty to one hundred weekly submissions from writers seeking representation, of which we accept about 1 percent. We sell most of the books we agree to represent because we are highly selective. Note that newer agencies might represent a higher percentage of submissions but may not sell everything. Changes in the publishing industry have not altered how many books The Jeff Herman Agency selects for representation. Still, we see books that would have sold in the past rejected due to the higher threshold standards and fewer opportunities.

While innumerable spiritual books are submitted for publication each year, clearly only the best rise to the top, many publishers now pass on some of the best books despite the quality of the submission. Although it is a blessing to become a published writer, you can see that it also takes a lot of hard work to get there and that there are practical considerations you can't ignore. Now that you are fully warned, approach the obstacles head-on. The more you know about the hurdles, the more accurately you plan to glide over them.

THE CONTENT

Be wary of writing about personal journeys, vision quests, and stories of survival and triumph if there isn't something in it for the reader. These books tend to be written chronologically and are filled with details that mean a lot to the author but have little market appeal. Many publishers and agents will not look at such books unless the story is truly extraordinary. However, I love memoirs and believe everyone should write one if only to examine the course of one's life. If the writing is compelling enough and the story is structured well with an eye toward a universal theme, it can be well-received. I have added a guest essay and some advice on memoir writing in the addenda portion of this book.

It is unlikely that a mainstream publisher will consider a reinterpretation of a great religious work unless you have relevant scholarly credentials. Nevertheless, the temptation to write about great religious works from a new perspective is not uncommon for spiritual writers because often, part of your journey is tapping into Spiritual revelation. You will see things when you read and study universal texts that speak to you in a personal way. Please review the Tolerance lesson as you will find in Chapter Two, Seven Lessons of Spirit. Sometimes the new insights are just for you and do not need to be shared.

Always remember that people who read books have a specific need. They want to be entertained, uplifted, motivated, or given new information. They choose books they feel are relevant to them. Books have the power to raise consciousness and reach people emotionally, but the material can't be so personal to you that it has no value to anyone else. Your mantra should be "what is in it for my reader." This is not the opposite of what I have been saying about finding your message and mission. There is what is for you and your Soul and what you are meant to share. Sharing something that is only for you will not fulfill your mission. However, you can reposition any book to reach an audience if you know who they are and what they need. Then if what you have matches their need, you have a winner. Your readers are the ones who are going to plunk down the cash. There is a lot of competition for those dollars, including the necessities of life. You need to make it worth their while.

Spotting Trends to Know if your Book has a Place on the Shelves.

Now think of spiritual writing as your job. You may write for yourself, but if you plan to publish, the next step is to pay attention to the marketplace and educate yourself about the climate of the publishing industry before you shop your book around. Writers sometimes see trends in sync with what they want to write. But if you notice a lot of books on your topic, you are probably well behind the trend. There may still be a window for a book that presents a fresh perspective, but if you sense that a topic has been exhaustively presented, move on to something else. Instead, aim to spot emerging trends so that the timing of your book will be just right.

You can notice trends by simply observing life. Spiritual writers are blessed with the intuition that can help them see beyond what is in front of their faces. Look beyond the obvious and see how everything relates to everything else. We are all connected. Observation is the key.

The internet is a wellspring of resources. There are ways to find demographic information and trends. You can easily research things like "what is trending on Twitter." If you become social media savvy, you have every opportunity to keep up with what is on people's minds.

Although you may want to be socially distant (a little bit of sarcasm with the hope that readers will soon forget what that means), you can learn what is important to people by talking to strangers. You probably already know how to strike up conversations in the checkout line and how to listen to other people's conversations. Just make sure you are discreet! Some of us are already considered weird. Okay, I am referring to myself. You can frequent bookstores and talk to customers and clerks to get a feel for what is selling.

Look at Amazon.com, Barnes and Noble, Powell's books, and other online retailers and booksellers for books in your area and see what is selling and at what ranking. However, this is not as easy as in the earlier days of the online retail behemoths. Keep in mind people can falsely elevate their ranking. It won't hurt to have your friend purchase your book or preorder it all on the same day, but that high ranking will ultimately fade if you do not have a good marketing plan behind it.

Many, if not all, popular trends started in an alternative subculture. To put yourself on the cutting edge of trends before they're trends, read blogs, tweets, and Facebook posts, and check out alternative magazines at your local independent book or magazine seller. You can do the same thing online. Many magazines and newspapers now only have digital editions. Read popular-culture magazines and watch television—but use discretion here because these types of media sometimes aim to create markets rather than cater to them. You can often learn more about what does not work from television and popular magazines. The shows that flop and the products that fail are good indicators of how the public is feeling. And don't ignore yourself. What is important to you? It is likely important to other people as well.

When you have completed an informal look at trends, check to see what books are coming up in the publishing pipeline. Bowker's "Books in Print" has all upcoming titles listed. It's available online or in print in the reference section at most libraries.

Request the catalogs of publishers that issue books similar in topic and scope to yours. Many publishers now typically only produce online catalogs of upcoming titles. However, you can visit publisher websites and get a sense of what they look for. These catalogs are usually available approximately six months before the books hit the stores and are sometimes available by calling or e-mailing the publisher. If you want to see the physical catalogs, you could ask your local librarian if they are finished with their copy. Most publishers send their catalogs to libraries hoping to make sales in this market, and librarians seem to have little need for old catalogs.

Go to the sources the publishing industry uses. Prominent review publications such as "Publishers Weekly," "Booklist," and "the New York Times Book Review" are filled with invaluable information about changes in the industry as well as books currently being highlighted by specific publishers. They also include some excellent general interest publishing articles, including analyses of popular genres and trends. If you follow me on Twitter @digitaldeborah, you can learn about changes in publishing and the marketing world because I try to curate these subjects. I stay on top of it by wading through a lot of material, so you don't have to.

Publishers Marketplace is also a resource agents and editors use to find trends. It is a paid site, but if you can join, you can see the deals agents and publishers report for each year in specific subject areas.

You can also learn about the independent publishing route by joining

Independent Book Publishers Association, IBPA.com, and reading their magazine. They provide a lot of solid information for all types of authors and publishers.

Another great resource used by agents and publishers is *Jeff Herman's Guide to Book Publishers, Editors, and Literary Agents: Who They Are and How to Win them Over* has been guiding the industry since 1990. It lists agents with surveys of their likes and dislikes and what they represent. It also has a database of all the publishers, their imprints, and the names of editors. The advantage is it puts everything in one place, along with valuable essays about the industry. Of course, I am a little biased, but the book has become a bible of the industry without my help.

When planning your book, you are like a detective searching for clues. People in the industry know things you need to know so you can navigate the waters. By combining keen observation with your link to your Spirit and intuition, you should be able to find your niche.

You know you must write—you need to find where your Spirit fits in and how to give it the best form in the spiritual marketplace.

Meet People in your Field.

If you want to increase your credibility, it will help to meet people who do what you do. Go to workshops. If you can connect with people writing the type of books you are interested in writing, you may find some mentors. Better yet, you may find some endorsements.

Many well-known writers teach at writers' conferences, and many of them hold workshops. You can also join a speakers' group, such as Toastmasters. I had already been speaking at conferences around the world when I joined. I was comfortable speaking in front of people but hoped to improve my organization. It is easy when speaking extemporaneously to get lost on tangents. Just as in writing, poor organization will lose an audience. I learned a great deal through Toastmasters and highly recommend it. I am not sure of the status of the Toastmasters organization post-pandemic. Most clubs moved to virtual meetings, eliminating some of the benefits of standing in front of a live audience. However, it is still an excellent place to hone your skills. I am the ultimate optimist, so I believe in-person meetings will be in the future. We all need to be adaptable to the challenges in the world, but it doesn't mean we should stop what we are doing.

In Toastmasters, you have the advantage of peers evaluating your speech to help you improve. If done right, the evaluations are like a sandwich. The evaluator tells you what is working in your speech and areas of needed improvement, and they finish with something positive. The purpose is not to tear each other down and take out frustrations. It is a strengths-based approach my team also adopts when we assess manuscripts. It would be great if writer's groups followed this system. I don't particularly appreciate when writers tear each other down to the point where a person gives up. It makes me sad. I see it in the same light as people making people feel unworthy in their spiritual pursuits. Spiritual snobbery robs others of their Faith and confidence in their path. Refer back to the Tolerance lesson in Chapter Two.

After you have developed your speaking skills and are confident in your presentation, speak to any group, who will have you. This is where a self-published book can help you build audience numbers. You can sell your book, and these "back of the room" sales figures sometimes impress publishers when you present your manuscript for their consideration. It shows that you know how to generate buzz and are savvy enough to have a commercial message.

If you can, get some media training (that is, training in speaking extemporaneously before a microphone or camera and using bodily and facial gestures to good effect) and develop a speaking "hook," a two- or three-line sentence that encapsulates what your message is about. You can create several hooks and topics that show you are an interesting guest. It is always best to have a book available when you do interviews, but if you are an expert on your topic, try to gain any exposure that will create an audience. Your "call to action" can invite them to follow you on social media or check out your fantastic website and blog.

In today's climate, you may want to learn how to look good in front of a computer camera. There are also lighting kits for smartphones. With so many meetings moving to the virtual world, you will do well to examine how you look and present yourself. Who cares if you wear yoga pants when people only see you from the waist up? However, bad lighting and a lack of consideration for what is behind you will ruin the ambiance.

I had excellent guidance from a media coach when I started to use video for conferences and recording. I got some professional lighting and purchased a backdrop for behind my desk. People often believe I have a massive library with wrought iron gates. You can find them online. They are worth the investment because the virtual backgrounds sometimes cause you to fade in and out. But I have heard there are apps to make people look more beautiful. That may be a bonus.

When you have a good hook or several topics you can use as talking points, you can promote yourself to radio and television producers and create a media kit that puts you and your message in an easy-to-digest format. (See Section Four)

The media are always looking for "experts," so let them know you're out there and available to comment on news related to your topic. In your media materials, do not emphasize your unpublished book; instead, present a show idea for them and demonstrate that you are an expert in delivering a unique perspective and wealth of information on that spiritual topic. Develop your spiritual credibility by studying with teachers who are name-dropping worthy. If that is not your thing, refine your message and consider what makes you unique. The best way to do this is through meditation, reading the spiritual classics (not just what is popular), and connecting to your own higher consciousness through prayer and writing. To "cook" spiritually, you must experience life and learn about yourself.

Learn to accept rejection and never denigrate anyone else's success. What goes around comes around. Focus on the positives of what you are doing, not how important you are for doing it. You are not the only one with a mission. Help others, and you help yourself. There is enough to go around. I am sure this sounds like an awful lot of work. I know. I taught spirituality and writing classes for over ten years before I was able to write this book. It is now twenty years later when I am finally updating it. It may not take you as long. I was busy with other things and waiting for the right moment to bring this second edition to life. Again, Divine Timing.

My spirituality classes helped hone my message as I taught others and gained the value of others' feedback and insights. I have also been teaching at writers' conferences for many years, some on strictly practical topics such as book-proposal writing, with no spirituality mentioned.

You don't have to wait until you are a household name before submitting a manuscript—although that can't hurt. Just do what you can to enhance your chances. View this groundwork as part of the excitement of the total picture. Every positive effort you make will benefit you down the road, no matter when you are published.

A Note About Self-Publishing.

In the face of all these challenges, self-publishing may seem an easy alternative to playing the "trying to get published game." One advantage is the immediate gratification of going ahead and printing your book without having to wait. Another is having control over every aspect of your work. In the first edition of this book, I didn't recommend self-publishing. At that time, the options were to do everything on your own or go to a vanity press. It was a costly process with little benefit. Now it is a very feasible alternative for you. The only caution is that you do not rush into self-publishing because you don't want to do the work required to pursue traditional publishing. Instead, make the self-publishing alternative a conscious choice. Comparison shop and do not be sucked in by author services companies that lead you to believe that you will have special status for their traditional publishing programs if they have one. They make money from their self-publishing, and unless you completely stand out so that any house would want you, self-publishing with them will not bring you any advantages you would not otherwise have.

There is now the hybrid/ Indie option. My company, Micro Publishing Media, Inc, is a hybrid Indie publisher with bookstore distribution and a spiritual imprint called Soul Odyssey Books. Many hybrid companies are doing a great job with their authors. But as you learn in the lesson of Self-Protection in Chapter Two, it is buyer beware. In Section Three, I will explain this publishing option in detail so you know the right questions to ask yourself when selecting a company to shepherd your book. That is what they should be doing. A hybrid company should offer you a menu of services that you would receive in a traditional publishing setting so your book can compete. The idea is you pay for the services in exchange for a high-quality book meeting the industry's professional standards. There is no guarantee that the book will sell, but it should have the access and support, so it has the potential to succeed. This is why you sign up with a hybrid publisher. They should be professional with experience and knowledge of what makes a good book.

Another perk of hybrid publishing is you should receive a higher-than-average royalty. Traditional publishers include the editorial, design, printing, and distribution services that you pay for with hybrid publishers and may pay you an advance. They will expect you to promote your book but may provide some support. In return, they will have the right to publish the book and will typically give you a 7 % royalty. If the book is a big seller, this makes a difference. However, most books do not earn back their advance.

I created a hybrid publishing company to accommodate the many new voices not being published in today's climate and to put the authors in a better position to earn from their labor. Fortunately, there are fewer vanity presses and more legitimate and high-quality hybrid publishers today. We adhere to standards, but some companies still do not offer personalized service at the high quality that authors need.

My goal is to educate you to become entrepreneurs. Many of the most talented writers had no idea how to sell their books. Therefore, other people benefitted from their talent. I have heard way too many times, "I don't want to market; I want to spend my time writing." If you are independently wealthy or a celebrity, that may be just fine. For the rest of us, even if we are guided daily by Angels, emissaries, and the Holy Spirit, we need to put in the effort to breathe life into our work.

You must understand how other people do it if you want your book to fly off the shelf. But don't worry; in the last section of this book, I will introduce you to the concepts and endeavor to demystify them for you.

Technology is our Friend.

This phrase should be added daily to your other affirmations. If you learn to harness the internet, you can target and reach your audience more effectively than a traditional publisher might do on your behalf. So do not look to the alternative of self or hybrid publishing as a default or second-string position. Keep in mind *Celestine Prophecy* began as a self-published book.

Another book set publishing on its ear was "Fifty Shades of Gray," which started as a self-published book. I can't comment on the content and why that book took off. I only know that it made publishers sit up and take notice of the self-published book.

Even the famous playwright David Mamet has chosen to self-publish a novel. When considering how to best share your voice, consider all opportunities and how you can make them work for you.

Make Sure you Give Yourself the Advantages of Traditional Publishing.

Many behind-the-scenes collaboration activities occur with traditional publishing that you must recreate to become a successful do-it-yourselfer. To produce the quality books you see in stores, you must ensure your book is ready. If you self-publish, you are your own boss. You are the most passionate about your work; you can get the most profit and do it your way. Just do not skimp on the editing. I can't stress that enough.

With hybrid publishing, you share the profit. Still, you have the advantage of a team of professionals behind you to keep your book at the highest standards of competitiveness in the marketplace.

Developing Credibility.

Writers of spiritual nonfiction have another obstacle: developing credibility so that someone will want to read what they have to say. No one will read a book just because the author claims the Divine Source of All Creation has given them a calling to write. If you are pursuing a traditional publisher, this is even more important. When traditional acquisition editors see a manuscript that makes unsubstantiated claims from a writer with no readily apparent spiritual background, they immediately throw it into the round file. They may not even send a rejection letter.

This may happen even if they like what you have to say. In rare instances, they may consider your submission if it is well written. Still, they will have to overcome the hurdle of convincing the marketing department that you are a writer who people will want to read. Before an editor considers a book, they will look at the author's bio and perhaps the book's marketing package to convince them that the author is qualified to write about the message that intrigues them.

So, in a way, before you can expect to be published, you need to grow into your message, whether you go a traditional or self-publishing route. Spiritual writers are often in a hurry. We feel an urgency to get it out even though our time and Divine time are very different. You may need time to grow and pay your dues, just like actors perform in summer stock and small theaters before they can work their way up. "Overnight success" only happens in the movies.

Once while working as an agent with an author to develop her book, I came to feel that she was not "ripe" enough in the spiritual understanding of her message and had not yet developed her credibility. We lost touch. Five years later, I ran into her at Book Expo America, the unfortunately now defunct annual trade show for the publishing industry. She had finally found a publisher to release her book. It had taken her five years to grow her manuscript and develop her credibility. We hugged, and she said to me with a knowing smile, "It was time." Her energy was relaxed and confident. When I knew her five years earlier, she had been frenetic in her need to have the book published. She felt it had to be published NOW. She had felt the rumblings in the universe and wanted to fulfill her mission. But it was taken care of when the time was right. Had she not been open to what she unknowingly had to learn to take her place among published spiritual writers, she might have become frustrated and given up altogether. If we do not open ourselves to the challenges we must overcome, we make it much more difficult in the long run. Understand, she was not necessarily having difficulty with her faith, or her spiritual path, which she pursued with love and openness. She was having trouble with the limitations of time, space, and the publishing biz.

How do you establish credibility as a writer and spiritual "expert"? As artists create portfolios, you can develop writing credits. Write for any publication that will publish you: magazines, newspapers (daily and weekly), newsletters—but don't expect to make your living this way.

Author branding and blogging are the best ways to build experience and an online platform. See Section Four for the specifics on how to do this. Remember to post your blog to other social media outlets that we will discuss in a later chapter so people can learn of it. Even though it might feel as if you are writing to no one, pretend that you have a roomful of friends interested in what you have to say. And enjoy it.

Staying Humble.

Worthiness is often a big issue for spiritual writers: either, like the Rabbi, we think we are not worthy of our message, or we think we are too worthy and too special. Beware of trying to gain credibility by drawing attention to yourself to the exclusion of your message.

This "look at me" attitude can come across as arrogance. Keep your focus and your faith. You do not have to sell God, and you do not have to sell yourself. Too much hype will backfire. While you must promote yourself to be heard, don't forget that you are a conduit for Spirit. Spirit will find its place and its audience if given enough exposure.

As the conduit, you are not irrelevant to the process. Still, if you are too concerned with making sure that audiences know how special and spiritually evolved you are, you will either alienate them or mislead them to think that you are more important than your words. Help people see their spiritual potential through you. If you are looking to be worshipped, then you may have difficulty progressing on your path. You may be terrific and successful, but you will not be representing a spiritual message or helping others build a spiritual connection.

We all typically go through variations of the "look at me" stage. God knows I have, and sometimes still do because it's human nature to seek validation. But if we are too needy in this way, we might end up trying too hard and instead work against ourselves. This is not the same as social media, which we will discuss in later chapters. People mistake marketing for broadcasting the "I am great, listen to me" message. Marketing today is about relationships and develops over time. If we look at this as a means of validation, we will quickly become very frustrated.

Many of the lessons spiritual writers learn, relate to this issue of accepting themselves without needing everyone's approval. If we seek only external validation, we will write for this purpose, and this self-consciousness will show in our writing. If we work toward self-acceptance, we are then building a better connection with ourselves and our God, allowing us to better accomplish our mission. When we can accept and love ourselves, we can write from a place with room for Spirit.

I struggled for years with a desire to share what I had learned about spirituality with others and to write about it. When I was a new writer and an even newer student of spirituality, religion, and metaphysics, I was jealous of anyone who had published a book on the subject.

In my grandiosity, I believed I could do as well as they and deserved the attention they received, although they had already paid their dues. I was in a big hurry and needed to grow and learn. The flip side of this inflated sense of myself was a total lack of confidence. While I could write articles and books on topics that did not reflect my deepest spiritual beliefs, I could not find the right language to reflect those beliefs that were most important to me. When we battle ourselves, we can't write, and we can't grow.

Spiritual writers can become caught up in the progress of our path as if it were competition. But we aren't going to "win" by owning the holiest relics, preaching the loudest, or wearing the most crystals. We can take ourselves too seriously, blocking us from writing in the flow. One time during a particularly grueling writing session, when I had twisted my hair into a spring, my husband approached me and whispered in my ear, "Stop worrying so much. You are not writing the Bible."

I felt like a woman in labor trying to resist the urge to fling a heavy object at his head. But he was right.

Finding your Divine Inner Voice.

We are all essentially on our own when it comes to our spiritual path. No two people occupy the same path at the same time. We may simply walk side by side and offer help to each other. But we are separate in physical form from one another for a reason: We each have a unique voice and spark to add to everyone else's light. The trick is to find it.

Writers who avoid a flashy, attention-getting style can more easily relax and write with a natural voice. Self-conscious writing is as evident to an audience as when an actor loses his character on the stage. While watching television talk shows, we are entertained because even though the host is the show's focal point, they welcome us as if we were part of an intimate gathering. We feel a sense of inclusion rather than the self-consciousness of an intruder.

When you write a spiritual book, remember that spiritual seekers will buy and read it because they need or want something. They want to be educated, they want to solve a problem or mystery, or they want to be inspired. When people buy spiritual books, they want to share an experience with the writer. It is like a student-teacher relationship. If the writer overwrites every sentence to make himself seem more knowledgeable and influential than he is, the reader will feel this and be uncomfortable.

Readers want to feel cared about and important. They aren't interested in reading about how important someone else is. They expect that a book written by a spiritual guru will be about how the reader can have a better life, not about how enlightened the guru is. Spiritual teachers whose philosophies have evolved through many turns on their paths do not have to brag about their specialness. They know where inspiration and wisdom come from. They know the secret that we all have the same potential and right to be awake and aware of the truth.

The further along on the path, the more information they may have to share. This has nothing to do with craft and success but has everything to do with conveying a pure spiritual message. The more we get out of our way and work through our human issues on the path to self-awareness, the better messengers we make.

I Know I Want to Write, but How do I Start?

You start. You jump in and take any opportunity you can to learn your craft. You wouldn't wake up one day and say, "I think I will be a brain surgeon," without going to school and learning how. I had education, but to learn how to write books, I had to jump in without knowing if I would sink or swim. I was fortunate not to know my limitations. I just did the best I could.

During my professional career, I have done a great deal of ghost-writing.

Although it would be interesting to write about ghosts, this means writing books for other people. My first book was entirely ghostwritten. An author of a medical humor trivia book handed in a manuscript, and the publisher rejected it. This doesn't happen often, but it can be complicated. The author may be required to pay back the advance, or if the publisher brings in someone to fix it, they may take it out of future royalties. They wanted the book, so they needed someone to rewrite it. I was an eager new writer and gladly took on the task. I jumped in headfirst and learned on the job. I was thrilled when they accepted it and probably earned ten cents per hour. But it gave me my start. My name was not on the cover but was buried in the acknowledgments. I was utterly invisible. But I knew I was there.

Many of the thirteen books I have written for traditional publishers were collaborations. I enjoy working with other people, and with one other exception, my name does appear on the cover. However, as my writer's journey and spiritual path developed simultaneously, I think I may have avoided writing from my inner muse. Writing the second edition of this book is my opportunity to share more of myself. I walk the same path as you and hope my examples help inspire and motivate you. All of you will find your place to begin.

Knowing When it's Good Enough.

We all know that life isn't always easy and is not a straight line. I often define spiritual awakening as being hit by a two-by-four on the head, and I describe the writer's journey as the process of wanting to tell everyone how it feels. To write good spiritual books, we do not have to be "healed" or achieve total self-realization. Our process toward awareness is often the most important thing we can share. This is how we help each other along the way. There comes a time when we must decide that our writing is good enough. If we wait for our perfection, we will not write.

Jennifer, a friend of mine, is a talented writer, but she doesn't believe it. She also doesn't think she is pretty, intelligent, or likable. She worries that she is not sufficiently spiritual—she doesn't meditate enough, doesn't go to church often enough, doesn't do enough good deeds, and on and on. She is a lovable and wonderful friend, so I haven't strangled her for her negative attitude, but I regret that she holds herself back from her other dreams and creative endeavors. And I know that her self-consciousness is typical and that many of us must overcome these obstacles because it's simply a life lesson—particularly with any creative undertaking.

Do not worry that you are not worthy of sharing your message—you are! You just need to learn the protocols of the publishing industry and work hard to take your place among the messengers. You can do it. There can never be too many spiritual writers. Your triumph benefits us all.

Part Two

From Inspiration To Manuscript

Having the inspiration to write and knowing what you want to write about does not automatically mean you have the slightest idea about the mechanics of writing a publishable book. No one is born with this knowledge, so do not be discouraged if you haven't been able to discipline yourself to write the requisite three pages per day that some books tell you to do.

Even if you have a clear idea of what you want to say, you can't begin a journey like this without a roadmap. When you have inspiration for a book, the first place to start is to focus on the idea. Let the idea germinate. Play with it. It does not hurt to put your business hat on if you plan a book you intend to publish. If you are writing nonfiction, this is a little easier than when writing a novel.

Writing a novel is a process that differs, but some of the same rules apply. You need to know where you are going before you set out to get there. The chapters in this next section will help you understand the process of writing a complete manuscript by breaking it into discrete steps. As discussed in the earlier chapters, it can be challenging for spiritual writers to transition from the excitement of inspiration to the tedious minutiae of creating a marketable, publishable product. Can your spirituality be squeezed into these publishing parameters? Of course, it can!

Chapter 6, "Transforming Inspiration into a Hook gives you pointers on distilling a spiritual message into a few lines of text. Those few lines, often called your angle or hook,

are the most crucial elements of the whole package that you will submit to an agent or publisher. It condenses your message so that the many people who will potentially read it will know instantly what it is you're writing about and whether you have a marketable idea.

Chapter 7, "What kind of spiritual writer are you?" will help you further tether your message to the realities of publishing by asking you to define yourself and your idea: What genre does your manuscript fall into, and where would it be shelved in a bookstore? At this stage, I recommend you use some marketing and branding techniques to help you zero in on your reader demographic. Some of these terms sound like they belong in a business book and not in a book about writing about Spirit. However, these techniques will get you there if you want to succeed and reach your audience. God gave you parts of the brain that you may have never accessed before. If I can use the business side of mine, you can too. It requires a balance between the creative process and the structure necessary to bring an idea into a tangible form. The marketing aspect of the business of writing is very creative. When you read the chapters about book marketing in the digital age, you will feel more comfortable with technology. I have become a digital evangelist because I believe it is the way of the future and gives spiritual writers the best way to grow a platform in the shortest time.

Many spiritual writers believe in the purity of their message and want to write with abandon and passion. That is a gift. It is an integral part of the process. However, sometimes there is so much you want to say that you will not know where to begin or how to organize your thoughts. A book needs structure and a place where it will fit in the bookstore if it is traditionally published. Even if you self-publish, you need to know your book's category. The micro/self-publisher needs to know how to describe a book and understand who the end reader might be. You do not write for the reader but do not write in a vacuum. If there is nothing in it for the reader you have in mind; then you may as well stick to writing a diary or journal that is for your eyes only. This is the same as writing a blog but having no way to share it. If no one is reading your blog, it is the same as a private diary—more about this in later chapters.

Chapter 8, "Can you contain Spirit in an outline?" will help you see how to keep the passion while creating an organized, logically flowing manuscript.

Lastly, in chapter 9, "Writing and Editing," we'll discuss how to make your now-finished draft the best it can be before you send it out into the publishing world.

6

TRANSFORMING INSPIRATION INTO A HOOK

*I*n your journal, you can allow your thoughts to roam free. You can ramble to your heart's content. However, when you sit down to write a book for someone else to read, you must harness all that free-floating inspiration and funnel it into a concise message that makes sense to other people. That message is your hook and the essence of everything you wish to convey.

A hook is as it sounds: something the reader can hang on to—one or two sentences at the most. This hook is your thesis, a position you will support with illustrations or evidence. It is about logic and structure. Anything you write is a type of persuasion. You have something to say that will lead your reader on a journey.

One of the most important things is to write a book people can follow. No matter how talented you are as a wordsmith, your reader will become frustrated if you do not have a logical structure to your book. This does not mean you cannot be creative. Keep in mind that you are taking your reader on a journey and although they might enjoy surprises, most people do not like being completely confused and in the dark. You would probably not bring a friend or your spouse into the wilderness without explaining why you are there and where you are going. You might want to, but I am sure your companions will ask many questions, each becoming more desperate and demanding as the path moves forward. It is human nature.

My husband has tried to plan surprises for me. The tradition started when our children were young, and he could not round us up to do something together without everyone arguing about it. He started mystery Sundays, secret adventures where he only told us what to wear and how long we would be gone. These trips always were fun, but we all complained and resisted every step of the way. And it took a long time for me to rise above my anxiety to allow him to make all the choices.

Your reader will not have the patience to wander into a mystery Sunday with you without knowing where they are going and why. As the writer and narrator, you still have complete control, but your reader is not married to you and can easily choose another way to spend the day. You need to earn their trust; the best way is through a strong structure and clear path.

If you begin with your hook and master it, you will form a strong foundation for your manuscript. The goal is to encapsulate your entire vision with pinpoint accuracy into one or two sentences. If you can't do this, your idea needs further refinement and focus. Do not be afraid if you start with a hook that seems to evolve. That is natural. The point of creating a hook is to make sure your thoughts are clear. From this point, an organized outline can follow. You need to know why you are writing the book, why the topic interests you, how you will support it with stories, facts, and anecdotes, and if you are the person best suited to write it.

Many spiritual books are written in a memoir style. Think about if there is sufficient reason for people to want to read about your experiences. What sets you apart. Remember, many people have transformative journeys. From where I sit as a former literary agent, I have read many query letters about people's stories. Your life is important to you, but you would be surprised how many people write similar books. Find what in business we call your unique selling proposition. What is different about you, and what can you give your reader that they cannot get elsewhere, or at least what they get from you is better.

Showing your authority and voice is part of honing your idea and creating a hook. Before you write, you will need to ask yourself the hard questions. It is tempting to jump in. But this preliminary thought process will go a long way in helping you write a good and readable book.

A clear hook puts you in control of how a reader will receive and interpret your message. Reading is an active process as writing, and every reader brings a different set of preconceptions to a manuscript. Still, a clearly stated thesis orients the reader to what you are about to say instead of what he thinks you are saying.

When you write the query or book proposal for submission to a publisher or an agent, remember that you have only thirty seconds to capture their attention. This is like meeting your dream editor or agent in line at Starbucks. I am tired of the elevator analogy. You have only a few minutes with someone who may be agitated while waiting for a coffee fix. That is a real challenge. Of course, most editors and agents do not enjoy having writers pitch them in line at Starbucks, at a private lunch, or on the way to the bathroom, but this is your fantasy. Make it work. This is a good exercise in learning to focus your message. You want to make every word count, and you want to make it look easy. Agents and acquisitions editors typically only scan submissions.

Most agents, editors, and interns will not dig through poorly organized manuscripts. They will not work that hard when they have so many queries, synopses, and proposals to consider; they will be more attracted to those that make their jobs easier. Some manuscript reviewers become so overwhelmed with the backlog of unread submissions that they are relieved when they can find a reason to reject a manuscript and move on to the next one in their pile or inbox. Don't let a lame or fuzzy hook be why your manuscript gets tossed into the "No" box, from which, eventually, an intern will retrieve it to send you a friendly rejection letter. They may not even do that, and you will be left wondering what happened to your great idea. Even with a great hook, there is no guarantee anyone will reach out to you, but at least you are doing what you can to increase the odds. Unless you are a celebrity whose name alone is enough to sell a book, an agent or editor will not spend time trying to figure out what you are trying to say, so at least remove that obstacle as best as possible.

Assuming you are focusing on your end reader, the organization of the book is what will create a great experience for them. Ultimately you are looking to write a good book and to make it stand out from those that are just mediocre. This is very true if you are planning to self-publish. There is so much noise out there now that a well-developed book with a solid structure and plans for how to reach the market will have a definite advantage.

Make sure you start with a good idea. The ancient editorial axiom states, "You can't get a good hook from a rotten idea." Be brutally honest with yourself; look your muse in the face and ask, "Is this book idea of mine something anyone else would want to read?" If your muse doesn't answer, do market research. We try to include the most updated lists of recent titles in various genres in *Jeff Herman's Guide to Book Publishers, Editors, and Literary Agents,* so you can look at the competition and get a sense of trends.

You need to be aware of other books on the topic you are considering. In the new digital world, you can also use the techniques marketing and public relations companies employ to see what the trends are now and where they are heading.

Although there are always new applications and places to find information online, you can look up trends using Google. You can search what people are looking for on the internet when they type in questions in their search bar. This is good information for you because it gives you a glimpse into the mind of the readers. You can also comb places like *Quora* and other online magazines or information hubs. See what questions people are asking.

I have read many book submissions where the author claims there is no competition and nothing like their book. Typically, I would have at least ten similar letters in my inbox. There are no completely new stories. But there are new perspectives, and there are always popular trends. We are a collective consciousness. You, as spiritual writers, can take advantage of your intuitive guidance. Follow the signs. If you are drawn to something, follow the path but be open-minded. The hook and, therefore, your book will reveal itself. Combining the process with your research, you will know how to structure things for ultimate success.

Publishers have seen a demand if you see other books on your topic. It also means that readers are reading about it. Your task is to distinguish what you are saying and how you say it so there will be room for you and your book. You can try this exercise. If God has a Divine spark in everyone and some are being called to write, would it make sense for everyone to do the same thing? Take the time to go inwards to see what your piece of the story is. How will it help people? Remember the Ego lesson by keeping in mind that you are not the only one who is helping. You don't have the entire burden of the universe on your shoulders. Remember, you do not have to have your book published yesterday. God's time and our time are very different. Think about what your contribution to the world can be and what your skills, passions, and experiences are. There are no accidents. If you think about it, the answers will come to you. Then you will know your very own assignment. Writing is challenging, but you should not choose to write about something that makes your brain hurt. If you are not suited to a subject, don't write about it because you think it will sell. Find your hook, not someone else's. Then all will fall into place.

When you have figured out your topic, work on developing your hook. Here is a possible hook for this book:

Spiritual writers must accommodate the commercial needs of publishers without losing sight of their missions. While focusing on practical aspects of getting published, the book is also part mystical journey highlighting seven spiritual lessons unique to this population.

This is a strong hook for two reasons: first, because it encapsulates what the entire book is about—every chapter, every paragraph, and even every sentence relates to this thesis—and second, from a marketing standpoint, because while there are many "how to get published" books out there, not one is specifically directed to spiritual writers and their unique needs.

Thirty-eight words. An entire book boiled down to almost nothing but a vapor. I am not a woman of few words, and it was not easy to develop such a focused thesis statement. But as you see, it can be done! If your idea has not evolved enough to boil it down to its essence, try outlining its major topic areas or even writing free-form. Inspiration is not static. If you play with your idea through journal-writing or writing a rough draft or outline of your manuscript, you may find that the real hook pops out at you. As in any writing, you may think you are writing one book when there is another book inside you waiting to be birthed.

Another idea is to speak about your topic. You will have to take it through many incarnations with feedback from the listeners. You can watch their faces to see how they react to your words. If they are glazing over or are engaged, you will see it in their eyes. If you are already a public speaker, use the opportunity to refine your message. It will help you in your publicity, and it will also help you eventually write a book that can support your speaking. The two go hand in hand.

Get involved in social media. Aside from helping build a following, platforms like Twitter help you practice writing in soundbites. Even on Facebook, people do not have patience for lengthy posts. There are always new platforms to explore. Use these to practice your message.

You will know you have found your hook when you can visualize or otherwise sense your manuscript in its entirety. You may see chapter titles and subsections within them and how you will build your manuscript, from beginning to end. Even though you don't know the specific words that will fill the pages, your search for a hook has brought you to the outline of your manuscript.

If you write fiction, the hook is just as important, but it is presented differently, typically in your protagonist's journey, who is changed in the end. Someone looking at a synopsis of your book needs to understand enough by your concise plot summary and description of the significant conflicts to be resolved to know immediately if they want to read further.

Here are some examples of hooks from successful spiritual titles:

Journey of Souls: Case Studies of Life Between Lives by Michael Duff Newton.

A controversial exploration of what happens after we die is based on actual cases where Newton regresses his patients to a point between lives—after death but before birth.

The Mystical Mind: Probing the Biology of Religious Experience by Eugene G. D'Aquili and Andrew B. Newberg.

Two leading medical researchers explore how the physiology of the brain is involved in the religious and mystical experience.

A Good Hook Goes a Long Way

The life of a good synopsis doesn't end with your writing the manuscript and proposal. Assuming your proposal merits a closer look, editors will read your manuscript to see if it delivers what the hook promises. Or suppose you're lucky enough to have your proposal accepted before you've written the entire manuscript. A strong hook ensures a mutual vision between the editor and writer, so the finished product reflects everyone's overall intent. It keeps things on track.

Your hook allows publishers and distributors to sell the book with clarity and enthusiasm throughout the sales process. When a new book is pitched to a publisher's sales staff, distributor, or retail booksellers, there is no time for long-winded explanations. Everyone is busy. Each book merits just a few minutes to establish its worthiness, or rather, its sales potential. A great hook gives everyone in the process a tool to describe the book entirely and succinctly to their customers.

As an Indie publisher, I now have the task of writing out the descriptions and metadata for the distributor to put into all the catalogs and systems. It is so helpful if the hook or theme of the book is clear and concise. I put these descriptions on a spreadsheet, and we are limited in how many words we can use. Everyone benefits from a clear statement of what a book is about. Think about a sales and marketing team presenting your book to store buyers looking at so many titles they all become a blur. Therefore, you want your hook to stand out. Even if you self-publish, when people search for something to read, you want them to know why they should choose your book over other options.

Your hook can also be used to write your cover copy. People read this on the back jacket and in the description listed in the online retailers or other distribution outlets. Your effort at this beginning stage will serve you well throughout. If you have difficulty with this exercise, think about your jacket copy. You want to say in a few words enough information to tease a reader into wanting to buy your book. You want to include the main characters and their struggles. For nonfiction, you will describe your core promise excitingly and compellingly.

When writing back jacket copy, I pretend I am describing a movie. What will entice someone to buy a ticket and sit through at least ninety minutes with or without popcorn?

7

WHAT KIND OF SPIRITUAL WRITER ARE YOU?

*Y*our writer's voice emanates from your inner muse, reflecting your unique style, perspective, and Soul. No one can duplicate your essence, but your writing must conform to what readers expect from your genre. There is a tone and style for different types of books. For example, a business advice book on how women can break through the glass ceiling would call for a friendly but authoritative and knowledgeable voice; details and specific advice and directives would be more critical than your revelations or musings. The audience would want to feel they were in the hands of an expert who had specific recommendations to help them.

On the other hand, a spiritual book can generally assume a more intimate tone, almost like one friend giving loving advice to another. The reader is seeking a relationship with you, as the author, and with the material. They want to know how your writing relates to their life and journey. Spiritual books that transcend the mundane require a greater connection between the author and reader.

No matter the topic you write about, strive to reveal your authentic voice—the expression of the contents of your Soul. When your writing feels natural and honest to you, you are writing from the place connected with your Divine spark. As a result, it will be easier for you to convey your whole meaning.

No one can write anything, not even the copy for a cereal box if they are self-conscious about every word. Let your voice emerge without editing. That part will come later. Engaging your intellect too early in the process will be like trying to water your garden while someone is kinking up the hose.

Self-Revelation

In any writing, the author's task is to help the reader enjoy the content without too much interference so that the reader can escape into it. There is a fine line, especially in spiritual books. In spiritual books, you want to reveal enough of yourself to establish the vital connection between you and the reader—but not too much. After all, the reader is looking in your book, not for insights into your life but for a better understanding of their own.

While a certain amount of self-revelation and a warm, inviting tone can help establish your credentials and voice, unless the work is a memoir or autobiography—self-disclosure can be overdone. There is no hard and fast rule, but self-revelation can also be underdone with a spiritual book. I have worked with a writer who presents a well-thought-out system for centering and evolving. However, in its first draft, the book did not explain how he came to know these practices he recommends. After a bit of probing, I discovered he had a fascinating journey of discovery that set the tone for why he was writing the book and why the reader should listen to him. The reader wants to know something about you but not so much that there is no room left for them. It is as if you are creating a persona who can share the journey with the reader. They don't want the role of the observer as much as they want to feel the experience with you.

Another word of caution is not to set yourselves above the reader. The tone for nonfiction self-help and transformation in the spiritual genre is most accessible with a heart-to-heart feel. The balance is to share but not engage in too much irrelevant personal reflection. If your experiences are illustrative and bring you together with the reader, they are often a plus for your book. I have edited many books as a consultant, particularly spiritual books, and I find that a lack of personal illustration makes for a dull book. The line you have to set is to anticipate what will interest your reader and support your thesis. As in any book, there should not be extraneous information. Anything you say should relate to some point or promise.

Readers Should feel they are Part of Things, Not Like Outsiders.

Similarly, the reader is looking to learn from your book but doesn't want to feel like a spiritual dunce. Try not to tell a story that makes it seem you are the only one with anything extraordinary to share. Instead, strive to include your reader as a welcome and respected participant. Remember the Ego lesson. Be the messenger and not the message. If this all sounds confusing, it is. I have curated many query letters and proposals about spiritual journeys and similar subjects. Manuscripts filled with ego elevate the writer so that if you met them in person, they would suck the life out of the room. Maybe they feel like narcissists even if they are not. It may be how they write because they go overboard trying to prove themselves.

If you need to get it out of your system, write your first draft this way. Indulge your desire to be the focal point of your book. Then set it aside and read it after it has had time to settle. Then you decide if it would interest anyone other than yourself and perhaps your mother.

When you write for your empowerment—in your journal or notes for your memoir—let your voice be big, strong, free, powerful, and personal. If you want to write for publication, remember to include the reader at your party and make your voice more inclusive of others' experiences. Later, when you become a household name, people might want to know every little thing about you. Until then, strive for balance.

Good nonfiction often includes anecdotes. You can use your personal experiences to illustrate your more prescriptive points. You can also create composite characters or circumstances to liven up your writing.

Techniques for Letting your Voice Emerge.

When you sit down to write, you may know so much about where you are heading that you could write your book practically overnight. You take your outline and place it on a bulletin board where you can see it. You stretch out your fingers, crack your neck, and begin to write. What comes out is something you do not recognize. You can hear it in your mind. It sounds like someone is talking while you write, but it isn't you.

Oh, but if it were any good! I can't speak for anyone else, but finding a voice that sounds like me takes a while when I write. I hear a voice in my head when I get started. Sometimes the voice begins as a stuffy lawyer or professor. After that, the writing can be beyond my understanding. If I don't know what I am writing, how will my reader? The more I relax and get warmed up, the more natural it sounds. Other times, if I am writing spiritual material, I hear a voice so ethereal that I need a spiritual translator to figure it out.

And sometimes, I practically glue myself to a chair and still cannot find my natural voice. So I repeatedly rewrite the same thing, hitting the delete key with mounting frustration. These rejects are not edited versions of something good; they are the product of total mental constipation. "Writerpation" could also mean a warm-up is needed before getting to the good stuff.

Or we get stuck because we lack confidence. We may worry inordinately about pleasing some fictitious reader who we believe wants to hate our work. (Reread the Self-Love lesson about worthiness.) It may sound a little paranoid, but we often think someone reading our work wants to find out what is wrong with it. Not true! The readers you're interested in having read your book want to like what you write. They are looking for insights. Publishers and agents also want to like what they read because they need to discover good books that can generate sales. So you may as well relax. If you are pursuing a spiritual path and are inspired to write, your writing stems from a place of truth. To find your voice, or as a warm-up practice, put yourself in the proper frame of mind by writing down or repeating to yourself these affirmations:

- I have something unique and special to say.
- My writing is inspired.
- Readers will love my authentic voice.
- Writing brings me inner peace.

Add to this list anything that makes you realize you have nothing to fear. Readers want and need to hear your message.

To find your voice, let go of control of the process. Don't edit as you go along. Instead, concentrate on revealing your message, not your life history. Then, after you allow your inner voice to emerge with all its enthusiasm and imperfections, you can go back later and correct any flaws. With its delete key and cut-and-paste function, computer technology is a blessing for today's spiritual writer who needs to unleash before tempering the Spirit.

A little tip: Stay organized with the versions of your writing. Always date your most current version of your manuscript, or you will be rewriting from older drafts. You can even erase older versions if you are not a document hoarder like me. You don't need them. But I am not that enlightened about such things and am also a notorious email hoarder.

If you find that everything comes out certifiably terrible no matter what you do, take a break and objectively ask yourself if you are caught up in the result rather than the process. Strong feelings always lead to a lesson or insight. You will only need to rewrite if operating on a voice disconnect. If this happens, set your writing aside and work on something else for a while.

I have already revealed my love of certain addictive computer games, the show *Frasier*, and my pets. Something physical also helps. As I was writing this, I needed a break. What did I do? I saw that the ceiling in my den/writing room needed repainting, so I have spent the past hour boxing up my books. It is amazing how many you can fit on your shelves. Ten banker boxes later, I am still only half finished. I call this productive procrastination! It cleared my head and refreshed my thoughts.

What is your Genre?

Knowing what kind of spiritual writer you are, helps conform your voice. Although you may push the boundaries, your book will fit into a genre and category. All booksellers, including online retailers, will separately categorize spirituality, religion, New Age, occult practices, psychic phenomena, UFOs, and ghosts. These are only some of the choices that may be relevant to your work. In addition, the publishers have now added mind/body, alternative health, transformational, inspirational, and new science. All of these genres appeal to vastly different audiences.

Christian books are a separate and substantial market; publishing uses this term to define books that deal with life issues and spiritual topics from a strongly Christian, often biblically-based perspective. Many are evangelical and typically must contain scriptural references and reflect Christian values. The Christian market, like many others, is in flux and specific authors and books dominate the market. However, some books cross over into the more mainstream bookstores. Publishers categorize Christian books differently than those they consider religious. Religious books are more scholarly or historical and well-researched. Inspirational books for the Christian market and mainstream often include gift books packaged as much for visual appeal as for content.

Naturally, many of these categories overlap because books often fit more than one description and because some types, such as New Age, are becoming less distinct as the topics become more mainstream.

The six most common nonfiction spiritual categories are spirituality, religion, New Age, Christian, inspirational, and Occult. Each religious tradition has a category, but the Christian market is a significant part of publishing revenue.

According to an article in Forbes published in 2019, Christian publishing grew in the previous years as the overall industry lost revenue. They named the leaders in the field Baker Publishing, Harper Collins Christian Publishing which also owns Zondervan, and Thomas Nelson, Faithwords, a division of Hachette Book Group, Tyndale House, and Crossway, with many denominations having a publishing arm.

At least 400 Christian bookstores closed when the pandemic hit, but that still left over 2000 such venues. If you write for the Christian market and follow the protocols, you have one of the largest audiences for your work. It is also a focused audience with particular interests. Many in the industry believe this market is underserved as they typically will only read books that are either bible- based or adheres to their belief system. Remember to be true to yourself. Don't write for this audience if you are not indeed a Christian. There is plenty of room in the general spirituality categories, inspirational or secular self-help with a spiritual underpinning.

This information brings up an important point. Spiritual writers do not need to only write about spiritual subjects. Many of my earlier books were not overtly spiritual. For example, I wrote a book about writing wills and one about fresh start bankruptcy. But I must have infused my spiritual leanings within the pages, as they were both reviewed as self-help. Keep that in mind when you choose what to write as you may have interests that are not directly spiritual, but you will add your Soul energy to them. That is just as important.

I don't want to leave out those of you who write fiction. There is a category of visionary fiction. In my research for a good definition, I found the Visionary Fiction Alliance, and their website looks pretty informative. Visionaryfictionalliance.com They describe visionary fiction much better than I can, so I will quote it here:

"Visionary Fiction embraces spiritual and esoteric wisdom, often from ancient sources, and makes it relevant for our modern life." They continue:

Gems of this spiritual wisdom are brought forth in story form so readers can experience the wisdom from within themselves. Visionary fiction emphasizes the future and envisions humanity's transition into evolved consciousness. While there is a strong spiritual theme, it in no way proselytizes or preaches."

They provide several fine examples, such as:

The Alchemist by Paulo Coelho

Celestine Prophecy by James Redfield (which started as a self-published book)

Jonathan Livingston Seagull by Richard Bach

I also love *Illusions* by Richard Bach and many others. Of course, many children's books fall into this category. But I think children are so close to their natural spiritual state that they will find vision in anything they read.

Our Agency does not represent fiction, so I had little experience with it as an agent. However, I would love to find the next visionary fiction classic as a publisher. As a new author, I think it would not be easy to break into the traditional publishing world in this genre, but I would never recommend you not try.

The most saleable books are typically practical and bring a new voice and perspective. Today, we are moving past the "what is it" to "how can we use it in our lives."

If your book doesn't quite fit into any of these genres yet still seems as though it should be under the general spiritual umbrella, spend some time on the internet or in stores to see where stores shelve similar books.

Publishers categorize their books by using BISAC. It is the acronym for Book Industry Standards and Communications. This list is the globally recognized categorization system used by publishers and booksellers, and the Book Industry Study Group determines it. The advantage of using the most current BISAC listing is it will reflect changes in Industry standards based on buyers' tastes. Today, books on spirituality fall under the general BISAC category of Body, Mind & Spirit. This high-level category is all-encompassing. Then it is broken down into subcategories that in the past might have been under "new age." But now, these subjects under Body, Mind & Spirit include healing, mediumship, parapsychology, Occult, shamanism, dreams, divination, and UFOs.

BISAC references religion under Body, Mind & Spirit as a separate category. It is helpful to review the BISAC website to see how the industry views your book, as it will help you understand where it belongs on the shelf. This system is all about positioning, which is the big concern of publishers and book buyers. They need to know where to put your book, so they know how to market and sell it.

BISAC may also list your books under Health and Fitness or Philosophy. You may disagree that your book belongs in that subject area, but this is the best way the Book Industry Study Group has found to put abstract ideas into some proper order. They use it, so do your best to see where you fit.

Familiarize yourself with book categories as you create your manuscript, even if it sounds very unspiritual. We often don't like to think of our work in terms so mundane. But BISAC and the term metadata are essential to help readers find you. Once you embrace this method, you will make these tools your friend.

BISAC categories represent readership. You will want to utilize these listings even if you self-publish. When you are familiar with these terms and categories, you can use them to help you with your marketing plan. In addition, these category terms can help you find blogs and sites online that will be useful in your own social media strategy.

What do Some of these Categories Mean?

Spirituality

Publishers define general spirituality books as those about self-transformation and a greater understanding of the divine or life force. This category also encompasses books that stress humans' connection to all aspects of life and the power of changing one's consciousness.

Religion

This category refers primarily to research-based books about the major world religions. An author's formal religious or philosophical education or training is essential. You will not find non-credentialed writers in this genre.

New Age

New Age developed as a catchall category for topics that did not fit anywhere else, some of which, like yoga or meditation, have become so mainstream in the past twenty years that they are hardly new. New Age books cover transformation, meditation, channeling, pyramids, ancient mysticism, shamanism, Native American spirituality, crystals, alternative health (which sometimes occupies its own category), energy work, and spiritualism.

In the late 1980s, New Age authors examined the existence of realities beyond our physical world and religious institutions, such as Angels, distance healing, and auras. Today, the shift from books marveling at these phenomena has led to books that show their application in our lives, thus creating the subgenre of "practical spirituality."

Christian

If you are a Christian writer, your faith, with its theology, dogma, and strictures, is integral, not incidental to your message. Many writers of spiritual or New Age material are practicing Christians. Yet, because their writing does not overtly reflect their Christian beliefs, it is not categorized in this more specific category. Readers of Christian material are generally churchgoers, and devotion to Christian teachings is paramount in their priorities.

Years ago, Christian material was confined to Christian publishers and Christian bookstores. However, today, some publishers will consider liberal Christian books if they can cross over into the mainstream market or at least into the mainstream Christian market.

Inspirational

I am not sure that even the booksellers know why inspirational material is separated. All books, particularly spiritual books, have an inspirational component to them. These books may be presented as gifts or kept for their inspiring and uplifting content. Personal stories with a theme of triumph over tragedy may be inspirational but will likely be categorized as memoirs. Booksellers will find inspirational books under several different BISAC categories. The common thread is they are encouraging with a positive message. They are uplifting.

Inspiration is an appealing category for new spiritual writers. It looks easy. But don't be fooled. Inspirational writing makes you easy prey for the "I am the center of the universe" monster. We are all inspired by our own lives. And perhaps other people might be inspired by your life. But publishers have been deluged over the years with so many "inspirational" stories that they are incredibly selective. You will have a better shot if your work creates compelling energy without seeming to be all about you. This is not a contradiction. Your story is about you, but your energy needs to be about how others can be helped by what you have experienced. It would be best if you become almost invisible. I realize I have made this point in nearly every section of the book, but that is because it should sink into you and become second nature.

Occult

Occult as a category has to do with esoteric, mysterious, or supernatural spiritual practices such as tarot cards, divination, psychic phenomena, mediumship, astrology (although astrologers would debate this), dousing, and astral projection.

Many publishers interested in spiritual material may not be interested in manuscripts on occult subjects. Research publishers to see where they stand. Look at their websites to see if they publish these books and what topics they have already covered.

Visionary Fiction

We have already covered this genre. If you have the skills, go for it. Learn your craft and use good fictional techniques while weaving your spiritual awakening tale. I have primarily limited my discussion of spiritual writing genres to nonfiction since this comprises most spiritual books published.

Research Publishers' Guidelines.

It would help if you had a sense of what genre you belong in to find your voice, ensure that your work reflects the appropriate protocol and style your genre requires, and determine which agents or publishers might be interested in it. I hope to create an ongoing directory of the Spirit-friendly publishers and agents on the Soul Odyssey Books website that I can keep updated. The first edition of this book had a listing, but things change very quickly. I would need to update this new edition every year to keep up with it. We have a group for spiritual writing and publishing on writersnetworking. com. I hope some of you will join and keep it active. You can share your recommendations and experiences to help other writers find their way to the right places.

You can find "Spirit-friendly" agents and publishers by studying books like yours. If you approach traditional bookstores or work with a hybrid publisher, you must be familiar with comparative and competitive books. This exercise will help you in many ways. You can create a lead list for later when you are ready to seek an agent or publisher. You can also find publisher's submission guidelines and current lists of the books they seek and publish in *Jeff Herman's Guide to Book Publishers, Editors, and Literary Agents.* That book remains current and updated either yearly or every two years.

Now that you know what you are doing and where it fits, let's examine how to write a great manuscript.

8

CAN YOU CONTAIN SPIRIT IN AN OUTLINE?

*P*erhaps the better question is, can spiritual books be written as a stream of consciousness without concern for structure? It is probably more fun that way, but without a roadmap, I doubt there will be a foundational structure that will carry out the goal. Writing is about conveying information to be consumed by another person. Just as you cannot expect your spouse or partner to read your mind, even if you can read theirs, you cannot expect your reader to fill in the blanks. This rule holds with creative writing and inspiration. Any time you are sharing ideas, you must be clear.

If you create a structure or a roadmap, you can leave room for the creative flow. I am a stream-of-consciousness writer within a loose structure. I have said many times that I'm not too fond of limits and do not want anyone, including myself telling me what to do. If I have created a table of contents or have a basic structure in mind, I find I allow myself the freedom to be creative without getting lost in the weeds. I have learned to be more disciplined with thirteen books under my belt, but I still prefer to have the illusion I am winging it. I am not.

I highly recommend you plan before you begin to write. I am not contradicting my earlier statements about the process of spiritual writing. This chapter is about how to put your universe into a jar. We are very expansive people and have difficulty narrowing down what we want to share. Here is where your intellect comes in. To be effective, your spiritual energy must be translated into the limitations of language. If you think this is challenging, you are right.

If you have already written your manuscript, perhaps these suggestions can help you revisit your structure to determine if it needs revision. I have never met a book that did not need some restructuring. On the other hand, if you are a new writer, I would be surprised if you did not automatically make some common errors.

For example, when I assess fiction, I find common errors that reflect inexperience. The writer may be talented, but we all start somewhere. In fiction, these seven areas are typically problematic. They are:

- Point of View
- Character Development
- Plot
- Showing and not telling through scenes
- Ineffective Dialogue
- Poor Structure
- Pacing

When writing a novel, planning and considering these challenges can help you write a better first draft. Many novelists start with a plot structure that will allow their characters to move along with the story.

- The typical structure for a novel begins with the characters in a relatively stable position. You introduce them and show who they are and what they are doing.
- Then, something happens to the main character called an inciting incident. It is anything that causes a disruption.
- After the change or inciting incident, the rest of the book will be filled with scenes showing the conflict and resolution.
- The most exciting novels usually have some major conflict that must be resolved.

This structure may sound too formulaic and may not relate to the book you are writing. But when starting, it may be better to stick with what works. For example, think about romantic comedy movies. They are formulaic, yet if you like them, you want them to all be about the same. There is comfort in knowing what will happen even though you marvel at the twists. At the beginning of these films, there is a meet-cute between the future romantic partners. A meet-cute is a film expression of when prospective romantic partners meet each other for the first time. These scenes are typically awkward misunderstandings, love at first sight, or an excuse for some physical slapstick comedy. Sometimes the first meeting is one of immediate dislike.

These films work because the formula is consistent. First, the meet-cute couple falls in love. Then, there is a montage of scenes showing them happy together. Then there is a misunderstanding or a rival that splits them apart. Then they find each other at the end, which leads to a kiss or a wedding.

Readers and filmgoers appreciate structure. So they do not want a book or movie to be too easy to figure out. But on the other hand, they want to avoid the anxiety of something new and unexpected. As with everything, it is all about balance. If you master this structure, feel free to play with it any way you wish. I would never discourage art.

Nonfiction Books Need Structure.

If you have not already written your manuscript, the first place to look in structuring your work is to revisit your hook. Be objective and try to create a table of contents. You may find you only have enough ideas or material for an article. You can't always expand a concept into a 200 or 300-page book.

For those who have not written your book, here are some suggestions for organizing yourself from an idea to a finished manuscript.

How to Begin
- Find the right idea
- Determine your core message
- Figure out your goal

Write an outline
- Plan out your book
- Develop a disciplined practice for writing
- Face the dreaded blank page or screen with confidence

Writing your book
- Decide what to Include and What to leave out
- Plan for how long it should be
- Determine when it is done
- In the next section, learn what to do when you are finished

Finding the Right Idea

You will want to find your passion and theme. (Reread about finding your authentic voice) Then find the common threads that will resonate with a reading audience.

Remember, readers want one or more of the following:
- To escape
- To learn something, they need to know
- To see themselves in the story
- To be entertained
- To be inspired, motivated, and uplifted

When looking for the right idea for your book, it is helpful to write a mission statement. This exercise is more than a hook as it forces you to look at your idea and why you want to write about it. While writing a mission statement, think about your audience. All books, whether novels, memoirs, or prescriptive, how-to nonfiction, need a through-line. This consistent and common element is the book's core theme, and everything you write will lead back to this.

Consider why you want to write a book when writing your mission statement. What do you hope to gain, and what do you wish to create for your reader? Then, when you are happy with your mission statement, I recommend you print it out and put it on a board or the wall near your workspace. This way, you will not forget why you are doing what could take a lot of time and create internal angst.

While doing this exercise, it would also be the time to describe why you are the person to write the book. You will need this for your book proposal and will want to develop clarity.

Publishers and Agents will Appreciate Good Structure.

A good message can get lost in poorly organized writing. Agents and publishers want a manuscript without tiresome digressions. Think about an excited child who tries to tell a story. You hear all kinds of extraneous details that might be interesting but take you away from the main point. There is more latitude in verbal effusiveness than in the written word. Most of your digressions will add color when you are bubbling over about something in a conversation. In writing, they can become confusing. Spiritual writing is not about the writer; it is about the message. Outlining allows our logical, ordering intellect to work with our expansive, enthusiastic Spirit so we can capture truth—universal energy—within this limited form of communication. When we do this successfully, our work can be understood by even the uninitiated reader. Organizing your message is the best way to avoid writing with an obtuseness that can be interpreted as condescension. It prevents you from alienating readers who are striving and searching. If you make it easy for readers to follow your ideas, you remove one more barrier to their understanding so they can move forward on their path. If you can create order out of Spirit, you are genuinely a co-creator with the Divine. No one can teach you talent, creativity, or God-connection. But you can certainly learn to write a good outline.

How to Write an Outline.

Writers tend to be perfectionists. We sometimes can't begin an outline because we do not have a feel for the "best" way to narrow things down.

You might have been taught how to outline in your high-school English class. For many of us, it was the antithesis of creativity. It's easy for creative people to view outlines as contrived and tedious things that inhibit artistic impulses; we may feel that by committing to a structure, we straightjacket the natural growth of our message. But, on the contrary, without an outline, you ensure that your writing will grow wild. You may write, and parts of it may be brilliant, but it probably won't move forward in a purposeful direction.

Unfocused creativity is like unharnessed electricity—it exists but has no grounding. Unlike high-school English, when you had to outline an assigned topic because you are passionate about what you want to write, an outline can flow logically out of your ideas, leaving plenty of room for inspiration and creativity along the way. Instead, it is simply a structural skeleton.

An Outline Creates a Path for you and your Reader.

An outline helps you identify the path you want your readers to follow. If you do not have a logical blueprint, you will not sustain their interest and, therefore, not convey the information as you intend.

Spirit links you to your creativity, but your intellect must usually partner with it to create balance. The purpose of using extensive outlining techniques is to make the book feel to the reader like it was easy, like the material flowed from a place of passion and logic, easily and purely. A good outline gives no hint of the writer's anxiety!

An Outline Gives Birth to your Table of Contents.

Unless your book is academic, you won't need many chapters. The more I have worked with book proposals, the more I am convinced that a strong Table of Contents, even if it eventually changes, will give you the foundation to write the book. Fancy titles are unnecessary. You want to think logically about how one point builds upon another to lead to the conclusion.

Here is the typical organization:
- Your Thesis
- Supporting information that grows to a crescendo like in a musical piece
- A decrescendo of information that leads the reader back to the beginning
- A conclusion that essentially restates the thesis or gives the reader closure.

Your Table of Contents is essential to your manuscript and will be included in your book proposal. If I start a book rather than restructuring one, I think of a tree. The table of contents is the tree trunk from which all chapter limbs will extend. When I first start writing, I often think I can begin writing with the branches, ignoring the tree and the roots. I then discover I am "out of my tree." Bad joke aside, your table of contents will follow the logic and chronology of your thesis.

The tree's roots are your thesis and what the book is about. The tree can represent the chapters. Nonfiction books typically have ten to twelve chapters with subheadings. The tree branches represent the subheadings, and the small twigs are the additional sub-subheadings. Today's readers like visual organization in the books they buy. They prefer the text to be organized into easily digested sections.

The internet and smartphones have changed the way people consume information. Nonfiction books, like mobile apps, should be designed to be user-friendly. Unless you self-publish, you may not have control over the final product's design. Still, as you structure your outline and manuscript, you can break up the material in a way that supports this ease of access approach to nonfiction books.

When you write your book proposal, you will see the benefit of a good outline beyond helping you write a well-organized book. Agents and editors look at the Table of Contents to see where the writer is going with the book.

The outline helps build trust that you, the writer, can fulfill the promise of your thesis.

The Mechanics of an Outline.

After you create your Table of Contents, you will add the two-line descriptions of the chapter. You will also use this in your book proposal, but for now, this is to help you organize your writing. Think logically. Although chapters may have many subsections, they focus on one main topic. Nonfiction book chapters are typically from 15 to 20 pages. Although page count and word counts vary, a sweet spot for nonfiction books is about 60,000 words, approximately 240 pages. Books can be longer and shorter, but as a small publisher, I have learned that page count translates into print costs. You should write until you feel you are done, but aiming for 15 to 20 pages per chapter will help you organize your outline.

Again, this depends on the type of book you are writing, the complexity of the subject, and your final page count. To review, the primary topics of your outline are your chapters; subtopics are the elements within the chapter that will enable you to create a logical whole, and you may have sub-sub topics to organize the content further.

Writing your outline

Begin by introducing your thesis, either in chapter 1 or in an introduction. Subsequent chapters will elaborate on specific aspects of your topic. Subheadings within those chapters will get even more detailed; when you get to the editing stage, these can be a handy way to check that you haven't strayed from your topic. The last chapter should summarize—briefly restate your thesis and the contents of the chapters—and then conclude, perhaps by inviting the reader to use this information to go forward incorporating your message into their own life.

A technique I learned from a high school English teacher was to use index cards. I don't always use them anymore, but if you are writing a book incorporating research, it is old-fashioned but still an excellent way to go. Some of my friends who do screenwriting swear by them because they can move them around on huge bulletin boards to get the sequencing of things just right. I cursed that teacher at the time, but she taught me some valuable techniques to tame my tangents.

Today, of course, there is software to help you with your outlines. My eldest daughter swears by Scrivener and always tries to get me to try it. I have adopted many techie ways but have yet to master this one. I am always looking for options to help with this process, so whatever works best for you is good.

Below is a sample outline that illustrates some of these points.

The book is: *Office Meditation to Enhance Your Work Life*

The hook is: Office meditation enhances your productivity, job satisfaction, and feelings of control over your work environment. This book gives you a humorous and inspiring guide to creating moments of intimate personal space and communion with the rhythms of the day even within an impersonal and hectic office."

Introduction: Set the stage for the book's premise by noting the stress and hectic pace of modern office life, a pace that is not conducive to reflection or feeling in control.

Chapter 1: Meditation as a Tool

Draw the reader into the book with a compelling scene: An important client is about to abandon the company because of their latest interaction with you. You've been called into an emergency meeting.

Chapter 1 a: Without meditation: Describe the scene, your composure, and others' reactions to you in the meeting.

Chapter 1 b: With meditation: Describe the scene, your composure, and others' reactions to you in the meeting.

Chapter 1 conclusion: Summarize the benefits of office meditation and invite the reader to learn more in the rest of the book. Introduce some simple relaxation techniques easily used in everyday life.

Chapter 2: Meditation breaks

Analyze the typical work day as having six opportunities to reconnect with the earth's rhythms and put your workday stresses into perspective:

Chapter 2a: Morning meditations:

In the morning, in your car, before you go into the office, as a way to center yourself and set a mood for the upcoming day.

Chapter 2a–1 After you greet your co-workers and sit at your desk, reflect upon what your co-workers add to your life and your place in the community.

Chapter 2a–2 Midmorning, do a stretching routine or take a walk to refresh your mind and perspective.

Chapter 2a–3 Before you eat lunch, focus on the abundance in your life.

Chapter 2b: Mid-afternoon meditations

Appreciate and take note of the fatigue and sense of accomplishment of a job well done.

At day's end, as you reflect and offer thanks for another day of life and your ability to contribute to it.

Chapters 3 to7:

These chapters discuss office problems such as co-worker conflict, challenging tasks, unrealistic deadlines, annoying bosses, and unsupportive staff.

The outlines for these chapters would be similar. They would include the problem, examples, some solutions, and meditation techniques as coping tools.

This is a rough example of how you might break down a book like meditation as a tool for the workplace. Still, it will likely not have enough information to sustain an entire book unless you bring in other topics like what is meditation, chair yoga as stress relief, and starting a wellness program in your workplace. We used this example of an outline in our first edition of this book, and I think today it would need to consider the home office due to the pandemic. Think about how you would further break down this topic into chapters with that new twist.

The idea of the outline is to tell a story in logical steps. Name the problem, how you solve it, explain the solutions, and then summarize everything in conclusion. As with anything, not all nonfiction books will follow this kind of structure. As you did with the genre, look at similar books to what you want to write to see how they are organized. I recommend examining successful books with a large following and high ranking. Analyze the structure and Table of Contents to see what is effective. You always want to strive to be the best. You may like a book that is not well-organized, but we do not want to settle for that.

Outlining Chapters

Outlining chapters is a way to start some preliminary writing. In book proposals, we call these annotations. They are short summaries of what information the chapter will cover. If your book contains anecdotes and descriptions, you can include them in the annotated outline.

At this point, you might only be working with topics rather than specific chapter titles. If you invent some titles, ensure they reflect the content you want to convey. It is easier to write what the chapter will cover. You can always be more clever later in your outline development. This is to keep you organized and on track.

Though the chapters should flow in a logical order (determined by your hook), also keep in mind that each one should be able to stand alone. If a chapter depends on the previous chapter to make sense, it probably does not warrant being separate. Of course, books are typically meant to be read sequentially, and each chapter builds on the previous ones. Still, each chapter should be a freestanding unit with a thesis, introductory statement or statements, support for your ideas, and a conclusion that summarizes and then leads the reader to the next chapter's topic.

For each chapter, elaborate on its topic with as many subtopics as a reader would need to understand the entire message you want to convey. If you're doing this manually, put one subtopic on a card and then lay these subtopic cards in the line below the card for that chapter. Proceed until satisfied that you've created enough detail for each chapter. Hint: This is called brainstorming! If you bounce ideas off another person, it is called "spit-balling." It's not so hard; in fact, it's fun. Write down your first thoughts, don't edit as you go, and work fast, letting the spirit flow. Later, when the Spirit has cooled, you can look at your outline with a cold eye, put it together and read it entirely. Does it still make sense? Do all your subtopics relate to that chapter, or are some better suited elsewhere in the book? Do you have a thesis for each chapter, and have you supported each one? All your chapters and their separate main points will return to the original topic. However, each chapter must make sense as a whole, beginning, middle, and end.

Writers can become intimidated when they consider the daunting task of breaking down their idea into an outline or organizing a random stack of index cards into a book. I have been told Scrivener helps you put it all together. I apologize if I am leaving out similar software programs. This is the only one my daughter has recommended so far.

Try to relax and remember that book chapters are like any other good writing: They all go back to the organization. The book has a structure that is followed in each of the parts. Paragraphs have topic sentences, supporting sentences, and a conclusion. Sentences follow structure, but I will not torture you and myself by explaining diagramming sentences. At this stage, I write instinctually and rely on grammar programs to point out my mistakes. Sentences can become second nature. However, the structure of books falls apart because of the logic in conveying the information.

In general, follow basic structure guidelines to avoid a confusing result. Viewed this way, you can see that even an overwhelming amount of information can be broken down into manageable bites. Memoir structure differs from the typical nonfiction book. I have included a guest essay explaining this unique structure to help you plan your book. The biggest issue I see with memoirs is the overload of details. Memoirs are similar to novels as they follow a story arc. However, the difficulty is for the author to be objective enough to tell the story without bogging it down in dullness. Refer to the Addendum for more information on memoirs.

9

WRITING AND EDITING

*A*fter you've outlined your book, the next step is to put some leaves on that tree. It is time to write. Some people liken writing and publishing a book to birthing a baby: some groaning, some pain, a lot of excitement, and a great reward at the end. And you have all the skills and preparation you need to birth this babe. Remember, your book already exists at some level. You can write it as only you can. It is your Spirit waiting to manifest itself in words. People will read it and love it. This should make you feel good. But I am a writer, so I know it may not. It might even make you nervous and doubt yourself more than when you had no idea how to write a book.

The Sacred Act of Writing

You write. Sometimes it flows fast and furious. Other times, each word has to be wrenched out of you, but you write until you are exhausted or finished, whichever comes first. Have you ever finished a project, and when you finally sit back and read it, you almost can't believe it came from you? You know you were there. You know you feel exhausted and blissful. You may even have a flare-up of carpal tunnel syndrome. But when the writing is finished, you also have a sense of awe that you were ever intelligent or wise enough to have written it at all. This is being in the flow.

The product may need refining, but if you are blessed to experience the deep connection of spiritual writing, you recognize how Spirit has taken you to a place beyond intellect, into the world of creation. It takes a certain level of faith to allow oneself to be lost in the process of writing. Humans have developed intellects that tell us there is something inherently unsafe or frightening about suspending time and space.

Now that you've understood the essential role the outline can play in helping you envision the shape of your book let it go. At this stage, the outline is a road map—but Spirit is your tour guide. Writing from your outline does not have to be linear; don't avoid unexpected detours in favor of finding the shortest distance to your destination.

Though you will eventually pare down your text and make sure every word relates to your thesis, so the end product is well organized, don't hold too tightly to your outline during the initial writing process, or you might miss some exciting adventures that you haven't anticipated. This may not be easy initially, but it will be vastly rewarding.

Your outline creates your boundaries, but they are not limitations. They provide direction and parameters, leaving it up to you to choose the route. This type of writing isn't for the fainthearted. It takes practice and a certain level of intimacy with your Soul to reach a state of writing bliss. But with trust and patience, anyone who truly wants to write can do so.

When you are ready to get into your writing, the first step is to discover which circumstances and environment most effectively allow you to journey inward on your creative quest. Some people like to write in silence. Some people want to have music blaring. As I am sure you have determined, or soon will, there is no one correct way. The only rule is this: No matter where you choose to write, look closely at yourself until you find the optimal way to maintain a sacred space as you work.

I work out of my home. I have a main office with my desktop. Sometimes I feel like I am working for NASA with two large screens surrounded by my equipment. I do my client work in that office and graphic design. I have done it enough to be reasonably proficient. Sometimes I write in that office, but I find too many distractions.

My writing room is more secluded. It has bookshelves and a partner desk (We put two desks facing each other in case we want to write at the same time). People ask how Jeff and I manage to get along in the same field. In case you are curious, we keep our territories separate. Hence two desks in one writing room. So far, our deadlines haven't overlapped. My writing room has fewer distractions and works well most of the time.

When I am under a deadline and find crickets belching from a mile away are pounding in my head, I take my laptop to the nearest library. Three libraries in my area have quiet rooms. You can book them for up to two hours at a time, and there are zero distractions. That is what I consider the big guns.

Only you know the best environment for your concentration. You will never find the perfect place. Figure out your minimum requirements and learn how to accommodate your needs with a measure of flexibility. Experiment with different situations to isolate what makes you more productive on certain occasions than others. For example, I have figured out I need to be in a closed space. I used to think I needed a clean desk, but I don't.

I need relative quiet. The television downstairs is fine, but my husband singing to the cats and dogs is out. Yes, that Jeff Herman! I am sure his secret is safe. We no longer have children in the home, so that is not a problem. I think if I am motivated, I can block out the world. Morning is my most productive time, and again, from about 8:00 to 10:00 pm. Mid-day writing is reserved for deadlines when I can't be choosy.

Many writers also find that they can write well only for a particular length of time. I need to take a break when the well runs dry for me after two or three hours. That is why I am constantly juggling several little projects at once. Some people, like my husband, think it is because I have an attention span the size of a piece of macaroni, but I am just priming the pump. Not always, I admit I am distracted by shiny objects. But sometimes, I am compartmentalizing.

When you have found the best way to reach your sacred writing space, use your outline to guide you back to the main road after any digressions or side tours. Without your map or navigator, you might drive around in circles. However, writers are sometimes surprised that a detour moves them in an unexpected direction. Don't resist the possibility that your book wants to move you toward an even better perspective than the one you have anticipated. Your book is alive, after all.

Once the outline is written, and the manuscript has been envisioned by your creative Source and the Divine voice, it already exists. Your job is then to capture it and give it form. Guidance can be mistaken for control. Just as with raising a child, remember that they have a separate path and that the more control you impose, the more resistance you will receive. Allowing some space encourages growth, so don't edit yourself too much at this stage. You can refine your words, but avoid squeezing your writing so hard that it can't breathe. If you find that you have extraneous ideas or concepts that don't fit anywhere within your current piece, write them down in another notebook or document. Later, you can patch them together or perhaps find you have the makings for another project.

When you let your ideas flow, don't look ahead to how many words you need to make it a book. Write as much as you feel you can in one sitting, and then forget about it. Live your life. Don't pressure yourself to produce a certain amount of material per day. If you write until your Spirit says you are finished, you will find that you have a book much sooner than if you keep checking your word count to see if you are done.

Modern life makes many demands on our time, and many of us are trying to start writing careers while emotionally and financially supporting ourselves and our families. When at all possible, carve out a time and place that is inviolable. You may need to sacrifice something or carefully negotiate to eke out a space, but it is part of the job. Some writers will keep their books hidden in their desk drawers to tackle them during lunch and breaks; some write during the short window after their children fall asleep and before they do. Writers who must "steal" time to write may keep a journal with them to keep creative thoughts fresh until they find a better time to give them life. Do whatever works. Finding time to answer your inner calling to write is not optional; it is a requirement for your spiritual wellbeing. You can tap into his inner voice to become a Divine writer.

The Values—and Perils—of Feedback.

Once you've written a good chunk of text, but well before you finish the book, it's time to gain some perspective on your work. Seeking and receiving others' feedback is integral to the writing process. It takes courage to expose your intimate thoughts and hard work to criticism. Still, this step carries you further toward becoming a professional writer who recognizes how the editing process strengthens your work. Perhaps the best way to get helpful feedback about your writing is to find objective readers—people whose judgment or intellect you respect—and ask them to read and comment on your work-in-progress. You're not asking them to edit or proofread the book for you; it's far too early. You are looking for impressions and global recommendations for changes in content or tone. Here are some questions to pose to your readers to maximize the value of their feedback:

- Is the subject interesting to them and addressed in sufficient detail?
- Does anything distract them as they read: redundancies; digressions; too much author presence; a tone that doesn't match the subject matter, or that is too preachy or didactic?

- What do they like best about the piece? Why?
- Is it easy to comprehend, or are there gaps where transitions or explanations are needed?
- When they read, what questions come to mind?
- Does the manuscript seem to carry through on its promises?
- Do they feel that you have said what you mean to say?

When choosing readers, try to match them to the subject matter. Envision your audience and find people who fit that profile. For example, if you're writing about the laying on of hands, with supportive anecdotes of faith healing, a left-brain, "where's the scientific evidence" engineer type of reader may not be the best choice; after all, they are probably not the target audience for your book.

Another great way to find support is by joining or forming a writing group or attending a writers' conference or workshop. Though it can be intimidating, writing groups have an advantage over simply showing your work to non-writers. If you choose this approach to feedback, remember the Self-Love and courage lessons.

Remember your worth, and don't let other people get under your skin for the Self-Love lesson. Critique is meant to help you improve. It should not tear you down. Do not let it.

If you remember the courage lesson, you will have enough confidence in your work and ideas to accept the helpful feedback while resisting comments that question what you know to be your Truth.

Keep in mind that all opinions are subjective, and when several people are involved, such as in a writing group, the dynamics of a particular group can be a blessing or a curse. Ideally, your most significant strengths or weaknesses will be identified by several people making similar comments. You will get various responses showing how the same work can affect different readers. Unfortunately, in some groups, decorum can take precedence over honesty, and you'll get no more illuminating feedback than "That is so great; I loved it." Others can become a cauldron of jealousy, with one person's good writing seen as a threat to the others. In groups like that, praise is given grudgingly or wrapped within a cutting critique.

It takes time to figure out who are your best critics. Seek people who share your passions, whose writing is at the same level or better, who have a healthy sense of self-respect, and who admire you for your accomplishments. They will neither be afraid to critique nor to praise.

When you have a friend whose comments you trust and whose edits make your words sing, you have found gold!

When you do hear negative or constructive comments, try not to give in to feelings of being personally violated. Don't cling to your specific words as if they reflect your worth. That is the mark of an inexperienced writer. But you are a sensitive artist, and if you do struggle with the Self-Love lesson, examine your feelings but do this in your journal away from other people. Remember Self-Protection as well. Don't show other people how to hurt you. If they are competitive and undermining, they will use it against you. The lessons are always lurking to help you become a better messenger. Accepting criticism gracefully and discussing differences of opinion will help you gain more insight into your writing and how other people might receive your message. You can develop this objectivity. It will take practice and internal reinforcement that you have what it takes and are worth it. On a positive note, good critique will help you see perspectives you may have never considered, helping you find new ways to enhance your work.

Keep in mind, however, that if you show your manuscript to ten different people, you will get ten different opinions—maybe even some that directly contradict each other. Listen courteously—you did invite comment, after all!—but remember that ultimately the work is yours, and you will decide on the final form. This is a true test for the "people pleaser" within many of us and a case where a strong sense of self and confidence in your message is vital.

You may want to pay an objective person to do the first read. This is not the same as a deep edit of your book and can be very valuable. I like to look at books for my consulting clients as if I were a consumer so I can give immediate impressions. I can't help doing some deep editing along the way, but the more valuable feedback is just what you will be asking your readers. I can determine when I lost interest or when I became confused. You want these things ironed out as much as possible before submitting to agents and Editors or, in the case of self-publishing, before presenting the book to your readers.

This information can significantly improve your work if you are working on a first draft. One of the primary values of feedback is seeing your work through others' eyes. You will gain a fresh perspective and a sense of renewal after you've sought feedback and gleaned the best from each reader. And that's a good thing because assimilating that feedback leads to the next editing stage.

Even Spirit Needs an Editor

Some of this is repeated in the chapter on the Publishing House and various people's roles. However, editing deserves a great deal of discussion whether or not you are pursuing a traditional route or are self-publishing. The digital revolution in publishing has increased access but has not relaxed the standards for good writing. When you write, the creative process is not bound by time and space, nor should it be. Creativity demands an unfettered mind. Only when you transcend the inner critic can your authentic voice emerge.

But now that your spiritual voice has emerged, it's exuberant, it's enthusiastic—and it needs to be edited! After getting feedback from others and perhaps by rereading your own words with an objective eye, you've found that, hard as it is to believe, this product of Spirit needs to be refined. Even if you have hired a first reader, you may need deeper editing of your book. When you are in the throes of writing ecstasy, the words often soar, even bringing you to laughter or tears as you read your words expressing what is in your heart. It is difficult at this stage to imagine that your writing is imperfect.

After the flow has ebbed, writers often forget—or haven't yet learned— the need for a collaborative effort and will try to own the words. So, it would be best if you allowed your words to leave the confines of your mind and the safety of your Soul after you write. You put them—and yourself—out there where everyone can see. When enough time has elapsed that you can read your words without your ego looking over your shoulder, you can go back to your manuscript and self-edit.

Self-Editing.

There are editing software programs, but you can't rely on them without scrutiny. They are better than they used to be, but human interaction is still the best way to refine a book. I don't recommend self-editing any more than I would represent myself if I were ever in court. Sometimes it is a matter of budget. Keep in mind the money we all spend on less important things. You are investing time into this project. You want it to look, sound, and be its best. I think self-editing is good if you are proofreading your work. It is always good to go over something to catch dropped letters or misspellings. But you want to give some time and space before doing deep editing. There are two possibilities with self-editing. You may love the work so much you ignore problems with the structure or flow. Or you look at something you have written with total disdain. You take that virtual or tangible red pencil and scribble all over your writing, "This stinks!" You crumple it up and toss it into the fireplace. The first is denial, and the second is not self-editing; it is self-loathing.

Save your pennies. Search your couch, the bottom of your wallet or purse, throw your change in a jar and save up to hire a professional editor. A good editor will look for ways to make your work better. They are on your side. Not all people who claim to be professional editors are qualified, but if you find a good one, you can have a great advantage. Don't accept failure. Give your book as many opportunities as you can.

The different Types of editing.

We will discuss the structure of a publishing house in the next section, "from manuscript to sale." There the editing is done for you or with you. If you are preparing a manuscript or book proposal to submit to a publishing house or to publish it yourself, you will also need to know about the different types of editing.

Conceptual Editing.

This is also called developmental editing. This type of editing is when you or a professional reviews the manuscript for overall tone and structure. Does the manuscript convey what you wish? When you look at a manuscript conceptually, you see both what is there and what is not there. Writers often believe everything is on the page because it exists in their brains. When you reread your own words, your mind fills in the gaps even if they are not completely clear to anyone else. The lack of transitions or disconnection of.ideas will naturally happen in a first draft, especially if, as a spiritual writer, you were in the flow. I recommend you hold off on a conceptual edit until you let your manuscript sit for days or weeks.

Another element of conceptual editing is analyzing a manuscript for what there is too much of. A common mistake is to rephrase and reemphasize critical points because they are so important. That is what we do in oral speech: we reiterate, restate, and emphasize to make our point. The audience doesn't mind the repetition, presumably because the speaker is there to engage them on other levels: facial expressions, hand gestures, bodily movement, and even props. But you are neither teaching nor giving a speech. Repeating essential ideas in your manuscript can distract your readers because even though you wrote your book in pieces, they may be reading it all at once. Their experience may be linear, so they are more likely to remember something you wrote in another chapter. So if I have done that, please forgive me. Or you can assume I did it just for illustration and not because I have overemphasized information.

Sometimes when a project is just finished, the prospect of reading it entirely is too tiring. It is essential not to skip this step of rereading, so I recommend putting the book down for a while. Pursue other things like sleep. I know from experience that hyper-focus on a manuscript can may you lose track of your surroundings. I have come out of a writing frenzy to find that I could barely recognize how the mess in my office happened. Coffee cups, unopened mail. As if I had been in a time warp. If you reread your book, you can often catch places where you might have rambled or unintentionally repeated yourself.

Readers can go back to other chapters if they want to reread key concepts. If you accidentally repeat a lot of the material, it may feel that you are underestimating the reader's intelligence. It is the voice of condescension that can creep in again. When you edit, cut redundancies and imperative language ("you must," "you should," etc.). Avoid, as much as possible, the use of "I." This is your book, and you are integral in it, but too much "I" leaves little room for the reader's "you."

Again, this is a "do as I say, not as I do." As any spiritual teacher, please take this information and become better than me.

Line Editing.

Many people think of this type of editing when they hear the word. It is when you review your manuscript, line by line, for grammar, spelling, and punctuation errors. Study the individual words. Are they necessary or redundant? Strive for tight writing. This means:
- Cutting words that do not serve a purpose
- Avoiding digressions that do not relate to your outline
- Eliminating flowery language that is there simply for its floweriness
- Not being too impressed with your cleverness
- Reducing the pomposity of grandiose statements that are unsupported or do not lead to reasonable and logical conclusions
- Releasing the bondage of overly tortured prose before you exhaust your reader
- Getting to the point before you lose your reader altogether
- Keeping paragraphs short

- After you have tightened up any wordiness, check your grammar.
- Do your subjects agree with their predicates?
- Have you spelled all proper names correctly?

You do not need to have the skills of a professional copy editor or proofreader. Still, you will naturally want your manuscript to be free of obvious grammatical and spelling errors. Refer to The Chicago Manual of Style (the stylebook used by most publishers) if you have any questions. Strunk and White's Elements of Style is widely regarded as the definitive resource on fundamental writing techniques and provides an excellent discussion of many common grammatical problems. The more you write, the more natural it will be for you to catch common mistakes.

When I wrote the first edition of this book, we were limited to word-processor grammar and spell checkers: They made many mistakes. They are not proofreaders. Now smartphones have autocorrect, which can create some hilarious results. Although the technology changes every year, I like Grammarly premium. As with any review software, you will want to look at the suggestions one at a time. My publishers have sent copyedited manuscripts to me with suggestions and queries. Working with Grammarly premium is very similar. The recommendations are typically improvements. But I never agree with everything. Software programs will not ask fact-checking- questions. Unless you work with a traditional publishing house, you should not skimp on this. Make sure your facts are as correct as they can be, or you will hear about it. This means spelling names correctly, dates, and factual information included in your book.

Lastly, before you submit your manuscript, format it so that it is double-spaced, single-sided, with page numbers, uniform margins of at least one inch on all sides, uniform chapter heads and subheads, and chapter titles that agree with your table of contents. Refer to the publisher's guidelines for specific directives, and follow them. It's like putting on your best clothes for a job interview; little details make a good impression.

Outside Editing.

When you reach a point where you have exhausted all of the standard self-editing methods, you might want to find an objective person to give you a more in-depth read than your earlier readers provided. The key word is objective—not someone who is your constant cheerleader, not someone who has no critical skills, and not someone who may be jealous and critiquing you too harshly. (Reminder: Courage and Self-Love with a bit of Self-Protection thrown in.)

It is also best if you find someone to edit your manuscript who does not have any stake in where you sleep at night (code: not your spouse!). Be aware that not everyone is supportive and that not everyone is right about everything. Again, as with your readers, please take in what people say, but take it with a grain of salt. If you find something useful, you can incorporate it. If the critique turns up something that shows you that the reader has no clue what you are saying, it doesn't mean the person is a dummy. It might be a flag that you have not made yourself completely clear.

I have friends who are, oddly enough, either Sagittarians or Taurians. They do not sugarcoat anything. However, knowing what I know now, I would consider springing for an editor if I felt I needed one, even though other people hire me to edit for them. That is a fib. My husband is a great editor at the right price, and I have learned not to throw things at him when I don't like what he has to say. I have also learned to warn him when looking for his business and publishing expertise or if I just want him to be a cheerleading husband.

I also know other excellent editors I would hire and am always happy to make referrals. We also have a group of professional editors on our social network, writersnetworking.com. We plan to set up a place where they can more directly list their credentials so you can choose for yourself.

What do Agents and Editors Say About Editing?

The answer to this question is simple: "Thank you for editing your work." When you hand in a well-edited manuscript, you save so much energy on the part of the agent or editor. It is easier for them to make an informed decision on whether to acquire a manuscript when they don't have to deal with content distractions and stylistic errors. Editors and agents look for submissions that have already been tweaked. A clean manuscript is just one more check mark in the plus column for you.

There is a practical reason for you to do your best to polish and professionally edit your work. Gone are the days when publishers dedicate editorial staff to fixing a marginal book. I was fortunate with my most recent book, *Member of the Family: My Story of Charles Manson, Life Inside His Cult, and The Darkness that Ended the Sixties* (William Morrow, a division of Harper Collins, 2017), because the publisher had a vision for the book, and we only had ninety days to complete it. This was the only time I had a dedicated developmental editor guide me as closely as the one assigned by Harper Collins. Although I wrote independently, the editor guided me along the way. The most significant thing I learned was about structure and pacing. The book is Dianne Lake's memoir structured in a three-act format. I wrote what I thought was a beautiful scene about the protagonist's last Christmas with her family in Act One, right before her family dropped out of society as Hippies and took to the road. The editor crossed it out, and I felt hurt. I took it personally, and the self-doubt monster crept into my thoughts.

I decided to ask him about it rather than stew. I meekly asked, "didn't you like my writing?" He answered with a definite yes. He liked it, but by the time the reader got to that scene, they wanted her to have met Charles Manson. Before this, I didn't understand the reader's experience and expectations and how that influences the structure.

I never had that level of hands-on editorial input from the traditional and large publishers that produced my previous books. Admittedly, this was a significant book on their front list, but in today's climate, I think this kind of editing is the exception and not the rule.

The takeaway here is as a first-time author, don't submit a manuscript to a publisher expecting that if they like it well enough, they will assign someone to edit it. Publishing houses are typically understaffed. They are looking for books that will have the most sales potential and require the least amount of in-house resources. Every dollar spent on editing incomplete manuscripts cuts into their profit margin. You want your submission to be as pristine as you can make it. Trying to exceed a publisher's expectations can only help you fulfill your mission. In other words, make sure your manuscript or proposal is ready to be made public, it is the best version you can achieve, and it adheres to the industry's guidelines before you bother sending it out. Do not look for second chances.

Part Three
FROM MANUSCRIPT TO PUBLICATION

DECODING THE PUBLICATION PROTOCOLS

When you are satisfied that your manuscript is the best it can be, it's time to send it out into the world. In this section, you will find information about who the players are in the traditional publishing industry, how to prepare your entrée into it by way of your query and book proposal, and what happens when an agent or publisher is interested in your work. As you know, nothing is guaranteed. You are not a failure if you do not reach a traditional publisher. I can't stress enough that today's publishing climate has made this more difficult even for experienced and already published authors. Not everyone will be traditionally published, but it does not mean you can't find a professional way to bring your work to your audience. Another thought is not everyone is meant to be published. Or at least not at the time you think is right. Try not to become so determined to control the outcome that you forget to see the lessons along the way. There may be other, unseen reasons for your efforts.

Although you do not want to be so stubborn as to miss inner guidance, at this point, think only of reaching your goal. You have read this far, so apparently, you have committed. Give your work your best efforts and vision, and listen to your inner guidance. When you have done that, turn it over to the universe. If you open to your Spirit, you will know what path to take. You'll give wings to your writing when you learn how to use the publishing protocols to your best advantage. So, engage your left brain and learn all you can. And do not dismiss self-publishing or hybrid publishing with real professionals. The entrepreneurial approach is not the last resort. Many writers choose this path for the many advantages it offers. Among them are:

- More control over the product
- A higher royalty or entire profit
- A shorter lead time to publication
- No middle person
- control over the outcome

A self-published or hybrid published book can compete in the marketplace if it is done with the highest of standards. There is enough writer education available to you through my websites alone to help you approach this professionally. You can be successful in achieving your writing goals. Embrace that belief and rid yourself of self-doubt. (Review the Self-Love lesson in Chapter 2) And please measure your success only with yourself. Think of writing as a lifestyle rather than a specific goal. Your experience on this journey will enhance your life on many levels. It is often challenging and frustrating, but the process also brings joy.

We will begin this section by setting the stage for how the publishing industry works. Then we will examine how to best present your work for submission, including book proposals and query letters. Many authors think too far ahead about publishing and do not spend enough time preparing for submission. If you take the time and create a compelling presentation, you increase your chances of making it to the top of the pile. My first writing mentor had many books successfully published. He explained that a book proposal should be better than the book.

Every step in the sales process should reflect your best efforts. There will be plenty of time for you to look for agents and publishers who will consider your work. For now, concentrate on your manuscript or book proposal before anything else. I always recommend building your platform as soon as you have your idea, but we will drill down into the steps in section four. Here we are only focusing on the submission package with a high-level look at the platform. Your platform is a significant piece of your proposal. However, work on the editorial piece, and when you reach section four, you can learn about proving your market and promoting yourself. You can go back to your proposal and add those things to finalize the picture of your benefit to anyone who wants to consider your work.

In the decades since I first wrote this book, I have worked with many authors either as a coach, editor, collaborator, or in building their brand. Many authors think a strong platform will make up for a weak book. A platform will put you over the top. It may be the deciding vote. But you can never forget this is a hard-copy business. Editors will still judge the quality of the writing and viability of the book. I don't mean you need to be the best or most literary writer. Your book must be well structured and well written to capture an audience and encourage word of mouth. You can get it into everyone's hands through clever marketing, but it will die on the vine if they don't enjoy it or see the value. If you are already marketing savvy, great. Just do not skimp on the editorial sections of the proposal, as they are equally weighted.

10

BEHIND THE SCENES OF A PUBLISHING HOUSE

*M*ost writers think of publishing houses as the Big Five. The dream is to find an agent and land a contract with one of these large companies so you can become a bestselling author. The vision of how this works is often limited. There is a lot that happens between manuscripts and shelves, and there are a lot of essential players along the way.

There are many options for publishing that did not exist twenty years ago, so we will break this chapter into traditional and alternative so you can understand the differences. Traditional publishers are not limited to conglomerates, and smaller presses should not be dismissed as viable options for your book. It is difficult to submit your book to a publisher directly without the benefit of an agent, but it is not impossible. We will save these discussions for the next few chapters.

The traditional publishing model is when the publisher pays an author an advance against royalties for the right to publish their book for a specific period. In the past, this publishing period was more defined and typically was from two to five years if the book was in print and actively being sold either from the front list or the back list.

Print on Demand technology made this publishing term more complicated as publishers can argue that keeping a small inventory or the access to printing the book on demand constitutes keeping it in print. When signing a publisher's contract, you must look at the term for the publishing rights. Arguably there should be a threshold whereby if the inventory or sales fall below a certain amount, the author can acquire the rights to their book.

Writers are only one part of the picture of bringing a book from idea to sale. Although publishing has changed and large publishers have become more prominent, the players are still basically the same. Here is the typical process. Presumably, your book has been submitted to the publisher by an agent, but perhaps you have been fortunate to be considered directly from your irresistible submission.

Who are the publishers?

You can find the listings of the Big Five Conglomerates through Publisher's Marketplace, *Jeff Herman's Guide to Book Publishers, Editors, and Literary Agents,* and many other resources. The process from acquisition to shelf is the same for them all, except that some editors have more authority than others, and some have much bigger budgets.

If you can obtain a contract with a large publishing house, that is a blessing. The larger houses have bigger budgets, can promote you, and can give you greater credibility. You will have better distribution and access to media. We don't want to create a reverse prejudice against the larger houses simply because they are Corporations. Corporations can do good things. They may be less accessible to you until you have a large following because, even though they have bigger budgets, they are risk averse. They want the sure thing.

The larger publishing houses often have imprints that accept transformational, inspirational, and spiritual titles. This was not the case when this book was first published. Readers showed the publishing world what they wanted, and the publishers followed suit. It could be great if you could meet the threshold for a larger house. However, you may also be lost in the shuffle. Large houses are prone to orphaned titles. If a Big Five publishing house gives you a reasonable offer, it would be difficult not to want to take it. So, say a prayer of thanks but still expect that you may be treated as the Golden Child upon publication and will then be asked, "what have you done for me lately." Like anyone else, your publisher will expect you to support your book's marketing and promotion.

We are all happy for you if you get a major publishing contract. Your success is the success of all spiritual writers. Just remember who you work for and try to pay it forward. Don't say what I heard coming out of the mouth of a marginal writer who was lucky enough to have gotten a contract: "I had to work hard to get here; why should I tell anyone how I did it."Remember the saying: "pride goeth before a fall." If you are privileged to get a contract, please share with other worthy Souls who may not have the time to waste before it is their moment to shine. We are all in this together.

Independent Publisher does not Mean Small.

Keep an open mind about submitting to an independent publisher. Independent can mean small, but size does not matter.

An independent publisher might only have a few titles and may have been created to support the work of its founder. That is how Louise Hay got started. Independent means a corporate behemoth does not own it. You may receive more personal attention at an independent house. You may get a modest advance, but if you follow the advice you can learn in this book and on the various sites we provide, you should be able to turn any published book into a success. If you have an independent publisher, you have something self-publishers do not. You can focus on your writing and promoting without production details; you also have bookstore distribution. You may never see your book in a bookstore, but the potential is there.

A Word of Caution.

If you are a starting writer, be grateful and follow the signs wherever Spirit guides you. Don't think you will give up everything and become a self-supporting writer. Even those published by large houses can't live on their advances forever. You are creating a new business for yourself that includes your book. It is not the other way around. Your book will not create the business for you. Spiritual Writers can move beyond the starving writer paradigm or the self-sacrificing servant of humanity. You can't serve if you can't eat. But all the pieces need to be in a row. If you are fortunate to find a legitimate and successful independent publishing house willing to support your vision, work with you, and pay you something for your book, pray about it and then do it.

You can become prosperous as a writer, but you should plan to grow your career as you would anything else. Be methodical and consistent, and you can move mountains. You can also create change in the world with your work. Therefore, finding a strong independent publisher to share your vision is a blessing.

Who are the Players in a Publishing House?
Acquisition Editor

The first person to have any contact with your query letter, book proposal, or manuscript is the Acquisition Editor, but it is more likely the assistant editor. These are typically young people who are paid very little but wield a lot of power in the path to publication.

There are so many submissions daily that the acquisitions editors who select books for the publishing house do not have time to screen them. The first screen is typically easy because many queries or submissions will automatically not make the first cut. It is likely to be the process we use at the literary agency. If a book is not something we typically represent, or it is not well written, or is simply bad, we reject it first round. Then the assistant will select projects that will go to the next level to the editor. Typically, out of courtesy, an editor will read a submission sent in by a literary agent without the first gatekeeper, which is why we all select carefully. If we send submissions that appear to use none of our discernment, we will lose the reputation we have established over many years. We try to make sure the projects we send in, even if they are not the right fit, have something to make them worthy of consideration.

If you are unagented, your submission to an editor should be as professional as possible. If you pass beyond the assistant, you are on your way.

The next step will be for the acquisitions editor to bring your work to the editorial or pub board. These are meetings where all the editors present their best picks. There are likely to be members of the sales and marketing teams present to express their concerns about particular books. Now, more than ever, the sales and marketing teams have a significant say about what is acquired. They know a great deal about trends and what their typical clients buy. If it looks like the author will generate some buzz or brings a great platform to the table, they will argue back and forth until it is determined that the book and the author will be a good match for the list.

There are only so many places in any given season. If your book is like something else and the other submission has certain things in its favor, your book will be nudged out. You cannot know what they are receiving, so you need to make your submission irresistible. Assume there is competition for your spot. Just don't become paralyzed at the thought of it. Spirit will help you, but you must do the work and as much research as you can.

Acquisition editors have some autonomy to decide what they would like to publish. However, the ultimate decision is made only after discussing it with other team members. An acquisition editor is responsible for making good decisions and will not make it on gut reaction alone.

Sales and Marketing

An editorial meeting where acquisition editors make decisions will include the sales and marketing people. Having an acquisition editor on your side will significantly increase your chances of an offer. Still, if the sales and marketing team sees problematic concerns, it could result in a pass.

The job of sales and marketing is to determine if they can successfully sell the book into the stores, including the online retailers, which are considered the same as the box stores. They need to see the data and figure it out in sales projections.

Publicity

Many larger traditional publishers have in-house publicity departments. The publicity team will be included in an editorial meeting to review their ideas for promotion. This is added to the equation of how much of a risk a book is and if the risk is reasonable. They will present how they would publicize the book, and the editorial board will consider their ideas when deciding whether to make an offer and how much.

What if a Publishing House Makes me an Offer?

Although we are getting ahead of ourselves, this will help you understand the process's inner workings. So, let's assume you have been given an offer. You know what to do—give thanks! Then get down to business. If you received the offer on your own, without the benefit of an agent, contact an agent to enhance your negotiating presence with the publisher. Agents often negotiate publishing contracts for books they have not sold; you will wind up with an expert to oversee the contract negotiations and editorial process for you, and you will pay a smaller commission than if you had signed with an agent before finding a publisher. The agent may also do it for a set consultation fee instead of a commission. But that is to be negotiated with the agent.

Another significant advantage is that you have now obtained an agent who will potentially consider you for future projects. Consider trying to get an agent to help you negotiate your publishing contract. Your lawyer may not be the right person for this job. They may not be familiar with publishing contracts, and it is their role to find flaws, not to close deals. On the other hand, an agent is there to craft a deal to your best advantage. The agent's fee is related to the amount of royalty income he can negotiate for you; he will want to see that the contract is weighted as heavily as possible in your favor and will try to retain appropriate subsidiary rights, such as audio or video productions that stem from your book. Agents are also far more familiar with what is negotiable and what is not.

Also, leave your "significant other" out of the process. Some writers have lost deals because they brought an overly exuberant, unsavvy, and nit-picking spouse into the contract negotiations. This situation can get very sticky for the publisher, and any bad past experiences with this situation may make them want to run the other way.

The contract defines your commitments to the publishing house and its obligations to you. It includes the deadline for the manuscript submission, approximate page length, the amount of your advance, your royalty percentage, and the retention and potential sale of subsidiary rights to your book. Resources for writers such as the Authors Guild authorsguild.org) contain copies of publishing contracts that you can review. You will see what terms are typically negotiable and are not up for grabs. Even if you have an agent, educate yourself regarding publishing contracts. But make sure to leave this to the professionals.

Don't expect a significant advance the first time around. By having a publisher, you have someone to make your book exist who will help you launch it into the universe and is paying a lot of money to do it. Remember that bookstores sell books by consignment and can return unsold books to the publisher anytime. Without a sales history to estimate from, a publisher is taking a risk on a first-time writer, and a modest advance—under $7,000—reflects that risk. Selling your spiritual manuscript is only the beginning of the publishing process. You will begin working with an editor who will critique your book and suggest changes.

If you sold your book on proposal, the next step is writing the book. You are far from finished, even if you have sold a completed manuscript. You will be working with many members of the publisher's team. Expect your final published text to look very different from your original manuscript. Accept that their input has value, and enjoy your ride!

What Happens Next?

After negotiations and a deal is made with a deadline in place, you will meet the team. A word about deadlines: your deadline represents when the manuscript is to be handed in and will typically be well before the publication date, as many things need to be done before it can be printed and distributed. Traditional publishing works on a list schedule two times per year with few exceptions. One of the reasons is that book buyers have their most significant budgets during those times. Publishing, in general, is always a year or two delayed from acquisition to publication.

There is a need for lead time in establishing lists. Some writers feel the urgency in their books and do not realize that acquiring a manuscript is only the first step. The book will not be published until another list or the following year. The book will need to go through contract negotiations, signing, scheduling, editing, copyediting, production, galley proofing of the final manuscript before it goes to print, and then the actual scheduling of the book to be sold to the bookstores. Many new books used to be presented to the trade during BEA, Book Expo America, but that no longer exists. Although there are other trade shows, the pandemic has left many of these gatherings facing an uncertain future.

Who Works Inside the Publishing House?

After the deal is made and you are in the system, the fun begins. You will be assigned a developmental editor, your project manager, who will evaluate your work. I have written thirteen books, and my experience with most developmental editors is they will connect with you at the beginning and maybe check in. I haven't had much involvement with my books until I hand them in. I don't know if that is typical.

My first twelve books were basic nonfiction. As I have described, my lucky thirteen was a book on the front list, which may explain why my developmental editor was more hands-on. Or maybe I was fortunate. Remember my first writing job? That author was given complete autonomy and handed in a manuscript that was not accepted. Lucky for me, not so fortunate for whoever had to hire me to fix the book. They could have dropped it from the list and asked for the advance back.

There are many kinds of editors at a publishing house. You can create this kind of team for yourself if you self-publish, but this is the kind of collaboration that goes into bringing your book to the consumer.

Developmental Editor

If a publisher offers you a contract, then the fun begins. You will be assigned a developmental editor and a deadline. If you have completed the manuscript, your editor will read it and send back "queries." These may be fact-checking items or questions of consistency. It may also be all kinds of editorial suggestions. You can certainly argue against them. However, in my experience, I have found most of the recommendations to be vast improvements. The developmental editors are not in the business to make you feel small or squash your creativity. They have experience in making good books better. Try not to let your ego get in the way.

Writing is a craft that a second set of eyes can always improve. On the other hand, you are allowed to object to what may seem to be ridiculous edits that change the essence of your message. Just try to be diplomatic about it. You may be assigned another editor if you do not get along.

When the book has been edited, handed in, and accepted, the book will go to production. You need to inform your editor if there is a reasonable deadline problem, even if it results from procrastination paralysis. Good communication on all sides will make this part of the process most successful.

Copyediting

The first part of the production will be a copyedit of the book. Copyediting means that it will be reviewed according to the stylebooks, whether Chicago or AP, to reach a consensus on proper grammar and spelling. It is amazing how many typos or missed words appear in so-called final manuscripts. Again, you will be given the manuscript with queries, particularly about facts and the spelling of names. Your copy editors will expect you to look at the manuscript to see if you can catch any elusive typos or mistakes. You can also sneak in changes at this stage, although they won't recommend it.

Then the book will be laid out for the print run; the editors will give you a galley proof before the book goes to print for a final review for typos or errors that might have slipped past everyone. In the past, the galley was a physically printed bound book. Some publishers still create these as uncorrected copies for review, but most of my books in the last decade have been done digitally. I like to print them out because it is easier on the eyes, but I have never received a bound copy.

This stage is the last time you can make any changes, and they should be limited to egregious errors or typos. As a publisher, I now understand the reason for this. After production has designed a book, any significant change will throw everything off. If the designer uses software to "flow" the text, they will need to do it again to maintain the pages and organization. This do-over costs money and will only be done if absolutely necessary.

Design

During this time, there will be a cover developed for your book. You might have input in the title and the cover if you negotiated for these things in your publishing contract. Here is another place where it is good to defer to the experts. Writers fall in love with their clever titles, but by the time it reaches publication, it is not even close to what they had in mind. I have seen contracts delayed over titles. The publisher often knows best. Unless they have had no success, they know what titles can grab a reader in 20 seconds. Be flexible here. But do not roll over and play dead. It just means do not become crazy and unreasonable, so they regret acquiring the book. There may be other more important battles to fight, and you want them to be thrilled to promote your book and tell all their friends about it.

The sales department is your friend. The publicity department is your friend. When it comes down to it, you need to be your book's friend and help give it life beyond what anyone else will do for you. Let the professionals do their job and only speak up if you fully believe there are not reflecting your true message.

What is Hybrid Publishing, and How Does it Differ from Vanity?

Vanity publishing was a mainstay of an opportunity to provide a publishing option for those people who wanted books to appeal to their vanity. They would pay a company to do everything for them and produce lovely books, but these companies had nothing in common with actual publishing. They would "publish" anyone who would pay them and had no actual means of distribution. These books were a way for people to create something they could give to family and friends, and although they looked nice, there would be an inventory in someone's garage.

Before print-on-demand options and online distribution platforms, self-publishing wasn't much different. Writers would need to wear all the hats to make a book happen. Some online platforms like Lulu, Smashwords, and Amazon made it easier to "publish" books, but without much help, the books remained amateurish. This general comment is not to disparage the books that find audiences. On the contrary, people make a lot of money with well-marketed books on Amazon, and all publishers, with few exceptions, distribute their books through online platforms.

In 2010 there was a proliferation of author services companies created with publishers who called these their self-publishing arms. Several of these were and are dedicated to spiritual publishing. However, I know first-hand from speaking with their executives that the self-publishing divisions are to generate cash. They are not there to "discover" titles to include in their main publishing catalogs. Instead, they are what they are, author services that will help authors create and produce their books.

If you know what you are getting, there is nothing wrong with using these self-publishing companies. They can get you started, and you can research what you get and how. These companies are a step up from complete self-publishing, but you are still mostly on your own.

Hybrid publishing is something that is growing out of changes in the industry and a need for authors to have options that include professional services. Although standards are still in development through such organizations as the Independent Book Publishers Association, they each seem to be evolving in the same direction.

Hybrid publishing involves monetary investment on the part of the authors. Typically, it is a menu of services such as editing, copy editing, design, and distribution. A significant difference is these titles are curated, and the hybrid publisher uses the same goals and standards as any indie press. They make money by selling books and not through their author services.

Although I only know how my company works, this business model allows the authors to pay for what they would get in a traditional publishing house in exchange for a much higher royalty. Hybrid companies are not passive. If they choose to publish a book, they provide everything needed for that book to compete in the marketplace.

Not all hybrid companies have traditional bookstore distribution. Micro Publishing Media has distribution, but we only select a few titles for the two lists we publish each year. Standard distribution is also part of our business model. We created a company we believe represents the way people buy books. Although we will discuss this in greater detail in part four, we discovered that people have a buying process that begins with researching what others recommend. We also realized that people are looking for a niche and a place to belong. With limited entertainment time, they look for books in specific categories. So, our model is to provide some books directly to the consumer through digital marketing, and we put other books with a broader audience into bookstore distribution.

The fees for author services vary, but when you comparison shop, don't stop at the prices. There are many companies with people who have not spent any time in the trenches of publishing, so this is the time to use your Self-Protection skills of discernment.

If you are entrepreneurial, the hybrid model could be perfect for you. You will be doing the marketing and promotion no matter who publishes you, but if you find a good match, you could build a thriving cottage industry for your work.

11

FINDING A LITERARY AGENT

*D*o I need an agent? As both agented and independent writers get published, the answer to this question depends on what sort of publishing path you want to take: If you are seeking traditional publishing, a literary agent is necessary. You can succeed without one, but a literary agent will give you the credibility and access you need to get past the publishing gatekeepers.

Any sizeable publisher is overburdened with submissions. While assistants can look for viable projects through general screening, it is more efficient for them to receive recommendations from agents whose profession is screening. A literary agent's job is to search through query letters, manuscripts, and proposals to find projects they can sell to publishers. It can take many years for an agent to develop the sensibility to know what projects are commercial. Part of their job is to form relationships with editors to know what they look for in their submissions. Editors rely on literary agents to bring the projects that fit their list and have the right platforms or credentials to support book sales. Literary agents work on commission, so if they want to earn a living, they need to learn their trade.

Literary agents are experienced publishing professionals. If you can sign with an agent, it is a game changer. As with anything related to publishing, it is time to use your Self-Protection due diligence to weed out agents who are not legitimate. You will want to avoid fee-charging agents or those who don't have any book sales to show you. You don't want to listen to whiney complainers on the internet who might disparage literary agents who reject their masterpieces or do not respond to them within a reasonable time. There are reasons to avoid certain people who claim to be literary agents but are money-making schemes. But all agents will give people reason to complain. The proof of their efficacy is in the track record with books sold. You can find agents' listings in *Jeff Herman's Guide to Publishers, Editors, and Literary Agents* or in many other places, including *Publisher's Marketplace*. There are other guides to literary agents, but since I am married to Jeff Herman, I think his book is the best, and I leave you to research the others on your own. Unlike other listings, Jeff has the agents fill out surveys giving you valuable information right down to what they have on their wish lists.

What is The Role of an Agent, and What Makes a Good One?

The role of a literary agent is to act as a writer's business representative. An agent who agrees to represent you will review your work, advise you about its quality and market potential, and devise a strategy to pitch it to publishers who they think will be the most interested in it. The agent will negotiate contract terms for you if a publisher makes you an offer.

Agents are the publishing world's gatekeepers, weeding out material that is not ready for the marketplace. They represent authors but also are friends of the publishing houses. Editors often contact agents who have brought them good manuscripts in the past and will share their wish-list for future projects. As with anything, an agent's assessment of a manuscript's quality is subjective. As do editors, experienced agents typically gravitate toward specific areas of comfort and specialization. If you can find an agency that specializes in your area of interest, you've got someone who can enthusiastically advocate for you. They may also bring you projects in your wheelhouse.

Agents want to discover new talent and must sell manuscripts to publishers to stay in business. They want to like your work if you have something interesting and can say it well.

Anyone can call themselves an agent, but a literary agent should have some prior connection with the publishing industry before hanging out a shingle. Or they should come from a career like public relations or marketing. An agent's value is their ability to advocate for your work and access to publishers.

An agent does not work for the writer but rather on behalf of the writer. Signing with an agent gives them the power to act for or represent your interests. They will become your professional face when dealing with publishers. Good agents know how to close a deal. While negotiating with both parties to create a mutually satisfying agreement, they will act in your best interests, working for the best monetary advance and terms possible.

As an author, you can, of course, submit your proposal directly to those publishing houses that accept unagented submissions. Still, even at those houses, an agent can give you more leverage. Individual authors can't have the access that agents have to publishers, no matter how savvy they are. A good agent should be able to pick up a phone and get through to an editor without having to plead with her assistant. Suppose the agent has a good reputation for bringing in quality manuscripts and working ethically. In that case, publishers will answer their calls, and the submissions will go right to the top of the editor's in-box.

Finding an Agent.

As writers, we are highly vulnerable to anything that seems to bring us closer to our goal. Reader's fees for literary agents are a red flag as they work on commission. However, the guidelines for agents have been blurred as they look for additional ways to earn a living. The key here is clarity.

Many agents are doing content strategy to help clients whose work is good but perhaps time-sensitive or is too niche for a large publisher. These agents or consultants guide the projects and package them so the writers can determine how to best bring them to market. These are not the same situations as fee-charging agents. If you are seeking traditional publishing, there is no reason for a literary agent to charge you anything. If you think about it, if an agent charges you to read your manuscript, there is no incentive for them to make a sale for you. If they feel your book is mediocre, they still make some money. This choice is not the same as hiring people with industry experience to consult and edit. Downsizing in publishing is forcing many professionals to change careers. They have years as in-house editors and are now working as independent editors or packagers.

Most reputable agents don't charge these fees; instead, they work on commission, typically 15 percent of the author's advance and royalties, meaning that the agent doesn't get paid until he places the manuscript with the publisher and the author gets paid. For such agencies, reading manuscripts is simply a cost of doing business, not a source of income. Therefore, you may not hear back from a literary agent immediately. If they receive many submissions, they are under no obligation to respond except out of courtesy. They do not get paid unless they sell your work, so they are looking for commercial projects. We will cover book proposals and query letters in the following two chapters. These are the vital tools for finding an agent.

The first step to finding an agent is to review the listings of who they are. You can also find them by reviewing books and checking the acknowledgment pages. Most authors will acknowledge their agents, so you will see who represents the types of books you are writing. You will want to create a wish list, but you won't want to reach out to any agents until you have perfected your submission. Contacting an agent to test the waters about your idea is a bad mistake. But if we assume you have everything ready to go, here is how you go about it.

The first step after you create a list of agents you want to approach is your query letter. Although we will discuss what you should include in the letter in the next chapter, this will be the first contact you make with the agent or agency.

Step One: Make a list of potential agents

Step Two: Research the agency

Step Three: Make sure you understand their submission guidelines

Step Four: Determine if they represent your type of book

These may seem logical, but when screening query letters for the agency, I was astounded by how many people sent in novels. In the 25-plus years that the agency has existed, Jeff Herman has only represented and placed three novels. It should have been evident from the titles sold list that most of the books are nonfiction, and it is written all over the website. Even before websites, any listing of agents stated The Jeff Herman Agency represents nonfiction. I think by now, writers should believe him.

The problem for you is you will be rejected by an agent immediately if you do not fit their typical list. There are so many opportunities for you to determine what an agent represents that there is almost no excuse for this mismatch.

Few query letters are sent by mail these days, so you will also want to review the online submission guidelines on an agent's website. Many of these websites will have a place where you can submit directly through an online form. This submission process improves your chances of hearing back one way or another more quickly, but remember the agency is under no obligation to respond. It is perfectly acceptable to make multiple submissions to literary agencies if you inform them that you are doing so.

Challenges for Spiritual Writers Finding an Agent.

One problem spiritual writers sometimes face in finding and keeping an agent is letting their sense of mission get in the way of following publishing protocols. As a spiritual writer, please do not fall into the trap of thinking that your book is preordained to be published. I can't stress enough that publishing, even spiritual books, is a business first and foremost; those who know how to play the game will win. You can undoubtedly use your intuition to guide you as to where to make your submissions, but this is where you use your know-how, savvy, logic, and brains. The Spirit may guide you, but you need to take the lead. And don't set your mind on one agency because you have a vision. Sometimes that vision will lead you to the right place. If you get stuck in one direction, you may miss other opportunities.

Because agents are inundated with submissions, many improperly submitted proposals are summarily dismissed. Spiritual writing has many categories, so refer to what kind of spiritual writer you are to ensure you apply to the appropriate agencies. Many nonfiction agencies or agencies that do fiction and nonfiction will look at books that fall into the practical spirituality categories. You will want to find like-minded agents if your work is more esoteric. If you find someone you feel has potential, don't let your enthusiasm get in the way. Be sure to review submission guidelines and adhere to all of them. Some agents' policies are to reject anything unsolicited, except for query letters automatically, so submit your proposal and manuscript only when asked to do so. Your book may be the next most extraordinary work of spiritual literature, but these agents will still not look at it if they have not requested it. Try to catch their attention by following protocols and showing that you are a serious professional writer who will be a good team player. Selling books requires teamwork. The partnership between a spiritual agent and writer can be a powerful one. As a spiritual writer, remember that the agent knows what they are doing. Let go and let Spirit work through both of you.

Things not to do when seeking a literary agent:
- Do not phone with an idea, especially if you do not have a manuscript or proposal ready.
- Do not phone us to find out if we have read your query.
- Do not send a letter to a literary agent addressed to "Dear Agent."
- There are so many directories with names and addresses of agents that there is no excuse for this.

- Do not send a letter to an agent meant for another agent. Authors do this more than you know.
- Do not send an email submission of a query letter listing the other agents to whom you are sending it. This email faux pas also happens more than you know. Instead, take the time to send separate submissions.
- Do not send a query or email submission that includes your proposal and/or manuscript. Agents have too much to read as it is. They will request what they would like to see.
- Do not behave in a hostile manner toward a literary agent for rejecting your work. You may see them at a conference and who knows they may remember you and your work. Could happen.
- Do not stalk your potential literary agent or your actual literary agent, who then has to drop you as a client because your behavior is so bizarre at a writer's conference that you are freaking out all the attendees. This situation has happened.
- Do not call a literary agent and bully the receptionist so you can talk to the literary agent. At least at our literary agency, I often answer our phone in my receptionist's voice. Do you think we want a client who does not respect the support staff?
- When given an offer of representation, do not immediately go Hollywood. While agents are hard at work trying to sell your project, you are welcome to tell people you have a literary agent. Just do not expect us to be available to now read all your friend's work so you can show off how important you are. Sometimes we do it but do not like anyone to expect it of us.

What do I do if an Agent Makes Me an Offer of Representation?

When an agent requests an exclusive look at your manuscript, they want the first opportunity to see the material in greater detail before any other agents have a chance to snap it up. And this means your query did the job of convincing them that you might have more there. However, expressing interest for a first glance is only one step in the process. Don't put a deposit on a new car yet.

You are not obligated to offer an exclusive to anyone just because they ask, any more than you should marry the first person to say they like you. However, if someone else is your first choice, ask if that agent has any interest. Sometimes telling an agent that another agent is requesting an exclusive can create just the right amount of competition between professionals. (Be warned, however, that fabricating interest can lose you the deal—most agents can spot it a mile away.)

If you agree to an exclusive, you should offer a short but reasonable period. If the agent is interested, you should hear quickly—from a few weeks to a month. You should follow up after the allotted time to determine genuine interest and to see if you can reel in an offer. Sometimes the lack of response is a matter of time constraint and is not a reflection of an agent's interest in you. Your project may not be an immediate priority unless you are a known quantity. If you tend to obsess and worry, try not to wallow in thoughts of rejection until you have received them.

Assume the best and politely check on the status of your submission. Do not nag; just inquire and make the agent aware of the expiration of the exclusive. If the agent who requests the exclusive is your first choice, there will be an underlying expectation that if an agent offers you representation, you will accept. There is a minimal variation from the standard 15 percent commission, and at this stage, we don't recommend you shop further even if you are still getting responses. If you receive other requests for material, you can use this information to leverage a more expedient offer from your first-choice agent. Still, we do not recommend sending out manuscripts after receiving an offer you are comfortable with. It is bad form.

If the first agent to respond is not your first choice, or if you receive several responses, it is best not to offer an exclusive even if one is requested. Be upfront and indicate that it is a multiple submission but that you will keep the agent apprised. Make sure you are diligent about contacting any agents who have requested to review your manuscript should you decide to sign on with someone else. Agents earn nothing unless they sell books, and it is not nice to waste people's time. If you are trying to hedge your bets by going behind people's backs, you may wind up with nothing.

Authors do not realize that although many books are published each year, there is a limited number of active agents. Eventually, most agents cross paths or hear about one another. There are also only so many editors. We had one client who had signed with us to represent one of her books. Unbeknownst to anyone but her, she signed a separate project with another agent. There is nothing illegal about this, as most contracts do not tie up authors for all their books, but there was something she overlooked that cost her representation.

As we were shopping her book to publishers, the other agent was also shopping another of her books to the same publishers. The other agent was even more shocked than we were and dropped her immediately. We were not thrilled with the client's deception, so we dropped the project we represented. Eventually, she realized it was her fault and requested that we represent her again. We are softies, and we like her, so we did take her back. We have since developed a wonderful relationship, and she has had a very prolific career. But you may not be so lucky. Writing is a business, but never underestimate the human factor.

When you receive an offer for book representation, this is the time you can shift the focus a bit from selling yourself to allowing the agent to do a bit of selling. There are varying opinions about this, but as I mentioned already, it is best not to put the agent on the hot seat—remember, you haven't made him any money yet. Unless you are already an established author, there is an expectation on the part of the agent that there will be a learning curve. The agent will factor how well he can work with you and guide you toward a sale and a successful career. Even though you have an offer, you are not entirely in the driver's seat. For every accepted author, many others are vying for the same spot. If you have done some research, you will already know about the agency you have targeted, but you may want to learn more. While you are justified in wanting clear information about the agency helping you shape your future, it's essential to hone your questions so they do not put the agent on the defensive. The last thing you want to do is cause them to question the decision to make the offer.

Some questions you can ask include:
- How long have you been an agent?
- How many titles have you sold?
- May I see your list of client books sold to publishers?
- What is your commission rate?
- How and when am I to be paid?
- Do you require a contract, and what is the term?
- Can your contract be terminated at any time?
- Do you have anyone who handles film, television, audio, foreign, or other rights stemming from a publishing contract?
- Do you charge any expenses?
- How will you communicate with me regarding the status of my project? How often?
- Where do I sign?

Most agents have a packet of material available that will answer most of your questions. We do not recommend that you ask overly technical questions when making your decision. The matter is to determine if there is a good match and to learn how things will work for you directly.

When you are offered and accept representation, you need to avoid trying to micromanage things. Most agents will keep you informed about status changes but may not contact you immediately with every rejection. There are a certain number of rejections anticipated with multiple submissions to publishers. The agent may wait to go over them with you all at once to establish an additional strategy for selling your book. This process also prevents the dreaded writer-insecurity backlash. There is nothing worse for an agent trying to sell a book than a hysterical writer. We had one client who became so enraged about the rejections she was receiving that she went behind our backs directly to the publishers, demanding an explanation. The result was embarrassing and not fruitful for anyone.

Agents assume a certain amount of risk in representing a project with a writer attached to it. Writers have the advantage of being able to thoroughly research an agency, while agents often must accept the writer's word. Google and social media have been an excellent help for agents and editors to learn more about their clients. Still, it is like the security announcements at the airport: "Has anyone unknown to you given you any packages?" and "Have your bags been in your possession the entire time?" If you were doing something you are not supposed to do, such as carrying contraband or leaving your bags unattended, would you tell someone? Similarly, agents can't ask, "Are you insane, mentally unbalanced, and liable to drive us crazy with your constant unreasonable demands?" Is anyone going to say yes?

So, if you are close to the edge and unwilling to admit it, at least consider that carefully building a relationship with your agent can benefit your overall writing career. A good agent is well connected and can help you throughout the entire publishing process, far beyond contract negotiations.

Agents can not only advocate on your behalf, but they can also find work for you. Agents often have projects that need good writers. Fiction writers can also benefit from a relationship with an agent that extends beyond the specific book offered for representation. Many novelists write nonfiction to maintain a steady writing career. Fiction writers also find creative fulfillment in writing narrative nonfiction and may find opportunities through their agent that they might otherwise not find on their own.

Agents are not entirely unavailable to their clients while they are submitting your book to publishers. If you do not abuse the communication, your agent will keep you apprised regularly. When a publisher makes an offer, your agent will typically and should contact you immediately. It is the agent's responsibility to inform you of any offers and help you determine whether they are acceptable. You are not required to accept any offer, but you can consult with your agent about whether the offer is the best for you. There are often factors other than the dollar amount that would choose a publisher advantageous to the book's success.

Working with your Agent.

Agent and publisher time can move even more slowly than God's time. Don't immediately drop an agent for not adjusting to your expectations. We recommend patience, as a good agent will tend to be busy. However, an agency contract should not tie you up for years. You should be able to terminate at will. You don't need to sign away your life just because you are eager to see your words in print.

Don't mistake your agent for your employee. Here are some additional dos and don'ts:

- Do not call your agent so frequently that he feels he needs to be in a permanent "meeting."
- Do not obsess about the status of your book.
- Do go on with your life and try to believe that your existence does not depend on publishing your book.
- Do not be temperamental.
- Do be willing to be flexible in the process of developing your project for submission.
- Do be willing to accept rejection.
- Do acknowledge your agent in all your published books.
- Do send presents, but don't feel obligated, as some agents don't like to feel beholden.

12

The Query Letter

The query letter is the key to opening the door to your publishing career. Although there is a temptation to jump ahead using assertive methods to gain the attention of agents or publishers, in the long run, following the protocols is the best approach. These methods are in place to make finding projects more efficient.

We have discussed the publishing house and how literary agents work. Your introduction to them is through the query letter. Otherwise, it is like crashing a party. You can show up uninvited and have a little fun, but the host will likely ask you to leave to leave.

What is a Query Letter?

A query letter is a sales pitch to an agent or editor designed to interest them in your book idea. It is typically one page, and every word counts. Your goal is to get that invitation to the party. Your letter should be very clear about what you are asking with a statement of what is in it for the recipient and how you can fulfill the promise.

The Tone.

Be straightforward and to the point, but not so concise that you entirely squash your personality. Finding your voice and balance for a good query letter is like finding your writer's voice. You may need several drafts to get it right, but it will be well worth it. If you are unsure, opt for clarity over charm.

It is sometimes difficult for spiritual writers to avoid being overly passionate in query letters. Be yourself, but if you tend to be effusive, rein yourself enough to fit on the page. Agents and editors see so many letters that they are not impressed with ecstasy or unsupportable claims. You will have as much success with hype as you will if you include a note from your mother saying what a special person you are. No gimmicks.

Agents and editors do not want to be wowed. They want something tangible to work with that they understand. Therefore, write in a respectful, relatively formal, and straightforward manner. You can be friendly, but do not cross the line into unearned familiarity, even if you have met the agent or editor briefly. If you have met at a conference, mention the meeting and include a detail that will help them recall your conversation. Be aware that often people you meet in a pitch session at a writer's conference or virtual meeting may show polite interest that should not commit them to your project. However, it is a good opening for your letter that may give it more attention.

One of the issues with query letters is the feeling you should cram every detail about why you are writing, who you are and your personal spiritual path. While you want the letter to be well-written and compelling, brevity is the most critical factor. Again, this is not a contradiction. It is about balance and care as you choose your words wisely. Agents and editors go through query letters very quickly. When screening letters for the literary agency, I would only dedicate a few minutes to each. If something caught my eye, I would put it aside and decide if I would move it on to the request pile or, after further review, send a rejection. I didn't have time to read through overwritten letters too challenging to comprehend. Many authors would write query letters as if they were literature. Other people may feel differently, but when I was screening, I was looking for particular things:

- What is the book about?
- Why should the book exist?
- Why is the author the one to write it?

Query letters do not need to be boring or written like a business plan, but the agent or editor should know what the book is about in the first paragraph. I have finished reading letters where this basic bit of information is unclear. Writers will then fill the precious space with hype and spurious claims that the book will be the next (fill in the blank) and a bestseller. If you have a unique plan that will ensure its bestseller status, you can include this. For example, if you are about to launch your own talk show on a major network and it has been green-lit and scheduled, this might catch an agent or editor's attention. It can go in your letter.

It can go in your letter if you have a significant platform or following. Anything factual and supportive of your project can potentially go in your letter, but even then, say the most with few words.

Those of us on a spiritual path seem to be attracted to kindred Souls and want to make it a point to communicate that we are somehow all a part of the same club. Rest assured that a spiritually oriented agent or publisher—especially one who says it out loud and in print—will sense who you are and your connection to the Divine. You speak the same language without saying a word. Just assume that there is a cosmic connection but stick to the facts at hand: your book and why it's a great opportunity.

NOW LET'S BREAK THE LETTER DOWN INTO ITS PARTS

The Content.

A good query letter answers specific, somewhat standardized questions, each of which is discussed briefly here and in more detail in chapter 13, "The Book Proposal." Both the query letter and the proposal need to address these questions, although you have more space to elaborate in the proposal.

What is the Book About?

You must make your hook clear right from the start. You can incorporate your hook in the query letter as it should encapsulate the project in a few sentences. You don't want the agent or editor to work too hard to assess your submission. You want it to go right away in the request more pile.

Your first sentence is the most important one. Write a creative lead that tells the reader what your book is about and hooks him into wanting to learn more about your idea. And don't forget the number-one rule in writing: Remember your audience. Consider the reader's needs; ensure you answer the implied question, "What's in this for me (or my literary agency, or my publishing house)?"

Who is the Market for the Book?

Have a clear idea of a defined audience for your book. Is it single women under thirty, office workers seeking spirituality in the workplace, or parents wanting to counteract the materialism in society? The one thing you should not say is, "My book will appeal to anyone seeking a richer spiritual life," or some other vague statement. Be specific, and if possible, back up your intended audience with data such as researching search terms or showing relevant statistics.

For example, for a book on nurturing children's spirituality, you might say, *Famous Parenting Magazine* recently noted that 70 percent of parents feel that their child's spiritual training is not as complete as their own." This statement establishes a need for your book and makes a publisher want to address that need.

How does the book differ from other similar books on the market? You may not have room for this in your query, but if you are writing in a crowded area, it might be relevant to distinguish your book. You will need to research comparable and competitive titles for your book proposal anyway, so you should have this information at your fingertips. Then clearly articulate how your book addresses the subject from a newer, fresher angle without rehashing previously published material.

If there are no books on the market on your subject, that can either be great or not so great. It may indicate a gaping hole crying to be filled by a quality book or a topic nobody is interested in writing or reading. Either way, don't ignore the competition. A publisher won't.

Why are you the best person to write this book? Include them if you have credentials such as a degree or other education related to your book's topic or relevant publishing history. Keep your cited credentials pertinent to your book, so you do not appear insecure and overselling. This query is a professional business letter, not an approval-seeking exercise. Do not allow a tone of neediness in your letter, or you will raise a red flag of being potentially "high maintenance."

How Will you Help Promote the Book?

Show your publishing savvy by indicating how you as an author are prepared to help market and promote your book. Add this if it is certain and you are not taking space from other essential facts.

Query Letter Taboos.

Your query letter will have a much greater chance of being taken seriously if you avoid the following statements:

- Ten other agents/publishers rejected my manuscript, but I know you will have the intelligence to see its value. An appeal to the reader's vanity will not overcome his sense of foreboding when he reads this.
- My book will be a best seller.

- I am the next Eckhart Tolle, Marianne Williamson, Paulo Coelho, Deepak Chopra, savior of the world.

These comparisons are meaningless to agents and editors. If you have good endorsements by some luminaries, that is another thing.

- My manuscript has been read and endorsed by Famous Author X. Some famous authors will give a complimentary book quote to anyone who asks them. Agents and publishers know who these people are— and so will you if you peruse enough book jackets— and their names mean little.
- Dear Sir or Madam.
  This salutation makes it seem like the writer lacks the initiative to find an agent or editor's name and title. They may assume the writer doesn't have enough ambition to be a professional. I've never yet met an editor or agent named Sir or Madam. In today's world, there are also too many variations with pronouns. I am too old school to figure out he/him, she/ her, they/ them. One time, while in Los Angeles, I stopped at a boutique that was giving out buttons appropriate to your chosen pronoun. I said, "do you have one that says "we" to accommodate all the voices in my head?"
- I got your name from Person X.
  Usually, a referral doesn't make much of a difference. Some publishing houses will, as a courtesy, read anything that comes through one of their published authors. This is not a set-in-stone taboo. We often get referrals from our major clients, and we will read them. Just know that we can see through something that is not true.
- God told me to write to you.
  This statement is a red flag, even if it is true. To the uninitiated, it can cause you to appear strange. Of course, I don't necessarily mind that. However, it could also put pressure on the relationship from the outset. Who wants to argue with God? Make sure your book is good, and you will be fulfilling your mission that way.

Here are some more don'ts:

- Don't forget to proofread your letter for typos or grammatical errors. Agents and publishers love words! Avoidable mistakes raise their hackles.
- Don't pack your letter so densely with type that it's difficult to read.

Editors and agents read all day, and their eyes get tired. Include plenty of white space and visual breaks like subheads to open your letter up and keep their eyes from crossing.

- Don't brag. You are writing to inform and to offer a mutually beneficial proposition, not to impress someone with how wonderful you are.
- If you are using the postal service, remember to include your SASE (self-addressed, stamped envelope)
- Don't handwrite your letter. Still happens. Get a friend to type it if you can.
- Don't call to pitch an idea or ask for a meeting. This is a breach of protocol. No matter how good you can make something sound on the telephone, you will invariably hear either, "I have to see it first; send a query," or "We don't accept phone queries." Such encounters are discouraging and can bias the editor or agent against you, making them remember you for the wrong reasons.
- After sending your query, don't call, e-mail, or write to ask, "Did you receive it?" or "Did you read it yet?" If you get no answer in what you think is an unreasonably long time (give them at least a month), mail or email another letter. It is possible the first one got lost. It happens all the time.
- Do not reprimand the agent or editor for not getting back to you. Remember, there is no obligation on anyone's part to even read your letter. Most agents and editors will try to get back to people within a reasonable time, so don't fret too much. Meditate, pray, or write in your journal.
- Don't insist the reader must read your entire manuscript because there's no other way to truly grasp the importance/beauty/truth of the message. The message of your manuscript is only one of several things agents and publishers learn from your query. They also learn how professional you are—an indication of what you would be like to work with—and whether you understand your writing well enough to convey the book's essence in the way you would need to as a published author.
- Don't bother begging them to read the whole thing. I can assure you; they won't

.

The Importance of the Query Letter

Compared with the task of writing an entire book, query letters are not complicated. You have already worked hard to bring yourself to the point where it is appropriate to send one, so be sure to make the query reflect the work you have already done. Every part of the process toward publication is important. Inspiration is a gift but knowing how to get published is a skill. Each step in the process forms a foundation for the next. Put your Spirit into this letter as much as you have the rest of your book but keep it within the parameters of professional business correspondence. Remember to relax, allow your inner voice to write, and then employ your inner editor.

If you skip the query letter and send an unsolicited proposal or manuscript to a publisher, you may never hear anything back. It is acceptable to send several query letters simultaneously. Just indicate in each that you are sending multiple submissions.

And remember, before sending off your query letter, have a proposal or manuscript ready. Nothing is more annoying to an agent or editor than getting excited about a book that doesn't exist.

When you write and send out any kind of submission, just say a prayer that your letter or proposal arrives where it needs to arrive. Other than that, you pretty much must let it go. Everything happens as it should, but we don't always know what the "supposed to" is. Remember that sometimes our writing is to grow our Souls. Sometimes no matter how hard we try, the universe has a different plan for us.

13

THE BOOK PROPOSAL

By now, you should be well-versed in the working of the publishing industry. Even if publishers would like to publish books to benefit humankind, their bottom line will be if they can make money doing it. Now that I have been on all sides of the industry, from literary agent to author to marketer and publisher, I am far more familiar with the economic realities. All the wheels must be turning in synchronicity for books to succeed. The conglomerates have the capital advantage, but it is economy of scale. They can lose money just as much as the smaller players. While it might not cause them to go bankrupt, a wrong choice could cause someone to lose their job.

Your concern is to prove through your submission package that your book is worth the risk. A good book proposal will answer all the questions an agent or publisher needs to make a good decision. The agent will use the proposal to support a decision for representation, which will involve an investment of time. They need a solid proposal to send to publishers to make the sale and close the deal. A good book proposal keeps the wheels turning as industry insiders choose the books they will publish and promote for their upcoming seasons. A polished book proposal can persuade a publisher to invest in you even if you have a completed manuscript.

Why leave it up to chance that an agent or publisher will see the potential in your work? If you write an irresistible book proposal that addresses all their concerns, you can find yourself in the top echelon of submissions. Of course, there are still factors that could lead to rejection, but you will remove the obstacles you can control.

Agents and publishers are always swamped. All that has changed in the two decades since the first edition of this book are writers can submit their queries and work digitally. The number of submissions has not decreased even while the opportunities have. The competition is greater, but the standards are the same. Agents and publishers don't have time to read every manuscript. They want you to condense your message and make it easy to determine if they will do business with you. An excellent proposal makes their job easier.

When I wrote the first edition of this book, I had experienced being a literary agent and was already a published author. I was a book proposal doctor and had co-authored the book *Write the Perfect Book Proposal: Ten Proposals that Worked and Why* with Jeff Herman, now in its third edition.

As an indie publisher, I can give more opportunities to those authors who are worthy but may not meet the threshold for the conglomerates and larger Indies. And in today's world, I work to provide writers with the tools to succeed.

All thirteen books I have written have been traditionally published. This is not because I am married to my literary agent, although you would think that would help. The advantage came because I learned to listen to the industry's protocols and saw firsthand how agents and editors decode proposals. The decision process is not rocket science. My law school training helped us create our format for book proposals, as everything we learn is about persuasion. We build our cases by stating what we will prove and backing it up with as much fact and evidence as possible. That concept translates into how you can break down the requirements of a book proposal. There is a slight difference between nonfiction book proposals and those for novels. But the goal is the same. With nonfiction, you want to prove to a prospective agent or editor that the project is viable and should exist. With a novel proposal, you also need to show the writing is compelling and you can carry it out. That is why you must complete your novel before submitting a proposal to an agent and publisher.

A good proposal is what an agent will use to gain the interest of an editor at an appropriate publishing house. It needs to answer all the questions the editor will be asked as the project is taken further to all the team members. As you know, even if the editor has autonomy, especially today, they need to show viability other than they like the book.

Even after your proposal has sold an editor on the merits of your idea, it does not get set aside. Instead, the editor will use it to sell your book to people throughout the publishing pipeline. First, editors pitch your book to their editorial review committee, where a good proposal gives the editors persuasion at their fingertips. They will be asked questions about the book's sales potential, and if you write an effective proposal, they can answer any question without hesitation. They will be confident about your book, and that confidence will be contagious.

Once the book passes a publisher's editorial review committee, it must be "sold" to the publisher's distributor, marketing department, or sales force to convince them that your book will be a moneymaker. Once that happens, the sales team will pitch your book to their national sales reps, who will then use the information from your proposal to advocate for your book when they present it to bookstore owners and buyers for the large chains. After a brief presentation about your book, these store owners decide how many copies to order. So, you see that, at every step, the information in your proposal can be used to generate buzz and interest and translate into sales.

Don't leave your book up to faith and good intentions when selling it. Master the craft of the book proposal.

What Comes First—the Proposal or the Manuscript?

Many nonfiction books are sold from a proposal even if there is a completed manuscript. Still, you might find yourself with an advance before you even finish the book if every element in your proposal is good enough. The agent or editor can be confident in your ability to do what you promised. It is risky with first-time authors. If you write a comprehensive book proposal, particularly the editorial portions, agents and editors will be less concerned about your delivery of a quality manuscript. Your outline will be a blueprint you must follow as it is what the agent and editor expect. So, avoid flights of fancy because you decide you want to write the book another way after it is acquired. The proposal is a commitment; you should only alter it by mutual agreement.

If your book combines prescriptive nonfiction with personal illustrations, you might want to have the book finished before writing the proposal. Prescriptive nonfiction has takeaways like prescriptions for your reader. Any time you include personal material to illustrate your points, your manuscript could fall into the category of a partial memoir. A good book proposal will help you. Always keep in mind the time constraints for agents and editors.

Memoirs are nonfiction, but it is a good idea to have the manuscript completed as it is considered more like fiction unless you are a household name or celebrity. Publishers review memoirs for the storytelling, writing, and a relatable through-line. (See the bonus material for advice about memoir structure.)

You should complete your novel before submitting it, and you can write a book proposal for a novel with a few twists. The importance of a fiction book proposal is to show you have a clear sense of your audience and how to reach them. You will provide a synopsis of the book as you would in any fiction submission, but it will be helpful in today's competitive atmosphere to back up your project with a platform. Publishers base decisions about fiction on the writing, but it doesn't hurt to show your marketing savvy and that you will be a promotable author.

For nonfiction, if you write and submit the proposal before writing an entire manuscript, you won't waste time on projects that are time-sensitive or have no market. If your proposal is rejected, the rejection might help you determine that your book's topic may need to be altered somehow. Another advantage of selling your idea by the proposal is possibly getting the input of the publishing house while you are writing the book. An editor may have a vision for the book that enhances its scope, substance, or marketability. If you haven't written the complete manuscript, you can incorporate this vision at an early developmental stage and avoid extensive revisions. The result will be a higher-quality, more saleable book.

If you sell your idea this way, you might also have the advantage of gaining the input of other members of the publishing house, such as its marketing and publicity staff. As a writer hoping to be published, you are only one player; you can't possibly know all the nuances of book marketing and distribution. It's hard sometimes to let go of the purity of your message, but if you can develop trust in your agent or publisher—or both—to hone your book and edit it so that it meets its broadest audience, you'll have forged a solid team, all intending to bring the best book to the most readers.

Why Write a Proposal and What Should it Include?

Here are your goals. Keep them in mind while writing the proposal. Your proposal will:

- organize your content, so an agent or publisher knows what you are offering
  - prove an audience exists for your material
  - show you can carry out the plan-proving credibility
  - show what you will do to make your project a success

You know that your hook is your best ammunition. Begin there and build your proposal around it. Statistics or factual statements will help you, but since that is not always possible for spiritual books, try to keep your credibility and promotability, the existence of a market for your book, and the quality of your message front and center. While you should not assume that the person reading the proposal speaks your same spiritual language, publishers and agents recognize the appeal of these books more and more. Write your proposal for the uninitiated. Your purpose is to find a publisher, not to convert one.

Do not include too much hype or fluff before getting to the meat of the book, or that may be all anyone sees. Make your writing tight and compelling, and be sure it clearly states your hook. Every section of your proposal is essential, so use the same energy on each; you never know how much weight your prospective publisher gives certain information. Everyone has their agenda when evaluating a project. Do not skip any sections, or you will be wasting an opportunity to persuade.

You want to control the information; you don't want the reader to draw the wrong conclusions because your proposal is incomplete despite your awesome message. And then there's the human factor—if the agent or editor is having a bad day, you are out of luck. An incomplete or amateurish proposal will merit a growl, moan, and a toss into the reject pile.

Proposal lengths vary. Some are short; some might as well be manuscripts. But longer is not always better, especially in the word business. Don't repeat yourself, oversell with hyperbole, or ramble. Find your balance, use your inner voice, and make your proposal at whatever length you feel will adequately address the points we'll cover below.

After you write your proposal, set it aside. Read it a week or two later when you can be objective. Then pretend you are an agent or editor. What questions might they have as they read? We have evaluated proposals where the only thing running through our mind was, what credentials does the author have to write such a book? The author did not address this question. Make sure you do not make the same mistake.

While there is room for creativity, stick closely to the following format to ensure you have not left out anything needed to present your book. Let's look at the standard proposal elements:

Title and Subtitle

Overview

About the Author

Market and Audience
Comparative and Competitive Titles
Promotions
Table of Content
Chapter by Chapter Outline
Sample Material

THE TITLE

Authors often get stuck on titles and fall in love with them. In most instances, if a publisher acquires your book, they will change your title. My experience has shown they are usually right about what will best sell the book. I was fortunate to have chosen the title *Member of the Family* for my collaborative true-crime memoir of the youngest member of the Manson Family. The publisher kept it and added a comprehensive subtitle. I am pretty sure that was the only time a publisher retained the title I recommended.

When writing a "working title" for your book, be descriptive and not overly subtle. Nonfiction titles are also helpful for Search Engine Optimization and a comprehensive content marketing plan. See Section Four. Create something clear, concise, and not overly long for your purposes. Create something that makes you feel connected to your book so you can see it as existing. Don't stay married to it if someone offers you a contract and a different title.

Even though publishers often change a book's title during the editing process, a bad one at the proposal stage can be a turnoff. A title is a key marketing tool. Don't make it confusing or depressing. Even if your book is on grief, choose a title that emphasizes hope or help, not despair. Avoid clichés. Don't pick a title so obscure that its meaning becomes apparent only after an extensive explanation. You will not be sitting next to the editor when they read your proposal to explain your title. If it needs explaining, it's not a good title. A title should tell and sell. If you choose a title that offers no insight into the book's contents but is still strong, then make sure your subtitle gives the reader an idea of what your book will cover. Study titles and subtitles at bookstores or online to learn what works. Titles are important.

Consider copywriting if you want to enhance your writing for a book proposal. Copywriting is simple but persuasive, using few words to create a mood. Copywriting is what is used in advertising. It is the style of writing that will help you with describing your book and your title. While you don't want your writing to sound like hype, you do want to use few words to convey the essence of your work.

OVERVIEW

The overview sets the tone. It should be from 250 to 500 words. These paragraphs are the first introduction to your work and should include relevant information in a well-written and persuasive style. If the overview is strong, it practically presells the rest. Your goal is for your prospective agent or editor to want to find things to like in the proposal. They are looking for a gem, and you can provide it for them. They want to see what is compelling and saleable in your overview right away.

Some of the questions they will have in mind as they decode your proposal:

1. Who is this author?
2. Are they proposing something unique?
3. Is the book a new angle on a desirable subject?
4. Does the author have a clear sense of the subject?
5. Is the proposal too obscure?
6. Does the author seem professional?
7. Does the author have an audience?
8. Does the author understand the audience and how to reach them?

You can't answer all of this in the overview. But if you have some answers that will make you stand out and anticipate their questions before they ask them, you can work them into this first section. The first step is to explain what the book is about. Sometimes you can include a scene if it is well written and will catch their attention. It is a good technique for creative nonfiction and memoir. However, it is best to stay with a simple description rather than risk the reader will come away unclear about what you are asking of them.

You can write your overview as you would your back jacket copy if it helps you think of how to explain the importance or sales potential of your book in a short amount of words. For example:

For this book, the overview might be:

When literary agent and spiritual teacher Deborah Herman first released the pioneering book Spiritual Writing from Inspiration to Publication, *the publishing world began to acknowledge a critical mass of writers and readers seeking this material. Herman was one of the first to coin the phrase "spiritual writer" as a special population worthy of recognition. Before this time, agents didn't know what to do with authors of alternative works and visionary books and relegated them to the category of "woo woo." Twenty years later, this prescient book, in its wholly updated new edition, is still the must-have guide for those writers who are called and wish to be chosen.*

"There are writers who write because they want to and those who write because they have to," says Herman.

Spiritual writers are drawn to the process by a sense of mission. However, the spiritual writer's mission and the realities of publishing are often at odds. This unique book provides the nuts and bolts and do's and don'ts of how to get published in this often- misunderstood arena. This second edition is updated to include the digital world and the expanded opportunities this brings for both traditional and nontraditional publishing.

This example is only one way to write an overview. If there are facts to support your book or you have a unique platform, you can include this information. Keep this part of the proposal focused on the key points of your book. It is a top-level view to encourage an agent or editor to read more. I have seen overviews that stretch into ten pages or more. There may be situations where this is warranted, but those would be the exception.

Here is a general list of what to put in the overview:

1. Include a clear statement of your book's name, thesis, and hook.
2. Briefly address the book, why it should exist, who will buy it, and why you are the best person to write it.
3. You can include a few of your very best—short—excerpts from the book.

If you keep the overview to between 250 to 500 words, you can say a lot to bolster your project. Although you want to grab attention, setting a concise, professional tone in the overview is best. There will be room later in the proposal to be more dramatic and creative.

I like a conversational tone in nonfiction if it is not too personal. Do not say things like, "I've been intrigued by and read a lot about subject x for years and have some free time now that my children are grown and have decided to share my discoveries." Amateurish. No matter what you say after that bit of personal revelation, you are climbing uphill. The overview is your first opportunity to persuade, to show you are a professional writer, so make it count.

ABOUT THE AUTHOR

When agents or publishers are intrigued by your overview, the next question they will ask themselves is, "who is this person?" I know that it is typically the next section I read even before I get into the meat of the proposal. The publishing professionals are reviewing your "About the Author" to decide if you have the proper credentials and are the right person to write the book you are proposing. We will not address the platform here as that is a different consideration.

From my experience, I want to see if there is a connection between the writer's goals and who they are. An interesting person with relevant background can pass this threshold even if we discover their platform is underdeveloped.

If a book is more technical, relying on data and science, such as a psychology book, even if in the spiritual genre, we often recommend that the author collaborates with someone with the credentials to support the work. A layperson with a great story combined with a co-author with a Ph.D. will go a long way toward overcoming a weak author bio.

Some authors have great book ideas but lack a track record. It often helps for them to partner with published authors to help them build their recognition. It is also a way for newer writers to enhance their skills. I am a firm believer in mentorship. If you are a willing student, you may find a collaborator who can teach you the ropes and help you launch your career. Be aware you will be sharing the credit and the proceeds. But in the long run, you will help your journey. Try not to be short-sighted. Every career path has a period of "paying your dues." Be generous and willing, and you will find a way to learn what you need and access the right opportunities.

Don't make stuff up to enhance your author bio. I did not need to say that, but it can be so frustrating to get over the initial hurdles that it can be tempting. You will find your way, and it will eventually be your turn. There is no harm in seeking a collaborator with the credentials you lack. Some people have the education or experience to support a book but lack writing skills. These are opportunities to build your resume, and mastering the art of the book proposal will help you along the way. People with doctorates connect with authors looking to build their reputations. You may share the billing on the cover or have your name in the acknowledgments, but you get a book on the shelf, which is the name of the game.

Be creative if your credentials and background are irrelevant to the book you are writing. But do not ramble and include things that are extraneous or stretch too far. You are presenting yourself with confidence rather than defensiveness. If experience isn't your strong suit, make up for it everywhere else in the proposal with stellar writing.

Include media experience in your bio and publishing history if it is recent. You can also add personal information but avoid too much cuteness or snarkiness. Your biography is a window into the person behind the words. As in everything you do, find your balance. Make sure your bio feels like you, but on a good day.

If your spiritual path is relevant to the proposal, you can include a reference to it as it relates to your book. Remember the lessons. This author bio is where you are selling yourself, and there can be all kinds of pitfalls.

Courage: Don't worry that you are stepping outside of the mainstream.

Tolerance: Try not to go overboard in preachiness. Avoid evangelizing.

Self-Protection: Stand in your power as a professional without leaving room for negativity.

Self-Love: Have faith in your worthiness. Then, when you write your bio, be confident that what you have to say has value.

Ego: Avoid statements like, "I am a prophet of the Lord." We have seen this.

Love of Humanity: Focus on what you do for others rather than how great you are. Then, even in a bio, you can write about what value you bring to the table.

God-Love: Write your bio with confidence but humility. Be a conduit for the universe, and you cannot go wrong.

I recommend you write three bios of different lengths. These can be used in your book proposal and reused for a website and media kit if you are going to build one. We will revisit this in Section Four. Here are the different bio lengths with an example of my bio. I change my bio all the time, depending on the circumstances. However, I include them here to give you an idea of how much information fits the various word counts. You will be surprised how if you use words wisely and efficiently, you can say all you need in even the shortest description of yourself.

Your author bio is different from a resume or curriculum vitae. Agents and publishers want to know if you are marketable and interesting. They also want to know you are credible. It is helpful if you write in the spiritual genre for you to appear grounded with your camel firmly tethered. You need to show you are a real person who resides on this planet, even if you take occasional astral excursions elsewhere. For our purposes, keep those to yourself unless your book is about astral projection.

Sample Author Bios

Short Bio-50 words: For example:

Deborah Herman is a gifted spiritual teacher, a former literary agent with a top agency, a publisher, and an author branding specialist. Herman, the bestselling author of thirteen books, has dedicated her 25-plus career in publishing to writer education. She lives in Stockbridge, MA.

Subscribe to her blog at www.micropublishingmedia.com

Medium Bio (Approximately 100 words) For example:

Bestselling Author and publishing expert Deborah Herman is a gifted spiritual teacher, a former literary agent with a top agency, a publisher, and an author branding specialist. Herman works with writers who need help navigating the publishing industry from idea to shelf. She is the Author of 13 books, including *Spiritual Writing from Inspiration to Publication,* now in its second edition. Herman lives (and tries to stay warm) in Stockbridge, MA, where Norman Rockwell had his studio, with her husband, three dogs, and the two cats who run the household. Follow her blog at www. micropublishingmedia.com and on Twitter @digitaldeborah

As you can see, the medium bio has room for additional personal information to show a bit of personality. Make sure the tone of your bio matches the type of book you are proposing. It is tempting to be snarky and sarcastic, at least for me. I also like corny groaner puns. I have to rein myself in sometimes because I may only be amusing to myself. Save the real personality for people you know or your blog, where your voice may be what creates a following.

Long Bio for the About the Author section or for your website can be about 500 words: For example:

Deborah Herman is an Attorney, Author, entrepreneur, former literary agent, developmental editor, and digital marketing strategist. Herman achieved a law degree in a dual degree major with the Graduate School of Journalism from The Ohio State University, and although she practiced trial law for a few years, she knew her future was in books.

Herman worked as a literary agent with her husband, Jeff Herman, curating thousands of projects and discovering that at least 99% of all book submissions cannot make the grade. During this time, she learned what makes a good book and took on nonfiction assignments to learn the craft. Twelve traditionally published books later, Herman got her big break with the bestselling book *Member of the Family: My Story of Charles Manson, Life Inside His Cult and the Darkness that Ended the Sixties* (William Morrow) with Dianne "Snake" Lake. Lake, the youngest member of the cult, did not participate in the crimes but testified against them at 17. That book was the culmination of a goal to follow in the footsteps of early pioneers of creative nonfiction. The book opened opportunities to appear in at least four documentaries, interviews on CNN and HLN, and speaking engagements at Crime Con and other gatherings. In addition, Boston College has featured the book in a college class as an example of true-crime writing.

Herman is a self-professed bibliophile and nostalgia aficionado. Her indie publishing company, Micro Publishing Media, has niche imprints, including T.V. Classics Press. Herman has created a unique book style called a pictorial memoir through that brand. These are like scrapbooks that the stars might have kept along the way. So far, she has published *Munster Memories: A mini Coffin Table Book*, *The Donna Reed Show*, TV Dinners with recipes from 40 kid stars of the 50s, 60s, and 70s, and a new title called *The Family Affair Scrapbook* by Kathy "Cissy" Garver.

Herman has achieved three MBA-level digital marketing and social media certification courses to further her marketing education through the Rutgers mini- MBA program. Herman is the co-founder of Writersnetworking. com, formerly Writers, Agents, and Editors Network, and CEO of Author Branding Solutions www.authorbrandingsolutions.com. Her online bookstore is aptly titled Deb's Book Paradise and specializes in unique used titles. www.debsbookparadise.com

Deborah Herman lives with her husband, three dogs, and two cats in Stockbridge, MA.

Books by Deborah Herman

Why my Funny Bone Doesn't Make Me Laugh (Villard)

Toasts for All Occasions (Career Press)

The Complete Idiot's Guide to Motherhood (Alpha Books)

Write the Perfect Book Proposal: Ten Proposals that Worked and Why (Wiley/ Turner Publishing)

Fresh Start Bankruptcy (Wiley)

A Simplified Guide to Creating a Personal Will (Wiley)
A Pregnant Couple's Guide to Sex and Intimacy (Citadel)
The Toughlove Prescription (McGraw-Hill)
Spiritual Writing from Inspiration to Publication (Atria)
Serenity Symbols Coloring Book (Soul Odyssey Books)
Member of the Family: My Story of Charles Manson, Life Inside His Cult and the Darkness that Ended the Sixties (William Morrow)
Inside the Manson Jury (Micro Publishing Media)
Contributor to *Jeff Herman's Guide to Book Publishers, Editors, and Literary Agents*

In my long bio, I stressed more professional achievements. I wrote this for a book proposal that was more serious in the subject matter. But as long as it seems, it is precisely 510 words, including the book list. That is about the correct length for your author bio. You can include relevant facts or descriptions about why you are writing the book you are proposing. If you are writing about trauma, you will want to mention your personal experience in a short synopsis if it is relevant to why you are writing the book. Your experiences are also part of your bio and credentials that agents and editors need to see.

Elements of your author bio for your book proposal:

1. 500 words are about the right length
2. Write it in third-person
3. Include your education if it is a plus
4. Include information relevant to why you are the one to write the book
5. Past publications are good if they are recent and impressive
6. Any unique experiences that make you stand out
7. Some personal information
8. Leave out any grandiosity unless you can back it up
9. Make sure to consider if the information you include would be interesting to anyone other than yourself.
10. If you have developed a personal brand (Section Four), writing a bio that fits that persona may be easier.

If you have a significant social media following, you should include it in your bio. However, you will have ample opportunity to discuss your following and efforts to build it in the markets and promotions sections.

MARKETS AND AUDIENCE

This markets section is where you identify who will buy your book. Saying that everyone needs it doesn't mean much to an agent or publisher. Identifying your market differs from your section on promotion. The purpose of markets is to show there are people who want the type of material you are writing. Promotion" is a proactive plan for how you will reach them and convert them into buyers. Try to be objective when considering your market. For example, if you have been speaking to spiritually friendly groups for many years and have a following in those communities, you may want to make them your primary market. The inclination might be to expand beyond what you have already built, but you may be overreaching. You can't be everything to everybody. It is more difficult to reach a new audience if your message fits a specific sensibility.

On the other hand, your topic may have a broader appeal. As long as you do the research, you may find you were targeting the wrong people at the outset.

Who Will Buy your Book?

Years ago, the only way to write about markets was to speculate. I don't blame people for writing broad statements about the market potential because we didn't know how to identify our readers and offer proof. We didn't have social media to estimate followers, and we didn't have Search Engine Optimization and keyword research to support our claims.

You can guestimate your market if you already access communities of readers who know who you are and who will support your work. For example, if you teach classes, belong to organizations, speak publicly, do a podcast, or regularly appear on television or radio, you can extrapolate a market description from there.

Don't skip this section even if you feel baffled. Identifying your market will help prospective agents and publishers see you have a viable book. Remember, you are building a case, and your markets section is part of your evidence.

The more specific you are, the more your proposal's recipient will have confidence that you understand the connection between books and business. Determining your market is not as difficult as it sounds. As you are considering all the possibilities, you may discover that you have affiliations that would represent a segment of your market. For example, people who attend seminars on your topic are your market. Check out Facebook pages and blogs.

Knowing your genre is so important. When you know precisely where a bookseller would shelve your book at a bookstore, you are more credible when you explain your market. It will also help you figure out where your readers hang out. I don't mean at the bookstore, although that is not a bad thought. I mean online and in what organizations or groups. Many writers indicate a broad market that has no real meaning to anyone. There are many permutations of spirituality. Know which audience is yours. For example, a Christian may be interested in spiritual growth, but it is a specialized market.

The book's last section will discuss the specifics of Search Engine Optimization and Keyword Research. First, however, take note that here is where that information is beneficial. When you know what your audience is typing into the search engines, you can determine how many people are searching for the subjects. For example, if you are writing about self-help, think about what problems or concerns your readers have and what they may be typing into google or other search engines to find answers. What problem are you solving for your reader? If you can determine that and show people are searching for the same things in the search engines, you can put that in your proposal.

I am not a keyword or SEO expert, but some people are. However, you don't need to be an expert to learn enough to see if there is a market that data can support. Yoast is a company that has software to help people with what is called optimization of their websites. It explains how SEO works. There is also SEMrush. They offer tutorials if you want to learn the basics of how SEO can help you persuade an agent or publisher that your book has an audience.

I know firsthand from speaking to publishers that they are impressed with large numbers of followers on social media platforms. But, to be honest, I think they are impressed because they don't understand how to analyze what those numbers mean. As we will discuss in section four, having fewer engaged followers will be more likely to lead to book sales than having inflated numbers on social media.

When you have determined all the ways to show your book has a definite market, don't forget to add if there is anything that could appeal to a foreign market. For example, does your book have the potential to be sold overseas or to "travel"? If yes, that's a big plus for you because the publisher could sell the foreign rights to your book as a secondary source of publishing income.

As you write your book proposal, do not confuse markets and audience with marketing and publicity. In your section on promotion, you'll describe ways you will help your publisher to sell your book and strategies and contacts you can bring to the plan.

COMPARATIVE AND COMPETITIVE TITLES

Your goals for this section:
- Finding comparative books to show your book has a market
- Listing competitive books to show they prove the market rather than eliminating room for yours

Don't worry about old or self-published books when looking for comparative and competitive titles. Your agent and the publisher are trying to determine where your book will fit in their publishing program. They need to know that other publishers have not exhausted the market for the topic or that other authors do not "own the shelf."

Denial is not a wise approach to this section. You want to be as thorough as possible, so you are not surprised by sending a query to a publisher who has just published a book on the same topic. There are ways to find out what books publishers have planned for future lists, but the first place to start is with online retailers.

First, familiarize yourself with popular books on your topic. If you are writing a novel, you can compare yourself with similar writers, but I am not an expert on how well this works. I have seen queries where novelists compare themselves to others in the form of a description of their writing. If a famous author is known for a particular style in your writing genre, you may be effective in using this as a comparative title. If you are a newbie, it may sound grandiose to use it as a competitive title, as thus far, you have not proven yourself.

Congruency with the Publisher's List

The internet has saved you time and hours digging through library resources. You can review a publisher's website to see what they have on their upcoming seasonal lists rather than taking a guess. Then, when you or your agent submits your proposal, it will show you have done your homework. You may even change some parts of your proposal to reflect the tone and personality of a particular publishing house you are targeting.

When you review a publisher's website, look for the overall brand, topics, and markets they cover with their books. Keep in mind that a web designer may create a company's personality that is not entirely in line with what they acquire, so it is best to look at the catalogs and lists for your best reconnaissance. Be a detective. Determine if your book can fit in with their list. If you can find titles that it complements, so much the better.

For example, let them know that your book would be a perfect complementary title to their recent release, Book X, or would fit wonderfully in their series on women who take a different path. Make the editor feel that your book belongs at their house and support your statements with details.

This section is where you face the other books like yours head-on. Before writing any book, be aware of similar books on the topic. If your book is similar to someone else's, you need to justify how yours presents a fresh perspective or how you are uniquely qualified based on your credentials.

The comparative and competitive title section is part of the hardcore business information the publisher will weigh. They will look at what you present and translate it into the number of books they can sell. Don't forget the costs involved in producing a book. If the market is already too saturated, it will not pay for the publisher to add another book to the feeding frenzy. You want them to see that your book could be part of a new trend, will fill a niche not yet crowded with other books, or has a unique angle that differentiates it from other books on the topic. Of course, this needs to be the truth. If it isn't, find another book to write.

Certain subjects can sustain only a few books in the marketplace. Other topics can always welcome new and fresh perspectives. And take heart— booksellers are in the business of selling new books. They need to have fresh takes, even on old subjects. There are only so many topics under the sun, yet booksellers sell millions of books each year. If you can say something in a fresh way, even on a familiar subject, you've got a marketable book— if you can get people to understand what makes yours stand out.

Check out bookstores, online booksellers, book clubs, and catalogs such as *One Spirit* to see current books in the spiritual market. Places like Goodreads list spiritual books and numerous blogs to help you know what is out there. Remember that traditional publishing has at least a one-year lead time before a book reaches the shelves. What you see as an exciting trend today could become too crowded in the world of the publishing calendar.

Things to remember:
- Most publishing houses have websites listing their upcoming books.

- Research existing titles to be persuasive on why your book will be filling a need.
- Show how other similar books establish a market for the one you are proposing.

Think of the competition in terms of how it benefits you. It is never adequate to say there is no competition, even if you believe this. There may be a good reason for no competition or anything remotely like your book. Maybe no one wants a book like yours. Lastly, avoid trashing other books. This negative speech does not reflect well on you and will come back to haunt you and not in a good way.

PROMOTION

Promotion is another crucial part of your book proposal. You have identified your market and explained your reach, but now you can describe what you will do to support your book. Again, the emphasis is on you. As you will see in the publicity chapter, your publisher will expect you to participate in the success of your book and not in the passive way of allowing the publisher to make you famous because your book is so great. For every book they accept, thousands of eager writers still hope for that spot. You do not need to be rich to persuade a publisher to take on your book, but it doesn't hurt. I have seen deals that hinge on the authors paying for a significant number of books to sell to their "constituents." But that is only one way to make a deal. I want you to see that there are things you can't control that put other people ahead of you.

What you can control is having a humble but strong attitude that includes some promotion savvy. If you can squirrel your pennies to hire a publicist to support the publishing house's work, this will help you in the long run. Most publishers have some in-house publicists who will help launch your title, but after two months, you will be on your own. So be creative but realistic in your promotion section.

When you develop your online platform and brand, as you will learn in section four, you can use the description in the promotion section as it is something tangible you are doing to support your book. Publishers want to see that you are working toward your success and that you understand the business side of things.

I used to read many proposals that said, "when the book is published, I will...." That is a nonstarter and gives the agent or the publisher the impression that you are looking to them to make you famous. They want to sell books. They are going to bet on relatively sure things because they can. Anyone in the book business likely feels gratification in discovering new voices. In the spiritual genre, professionals may also feel a sense of mission. However, you can't forget that this is a competitive business.

I hate competition. It grates on my spiritual nature. I don't want you to feel derailed by the realities of the industry. I want you to be strong and focused on learning how you can be the best you. Focus on how to build your following without worrying about the competition. However, I suggest you do not reveal your concerns by writing amateurish promotion plans when I have told you how you will be perceived.

Writing a book is one piece of the publishing puzzle. Showing you understand how to promote your book is another hugely important piece of what you bring to the table. Editors look for writers who are savvy about the business side of publishing. Your input is valuable, especially if you are an expert on your topic. If you're a first-time author, the publisher needs to establish your credibility with book buyers, and they may also be looking at whether you can promote the book in the media.

Following are some possible ways to highlight your ability to promote your book. Not all will apply to you, of course, but the point is that the publisher will expect you to participate in publicity actively.

- Speaking at seminars connected to your book's subject or holding your own
- Teaching classes on your topic, either in person or online
- Having radio or television savvy for interviews about your book
- Being a recognized expert in your field, one whom the media may call on for quotes or analysis on your book's subject
- Getting connected to influential (sales-enhancing) people who could provide a quote or foreword for your book
- Hiring a publicist or purchasing a certain number of your books
- Writing a blog to stimulate interest in your book
- Being a member of an organization that could offer opportunities for you to speak and promote your book
- Having a viable connection to any facet of the media

Don't say things like this will be perfect for all the talk shows unless you have already been a guest. Saying you are hiring a publicist is better. If you can't afford one, there are ways for you to reach out to media people with professional P.R. releases that can get you noticed without the significant investment.

You may find a good publicist or build yourself to the point where you can make it yourself, but do not rely on miracles. Book proposals need facts or at least tangible possibilities.

If you have only a few hard leads to offer in this section, at least show that you're willing to do whatever it takes to promote your book. You can contact organizations or bookstores to see what it would take to set up book signings. Be creative. Moxie costs less than spending money. The more practical your book is, the more forums there are through which you can sell it. These promotion ideas are what agents and editors want to see. Your ability and willingness to market your book can elevate your project above the others in an editor's in-box.

Social Media as a promotion strategy.

The social media explosion did not exist when this book was first published. Remember that social media differs from what you can do with your website to establish credibility and a following. You will learn how to do this in the chapter on platform building in the digital age. You should include your social media following in your promotions section, even if it is not enormous. While publishers are still behind the curve with understanding social media, they are impressed by numbers. If you have a following of real people, even a small following can be impressive. If you show you understand social media and have a strategy to build your engagement, that should fill in for the lack of numbers. My personal bias is to have a smaller engaged following than an inflated bunch of bots.

This process of gathering followers is called organic social media building. Even if you don't know all the people, they can ultimately turn into book buyers if they have chosen to connect with you—more about this in section four. People used to pay for a following. I am not sure if that even exists anymore. It may not even be possible anymore to purchase a following. You also don't need to be on every platform. When you review the section on social media, you can choose what feels best for you. The importance is consistency in your posting, so you will want to choose things that feel relevant and comfortable.

Agents and publishers finally understand that a presence on the internet will influence book sales because it represents your community and your platform reach. You do not need to go into too much detail in this section.

You want to show that you have a basic understanding of social media and are utilizing it. If your numbers are impressive, use them. If you only have 54 Facebook friends and they are all cousins, do not.

In the section on promoting your book in the digital age, you will learn more about how to set up a strategic system to market and promote your book online. You can start many of these things and should before you even submit your book to an agent or publisher. Do not be overwhelmed. This process is a journey that many writers have tried to avoid. However, I guarantee you that if this technology had been available in ancient times, we would see a tremendous difference in how religions spread throughout the land. Technology is not a good or bad thing. It is truly good if utilized for the benefit of people finding you and your message.

I recommend you start your online presence while you think about your book. However, many of you will already be very far along with the writing process. So don't worry about it. You can start any time; there is no time like the present. Be patient. Whatever you master now will help you, so don't become intimidated by what other people are doing. Do not spend a lot of money on things that promise to make you the most famous person on the internet. While some are useful, they can overwhelm you to where the loudest and most hype-driven offer will seem appealing. Learn about how to use the internet before you invest in it. There may be much better ways to spend your money. The beauty of social media marketing is it is primarily free. You can pay someone a lot of money to do it for you, but they may only be a few tutorials ahead of you on "YouTube" in learning how to master it.

They may be using buzzwords that make you feel stupid because you don't even know that a tweet is not the sound a bird makes, or TikTok is not the sound of an old-fashioned clock. So relax. If you have a social media presence, include it. If not, let's get you up to speed.

NOW FOR THE EDITORIAL PORTION OF YOUR PROPOSAL

While every section of the book proposal is essential, you must never forget that a book must stand independently. Editors love books or would not be working in the publishing industry. Therefore, what you present in these sections is significant. Editors need to fall in love with your book or at least see it has merit.

TABLE OF CONTENTS

As we discussed in chapter 6, the table of contents is the backbone of your book. It will serve as a blueprint for you when you write the manuscript and give your agent or editor a quick view of where the book is heading. It indicates your logic and how well you have developed the structure. You will find that some agents and editors skip from your overview to the table of contents. Do not skimp here because it is yet another opportunity to influence their decision.

You can include each chapter's subheads in your table of contents for the proposal. Chapter titles are sometimes not informative, so including subheads gives the reader more detail about the book. Another effective technique that requires strong writing skills is to include the first sentence in each chapter after the chapter title in the table of contents. If the first line is strong and compelling, the editor will want to flip right away to that chapter to read "the rest of the story."

CHAPTER-BY-CHAPTER OUTLINE

Another way to provide a quick overview of your book's contents is to include a chapter-by-chapter outline—a paragraph or two summarizing the contents of each chapter. Think of each chapter as a magazine article, with a beginning, middle, and end. Use your most compelling writing in this annotation; it may be all an editor has time to read. Don't include too much detail in each summary. However, this is where you can include some sample material like an anecdote or two. It is similar to an abstract.

When I wrote the proposal for the *Member of the Family* Book, I chose to write extensive annotations. Each chapter summary included a writing sample and an excerpt of the story. I had not written a proposal in this manner, but it seemed to fit. It was a memoir couched in historical context. We took a chance with a comprehensive proposal outline, and I am unsure if I included sample chapters. There are many reasons we "got away with it," not the least of which was the story. I also had a track record. The funny thing was that the editor said, "we are not going to use your outline but will be completely restructuring the book." That happens.

I recommend you stick to the formula of shorter chapter summaries and sample chapters. Otherwise, an interested publisher will likely ask you to submit more material.

SAMPLE CHAPTERS

The publisher must receive sample material if you are an unpublished writer or are writing about an unusual subject. One to three chapters is standard. Many editors prefer that you send chapters in order, but that is your call. In nonfiction, chapters are typically self-contained. You are welcome to select chapters that best represent your writing. Try to make the sample chapters better than anything you have ever written. Speaking from experience, if I have put a lot of effort into a book proposal, I can lose my steam by the time it gets to the sample material. Be better than I am and write your sample chapters with as much energy as possible.

This advice is critical. Even if everything in your proposal up to this point has been strong, if you're not able to deliver well-written, supported, clear, organized, and thought-provoking material in your actual book, that'll be the end of the line for you. Publishers see many great ideas in proposals that make them excited. They are often disappointed, however, because, in the execution of the idea, authors fail to deliver on their promise.

It takes practice, but it is essential for your proposal to show consistent quality and effort from beginning to end. Please don't assume that the agent or editor will have enough insight to take your word for it because you know what you have to say. Always have someone with a cold eye read your chapters and point out where you need to clarify, organize, or tighten before you send your work out into the world.

Many freelance editors will do proposal doctoring or coaching for a flat fee. If you want additional samples of proposals and sample chapters, see our *Write the Perfect Book Proposal: Ten Proposals that Worked and Why.*

The Tone for your Spiritual Book Must be Balanced.

I know I am repeating myself but never say, in your proposal, "God told me to write this" or "My psychic told me it would be a bestseller." Even if your claims are valid, I doubt editors are ready to believe you, or they may have heard it before. You may also have had a vision of the Blessed Virgin but keep this to yourself unless it is relevant to your book. This zeal will raise a red flag even with Spirit-friendly agents and publishers. Wide-eyed naïveté and unchanneled enthusiasm can be charming—but not when it comes to selling your book. Even if your subject matter is esoteric or channeled, highly interpretive or intuitive, your book proposal needs to be rooted in the realities of the publishing business. Faith and connection to your inner voice will give you the creativity and inspiration to write, but do not count on people understanding your internal language. Agents and editors do not have to be "on the path" to be effective. Be clear in your communication. Stay grounded.

Presentation

If you send a digital version of your proposal, ensure it follows good formatting. Do not send it unless it is requested. Knowing graphic design allows you to utilize more interesting covers and easily incorporate photographs. However, this is not necessary. It won't make up for a poorly written proposal.

If you send it in by mail, you do not have to spend a fortune on fancy binders and expensive paper for your proposal. Just make sure everything is neat and professionally presented. Also, please leave your proposal unbound because if it generates interest, agents and editors will make copies of it.

Do not package your proposal so that no one can open it without a crowbar or a bomb. It's unlikely that anything will happen to it in the mail. And as with query letters, do not use gimmicks. One agent once received a proposal packed with dryer sheets to make it smell good, and she almost passed out with an allergic reaction. If you smoke, have a copy made somewhere that will smell fresh, and do not anoint your paper with essential oils or perfumes. Finally, never send originals of artwork, photographs, or your manuscript. You are setting yourself up for unhappiness if you send a one-of-a-kind original or your only copy. A publisher or agent has no obligation to guard your originals carefully. When you deal with hundreds of pieces of paper daily, things get misplaced. Some publishers and agencies are remarkably organized. But you can't count on that. We don't know of any firm that lists "organized" as one of its credentials.

Remember to wait until someone requests your proposal before sending it. Most agents and publishers have ways to submit your projects digitally, making everything a lot easier and cutting down on paper clutter.

How Can I Avoid Rejection?

Stay under the covers! Rejection is a part of life and an inevitable part of the writing journey. The only way to avoid rejection is not to submit your work anywhere. Those working on a Self-Love lesson may need to do a lot of journaling during the submission process. Even if you do everything correctly, your proposal and book will not be for everybody. There could be a million reasons why an editor rejected your proposal, none of which reflect on you as a person. Selling any product is simply a matter of numbers—you have to get it out there to as many likely prospects as possible before you get any nibbles. Any salesperson will tell you this. For instance, a two percent response rate is considered a success in direct-mail marketing campaigns, even those targeted to probable product buyers.

Rejection letters are a good thing. They give feedback. You may want to reevaluate your submission if you get enough of them. You can also learn from a kind editor's specific comments as to why your book won't work for them. You don't have to contact that person again so that you can take their advice in the privacy of your ego.

Every time you put your work out into the universe, you receive something to help you achieve your destiny. Ask, and you will receive. For example, if you put your manuscript out there, you ask the universe, "Should this book exist? Who will benefit most from it?" You will get an answer one way or another.

Creating a successful proposal that generates interest is like putting together the pieces of a puzzle—the more details you put into place with solid writing and content, the more checks go into the mental "plus" column in the editor's heads as they read it. Enough checks, and you may be getting an offer.

Sometimes strange things happen to bring manuscripts to the right people at the right time. So maintain your faith, dignity, and tenacity because you never know when it will be the right time for you or when the right people will converge.

TEN THINGS NOT TO DO WHEN WRITING A BOOK PROPOSAL

- Do not forget the purpose of a book proposal. The proposal is not a mini manuscript. Instead, a book proposal is akin to a business plan where you can introduce your project to the appropriate agent or editor.
- Do not think you will put all your energy into the manuscript and whip out the proposal just because you have to. In many cases, your book proposal needs to be better than your book. This document is what will get you in the door.
- When writing your book proposal, do not pontificate. Your overview should only be 250-500 words. You are enticing the agent or editor to read more. You do not want to waste this space with fluff about how it will be a bestseller and change the world.

- Do not weigh any proposal section as more important than the others. Every section is there for a reason. You are anticipating questions the agent or editor will have about your book's potential and answering them in ways geared to support you.
- Do not write a disorganized table of contents with fancy chapter titles. • It is better to have clear and explanatory titles that allow a reader to completely visualize the book than for someone to think you are clever but unfocused.
- Do not forget to do your market research. Know who your audience is. Saying that every woman in the world needs to read the book is not valid even if it is true.
- Do not forget to research your competition thoroughly. You may not find all the books in the works at a publishing house, but you should be familiar with books already in the marketplace.
- Do not write a chapter-by-chapter outline that is non-persuasive. In other words, use good writing skills to show that the book will be a good read.
- Do not forget to describe what you bring to the table. If you have a reach to your audience, include it in your proposal so the agent or editor can be sure that your book is a reasonable risk.
- Do not get lazy when it comes to including sample chapters. You may not need to write the entire manuscript, but the agent or editor will want to know that you can write. Again, you do not need to be the best writer, but your sample chapters will show follow-through.

- Do enjoy the process and show that you are passionate about your book. Try to be patient with this part of the journey. It will pay off in the end.

14

THE OFFER

So you've created a proposal and manuscript in which every element shines. Let's look at what happens when an agent or publisher expresses interest in your manuscript and discuss how you can continue to build, during the courtship stage, the professional aura and attitude that will make you look like a sure bet as a publishing professional.

THE REQUEST FOR MORE INFORMATION

The first step when you send a query letter will be a request for either a proposal or a partial manuscript. It is exciting to get to this stage, but it is not a time for you to start emailing and calling the prospective agent or editor. If you receive a request, follow the directions carefully and send whatever material will bring you to the next level. If they ask you to send a proposal, you know how to create one and should have it ready at a moment's notice. If you are submitting a novel, the protocol is to typically send the first fifty pages, a synopsis, and possibly a bio. Don't send the entire manuscript unless you are requested to do so. Experienced agents can look at the first fifty pages and determine if they want to see more. Make those first fifty pages count because they will be requesting the pages consecutively, unlike sample chapters in a proposal.

As much as you will be bursting with impatience, play it cool. Agents are busy people, but they have invited you to submit your work. You are at a higher priority, but it doesn't mean they will not take a while to get back to you. Reaching out to them after two weeks and then again after a month is perfectly reasonable. Do not write accusatory or manipulative letters. Always remember the human factor. If an agent has not gotten to your work and you continuously contact them, they may decide you are too high maintenance. It is unfortunate, but since they are in the position to influence your future, work with their schedule. If you have had others requesting your manuscript, you can let each know about it. Let them know if you receive an offer for representation, as we said in the chapter on agents. If they are your preferred agent, it might move them to prioritize your work and make a decision.

Make sure that you put your contact information on every submission. This information should include your phone number. I can be an impulsive person. When I worked for the agency, I might just pick up the phone if I liked something. Agents also compete for the best material, so they might want to reach out to secure representation.

Be prepared with information about the agents you have queried. If you receive an offer of representation, you should be sure if you want to accept it. Sometimes it is more difficult to find an agent than it is to find a publisher. If you have selected agents who are all qualified, the first person to offer representation is showing enthusiasm for your work. It might be a wise plan to accept their offer. Do your research first. I know from experience that it is not always the best move to turn down the first offer you receive because you think something better will come along. You may not get another offer. This opinion is my perspective from working at our literary agency. If you receive an offer of representation, you can be sure the agent has spent time evaluating your work or has the experience to know if they can sell it to a publisher. In all honesty, you are not in the driver's seat regarding literary agents.

Some people in the industry advise writers to ask a list of questions if an agent offers representation. Some questions are reasonable to ask before signing an agreement, but you should know a lot about the agents before you ever approach them. The bottom line is that if an agent offers you representation, do not put the agent on the defensive. Unfortunately, unless you are a celebrity, you don't have the leverage you think you have. If you are a new writer and a reputable agent is willing to take a chance on you, say "yes" and "thank you."

If you are Fortunate you may have a Publisher Meeting.

If an agent represents you and they have a publisher interested in your work, the publisher may ask to set up a call or a video conference to discuss the project. In the past, we have also set up publisher meetings with authors who make the rounds to the possible prospects. This pre-screening process can lead to an offer or a pass. It is a flattering step toward publication, but you must be at your best. In most situations, your book is just a part of the total marketing package; you are the other key component. Publishers may want to know how well you can speak extemporaneously and how enthusiastically you can describe yourself and your book. In short, they want to see if you are marketable. Whether they set up events or you do them on your own, they want to know they will succeed.

If you meet with a publisher via phone or video conferencing, don't come off as blasé. When a publisher calls you to discuss your book, they have a plan—maybe they want to hear how you sound, how enthusiastic you are, and how amenable you are to their suggestions for the book. Believe it or not, when asked about her topic in an initial phone call, one prospective author answered, "Oh, I don't know, it's just something I've sort of been kicking around for a while. I'd actually forgotten about it—I've been working on this other thing." Maybe it was just natural reticence, but her lack of passion for her book was a major red flag for the editor.

If you are a quiet or shy person, don't reply to the publisher's or editor's comments with monosyllables like "OK," "uh-huh," and "right." They want to hear multi-paragraphed, enthusiastic answers to questions. Now is not the time to be overly timid, hesitant, or modest. Publishers are looking for a self-promoter but not hucksters. As you would in any job interview,

pause appropriately to see if the caller also has something to say. Try to have some new information that further illustrates your book's contents. A publisher will see this as great fodder for interviews to publicize your book. Be open to suggestions for your book's direction. You won't necessarily receive this type of personal attention, but if you are fortunate enough to have someone to give you feedback and nurture your vision, it is a good idea to take it in without focusing on the sale. You are already in the running if they are taking this time for you. They want to like it, so help them. This strategy can help close the sale.

Unless you want to publish it yourself, show interest and enthusiasm for a publisher's vision for making your book more marketable.

One last point, stop selling when the sale is made. Overselling yourself might lose you the deal as well. I love the expression: "What part of yes do you not understand?"

What do I do if a Publisher Offers a Contract?

As we discussed in the chapter on literary agents, your agent will negotiate the publisher's agreement on your behalf. You are not obligated to accept any offer, but your agent will present them to you and discuss the pros and cons.

Your agent will review the contract with you and explain all the clauses. Most publisher contracts are similar, outlining your responsibilities and their obligations.

It bears repeating that it is not always wise to involve a personal attorney unfamiliar with the publishing world or a spouse in the negotiations. While you should always share important decisions with your spouse, sometimes spouses or well-meaning friends can derail negotiations by whispering in your ear that you can do better. A good agent will try to leverage the best advance and terms because that is how they earn a living. And no agent will negotiate their commission unless they are taking on contract negotiations for a book they did not shop. This is a time to be an individual, work with your agent, and trust yourself. You don't need to involve the entire greek chorus.

Part Four

PROMOTING YOUR
BOOK IN THE DIGITAL AGE

This section was not in the original book because the word "platform" was just beginning to seep into the publishing lexicon, and at the time, there was only one way to create one. As the conglomerates continued to conglomerate, they looked for books that could give them less risk. Twenty years ago, people-built platforms through media appearances, speaking engagements, hard work, and money. Authors might include in their promotion plan a significant purchase of books to show their commitment or would agree to hire a publicist.

Publishers always like celebrities but would also look for people who had regular guest spots on talk shows, such as *Oprah* or *Montel*. This notoriety would all but guarantee a significant book deal.

Well-crafted mid-list books continued to sell, but it became more difficult for people to break new ground. In addition, as the large corporations absorbed the smaller publishers, agents had fewer opportunities to place these books. As a result, many agents closed their businesses or moved into consulting.

In this section, first, we will review your role in the promotion if you are under contract with a traditional publisher. Unless you are front list, and even when you are, you will be the one to keep your book sales growing. It is by necessity that your publisher and the editor you thought loved you will move on to the next big thing. I said it once and will repeat it: "it is business, not personal." So move on and take advantage of having a book that you can promote on your own.

We will also cover how to level the playing field before you submit your proposal or book to an agent or publisher. There are methods through strategic author branding where you can have enough of a platform to prove you have an audience and can reach them. I found many publishers do not understand how digital marketing works. You will need to explain to them how what you can show through your efforts can convert into book sales.

Writing is only one part of being an author. And being a spiritual writer has a higher purpose altogether. I believe I learned about these things to share them with you. I never expected to learn about anything remotely techy. When I first got a desktop, my son needed to help me turn it on. Computers were big scary things. I got my first word processor during the time of dot matrix printers, and if you made a mistake with those babies, you could wipe out your entire hard drive. It took me a long time to learn to trust again. But if I could do it, you can too.

15

BUILDING YOUR PLATFORM IN THE DIGITAL AGE

*N*ow comes the part that you have been dreading or eagerly anticipating. The internet is a miracle, and technology is something that everyone can master if they do not allow themselves to become overwhelmed. My son had to show me how to turn on my computer a few years ago, no joke. Now I run a social network; I am a busy book marketing consultant and CEO of an indie hybrid publishing company with over 25 titles in direct-to-consumer or traditional distribution. I also have an author branding company utilizing digital marketing. Understanding how to promote online is an ongoing learning process as the platforms and algorithms change. An algorithm is a mathematical set of rules to analyze data behavior. Social media platforms use

algorithms to organize the data, such as how something will display. When used for marketing, it can influence how you can get noticed. But let's back up a bit.

I am learning every day about the nuances of internet marketing. I had the advantage of studying with some of the top thought leaders in the field of Digital Marketing Strategy and Social Media Strategy when I obtained three graduate certifications through the Rutgers University mini-MBA program. What became most apparent to me is that when people say their social media is fine, but they can't tell me how they analyze those numbers or do not think their online presence is essential, I know right away that they do not understand what this stuff is all about. The best strategy is to build an online book marketing plan using social media, your website, and all the tools to help people find you. It helps to calculate everything you do for how it supports your brand. Everything you do should be shareable and should relate back to your hub, which is your website, including an optimized rich content blog. No groaning allowed. I hear you thinking, "but I don't want to take the time to write blogs." And this is not because I am psychic, even though I am.

Most book writers do not want to take the time to do anything other than write. You are not alone if you think the marketing part of things will magically happen when your book is published. I can't count how many book proposals I have read that say in the promotion part how their book will be perfect for talk shows and radio and will be a bestseller without spelling out anything they plan to do to make this happen. There is no law of attraction, manifestation affirmations, or anything strong enough to sell your book without you planting the seeds and exerting some effort and strategy. The good news is I can explain how to get this started. The rest is up to you.

THE PURPOSE OF YOUR ONLINE STRATEGY

You can build a community of readers primed to buy your book with a good strategy. This strategy is what marketers call creating a funnel. Think of it as a buying cycle or how you decide to buy something. If you are like me, some of your purchases are impulsive, but here we are discussing the more thoughtful, planned-out approach. In the pioneer days before advertising, or maybe we need to further back for this analogy, people relied on their neighbors and friends for recommendations. It was about learning who you could trust to fix your outhouse or help plow your field. If you trusted your neighbor, you would value their opinions.

Then came products and advertising. Manufacturers of such things as soap products figured out they could sell their wares if they made you think you needed them. You may never have worried that you smelled bad until you went into the general store and saw a display saying if you don't want to offend anyone, use this great-smelling soap. Medicine shows would convince you of all kinds of ailments they could cure if only you would try their magic elixir. You may never have had these ills, but you likely felt better after drinking the potion. They spiked most of them with alcohol or even cocaine. Coca-Cola, anyone? Or maybe it was a simple placebo effect because all of your friends and neighbors were buying the stuff. Thus, advertising was born. You were no longer turning to your neighbors for advice; you were trusting someone else to tell you what you needed without questioning their plan to sell you stuff.

Now companies would advertise in newspapers with the latest gadget, fashion, or convenience. This print advertising was the new word of mouth until the invention of the radio.

Radio was a boon for people wanting to sell stuff. It was a form of entertainment that could simultaneously get many people into the same room. For example, soap companies or other manufacturers would sponsor radio shows and integrate their product endorsements. The term soap opera was coined because of the melodramas sponsored by the soap companies. The idea was to reach as many people as possible at one time and convince them they needed what you had. As a consumer, you may never have considered you had bad breath or were unattractive without face cream until you heard the show's star tell you so.

Next came television. If you are a fan of early and classic television, it is evident that Lucille Ball and Desi Arnaz had cigarette companies as sponsors of their top show, *I Love Lucy*. Phillip Morris was a major sponsor, and there would-be advertisements that looked like part of the show. So when Lucy and Ricky would enjoy a cool, relaxing smoke, Phillip Morris could count the increase in their bottom line.

Later, advertisers would buy time during popular shows with campaigns like "Where's the Beef" and "Take it off, take it all off." What about "I can't believe I ate the whole thing?" I am indeed dating myself, but if you are a baby boomer or student of classic advertising, you will note these advertisements became part of the American lexicon and were very successful. The key was to run the ads according to how many eyeballs they could count on. If the show was successful, the higher the cost for the time. Advertising dollars were vital to the success of the networks. If sponsors were offended, it could mean the death of the show.

Now jump ahead to the invention of cable television. With its many channels and reduced restrictions, Cable diluted the number of people an advertiser could count on for any particular show. As a result, the shows like the Super Bowl and the Oscars became cash cows for the producers and advertisers because they could count on more viewers tuning into the same shows simultaneously. It also became more important to television programmers to have highly rated shows to guarantee the advertiser's money. If they had a hit like *Dallas*, the last episode of *Mash*, or other iconic moments in television history, their advertising income would be through the roof.

As cable television grew, it became more challenging for broadcast advertisers, but it was still viable. The rapid growth of the internet blew everything into this new paradigm of pull marketing. Before the internet and social media, advertisers relied on push advertising. That is the same as political candidates trying to gain name recognition by constantly barraging you with their faces and message. Until recent years advertising and marketing relied on push advertising to gain the attention of buyers.

We are now in a period that is more akin to the pioneer days when people want to hear the opinions of their peers rather than trusting the push, push, push of the advertiser's hype. Therefore, a good content strategy that offers engagement will do more for you than simply announcing your presence in a crowded room and telling people how great you and your book are. Audiences today are more cynical, burned out with all the noise, and frankly don't want to hear it. Instead, they want to make their decisions through trust and information gathering, which is where your content strategy comes in. You can draw in your audience by providing relevant content that will build engagement and trust. Once you establish these relationships, it is an easy next step to tell your readers and followers about your fabulous book. There is a reason for your book to exist, and you need the patience to help your readers see what that is. (Remember Tolerance? Building a digital platform takes patience.)

When I first noticed the changes in marketing and the growth of the social media platforms, I got very nervous. It all seemed like snake oil, and I think I was correct. There are still companies that will offer to get a ton of likes for you on your Facebook page or other social media platforms, but this is not the way to do it. Instead, internalize the following: you want to build engagement with your ideal followers, who will ultimately become your readers.

This concept is the true meaning of social networking. With a strategy, you can create an organic following. Organic in this context means people choose to follow you and engage with you because they like what you offer. These do not need to be your friends. Instead, you are building a tribe of people who will be like-minded and who will want to hear what you have to say. If no one wants to listen to what you say, you are not doing this right.

You are a brand. Your brand is your persona, and your book and message are your products. Therefore, they need to align with the minor details, such as the colors you choose as your website palette. Even though you may not be *Nike*™, you will want to be recognizable to your readers.

What is Social Media Marketing and Why Should I do it?

Social media marketing takes time and consistency. You can plan it ahead of time, and you can automate it. However, it is best not to plan too far ahead because you want to stay aware of changes in the news. As I have said many times, I avoid the news, but you want to be careful not to post something if there is an unfortunate tragedy that you need to address. Or just don't post on that day. People can be sensitive, or maybe they are looking for a reason to vent. You don't want to encourage internet trolls by being unaware. That goes for anything you post. While I have told you to find your authentic voice and stick to your truth, the internet has become very strange. This era of online combativeness is a time for Self-Protection. Therefore, do not let your guard down when you post. If you want to vent, do it on your private page with people on your side. Did I mention yet that you should have a personal page and an author page for Facebook?

When you set up social media, you should not rely on other people to do your posting. Your readers want you and will see through inauthentic updates by people you hire. Here is why you should do this if you still have any doubts.

People mostly buy on the internet. This behavior started long the pandemic and is truer now. Book buyers make decisions online because of convenience and the closing of many box stores. They also have the advantage of being able to read reviews to help them make their buying decisions. In addition, there are websites dedicated to book recommendations. They are listed in the resources section of this book but will likely constantly be changing.

Box stores and my favorite indie out-of-the-way bookstores still exist, but they are much fewer than ever and closed their doors at the beginning of the pandemic. I know the implications of this firsthand. I had just launched a book in 2020, and Barnes and Noble ordered a second printing. Many of those books are now sitting in my storage shed. The pandemic impacted the supply chain, which the industry will feel for many years in unimaginable ways. We even had a paper shortage, and smaller publishers couldn't get their books printed on time. The large publishers had the same issue but were given priority or did in-house printing. An unexpected positive side to this limitation on new printing was the focus on gently used books such as the ones I sell on debsbookparadise.com. People could get these easily and quickly, and I also have a fantastic selection of niche and quirky out-of-print titles. See, that was an advertisement but targeted to what I hope is my tribe.

You may be concerned that this marketing will be a time suck that will keep you from writing and teaching. Your mission is to write your manuscripts well and make sure people know who you are and what you have that can benefit them. Marketing can help you rise above the noise so the Creator can use your vibration as a spiritual messenger to help change the planet's circumstances. If that is not a worthy reason to do digital marketing, I don't know what is. People over forty or maybe fifty may feel alienated by a world of technology that changed too quickly. Every day there is a new app or a new social networking platform. It is daunting and intimidating. However, it is manageable once you understand the marketing mindset. All it is is a return to pull marketing. You are drawing people to you to build trust and engagement. You want them to resonate with your message. You will be giving them valuable things like information or new perspectives. Then you can offer them something to buy from you. That is the process. And that is how you build platforms and brands in today's world.

I do not want to assume that everyone uses a computer, knows how to type, and has ever used social media. However, I can't stress enough that not utilizing these tools puts you at a significant disadvantage. You can hire people to do these things for you, but at a minimum, you will want to know what questions to ask them. It is an integral part of your empowerment as a spiritual messenger that you understand this digital world. You need a website as the hub of your strategy. It is your virtual office and establishes the impression you give your readers and any publisher who will consider you. The first thing a prospective agent or publisher will do when you present them with a query letter is to look you up on the internet. You want to be in control of your image well before you submit a letter and submission. Writing the book is only part of the equation. If you are writing nonfiction and have a proposal, it is still only part of the equation. It would be a game changer if you had an online presence before asking any traditional publisher to consider you. You need to exist in cyberspace as it becomes part of the due diligence an agent or publisher will perform to see if you are a worthwhile investment.

Step One: Learn to use a computer
Step Two: Learn to Type
Step Three: Get over any fear of using technology

Some of you may judge this as "we know this already." You would be stunned how many people do not know this. Some writers rely on others to type their work, who are not comfortable with computers and who avoid social media or other technology tools like poison. Agents and publishers will not take the time to look at anything that is not at least meeting the minimum protocols of submission. Young writers have grown up with technology, so it is foreign to think this would be an issue. However, young writers may not have the spiritual experience to write a good book. We can all learn from each other. We want to bring everyone along who has something important to say. This world needs positive vibration, so we need to make sure it is not technology or the fear of using it that stands in the way of success.

We all know people who grew up without a television. It is admirable that parents want to limit their children's exposure to things they believe are not fit or positive. However, staying off social media is not a good choice for writers who want readers to notice them. You don't need to post your food or other "look at me" things. When you have a sense of your audience and message, you will know what to post to stay relevant and engaged.

There is something to be said about privacy, and a legitimate concern, about how companies use our data. However, if you are using these tools for good and to connect with like-minded people, does this really matter? Have faith that positive results can come from a spiritual messenger using social media for higher purposes. Think of Mr. Rogers and his thoughts about television. He knew some producers would use it to numb people's minds and for avarice. He dedicated his life to providing television to children that would enrich their lives and teach them good values. Tools are as good as how people use them. So learn to use these tools to spread high vibrational messages.

The first and most important steps are to create good books. You can have the most robust marketing strategy, but your efforts are futile if the book will not garner praise from readers to recommend to their friends, acquaintances, and neighbors. Spend time re-reading the chapters about the writing craft and the challenges of the spiritual messenger. Make sure your ego is out of the way of your writing and that you have done all you can to make your product something solid and competitive. Engage objective editors to use professional standards when evaluating your work. Many author services companies, including those that are part of some of the most significant spiritual publishing houses, are not looking at your book for publication. Instead, they make money publishing you and offer what appears to be good curation, editing, and marketing. You can ask people who have gone this route. They are invariably disappointed when their target publishing house doesn't "discover" their books and the author services company does not sell their work beyond marginal numbers. If you know the limitations at the outset, you can still make these services work for you. Be sure to note what kind of distribution they offer. However, It bears repeating here that passive placement on the retailer sites or in the Ingram catalog is different than being distributed by Ingram. If you build a good platform, these author services companies can give you the product to sell on your own. No matter how your book is published, it is up to you to ensure its success.

BEGIN WITH A WEBSITE

Whether you are on your own, have chosen to self-publish, have used an author services company, or are given a contract by a more traditional indie or large publisher, your branding will begin with a website. I recommend getting the URL for your name rather than the book title. You can do both, but author branding should be about you and should build your reputation and readership. There are many places to purchase your URL. If you can't get your name with a .com, try some variation or use authoryourname.com. If you are trying to sell a particular book with a precise topic, the website should focus on that project, with you as the author. You can have additional pages to reflect other books or things you do, but the primary content will be for the book you are promoting. You may do many things but try not to dilute the website to be all things to all people. This hub is your author website intended to build an online platform and draw your audience to you.

There are many excellent and simple website-building platforms. I recommend you use wordpress.org even though it has some complexity. I prefer Wordpress because it is also the most easily ranked for Google. However, other platforms improve all the time. If they offer optimization for the search engines, do not rule them out. Website development can be expensive. I think it is worth the money to get it right, but having one is more important than not having one. Shop around if you plan to engage a web person to help with your website. As you would with anything, try to get recommendations from people before you invest. I have had terrible experiences where my Self-Protection lesson reared its head. Lesson learned I hope. Never give anyone complete control of your website without maintaining equal access. And never buy into the excuse, "you are not techy."

I have also had some exceptional experiences with reliable providers both in the US and offshore. Fortunately, the bad experience caused me to learn a great deal about the technical stuff so I could hold my own. Of course, I do not wish that on anyone. But as I said, sometimes I need the two-by-four method to have anything to teach others. Arghh!

By default, I have had to learn far more about technology than I ever cared to know. However, I will try to give you some basics so you are not in the dark about the purpose and benefits of a website.

Most websites are invisible in search engines. This fact is surprising but true. If you are not driving the traffic to your website by handing out dozens of cards daily or constantly posting on social media, you will not have any "organic" web traffic. The only way for a website to be visible to search engines is to optimize it. Optimization is a techy-sounding word, but all it means is the content on the pages of the website is optimal for the search engines to rank it. Search Engines like Google do what it sounds like they do. Google, for example, sends out little spider things like little bots looking for good content. If you have content of little interest to anyone or the titles on the pages don't match what you write about, it is unlikely the bots will see you.

Our company authorbrandingsolutions.com uses an intake workbook for new clients starting a digital marketing strategy. I will share some of this with you here to get you started gathering the information you need for a website and a media kit. Then we will break down the actual website pages and finally discuss how to optimize your site using Search Engine Optimization, your Blog, and social media.

WHAT TO GATHER FOR YOUR AUTHOR WEBSITE.

We start with your book

Your author branding site will use your book as the center of your design and content. While you can promote your previous works, the first step is to gather either a mock-up cover with a working title or your actual cover. We often suggest creating your website color palette to coordinate with the book cover as it creates a uniform look and feel for the site. We have fun with palette-creating software like www.coolors.co, but there are others like www.canva.com and www.colorkit.co. We have mainly used coolors. co, so it gets our vote. Next, you can choose a base color and figure out what contrasting shades will look good. Although we creatives like color, your user interface should not be so crazy that it is difficult to read. Stick to a primary color and some contrasts so your fonts can show up easily.

Your book cover image should be clear and high resolution; however, websites only need images that are 72 dpi. Therefore, as long as your images for all of the website are clear and large enough, they will look good.

When you have your cover, you will need a synopsis. As with your author bio, we recommend several versions of your synopsis. Each description should read like a book jacket copy. It should be persuasive so your site visitor will want to know more.

Here is what your book synopsis should do:

- It serves as a summary of your book to market to potential readers or media.
- It shows what the book has to offer.
- It intrigues the reader to want to know more.
- It tells the reader what to expect without giving it all away.

A good synopsis considers the audience and what would be of value to them. For example, if your book is nonfiction, think about the problem your reader is trying to solve and show how your book solves it without too much information. Suppose your book is for people who want to learn more about Search Engine Optimization. In that case, you might say, "my book demystifies Search Engine Optimization so anyone can use it to their benefit."

When we begin a project, we suggest our authors provide the following:

1. A two-line summary (140 characters) You can use these two lines with reviews or articles. This short summary concentrates on the book's strongest storylines or marketing niche to attract readers.

2. A short Synopsis (50 words) Fifty words is ideal for a caption or thumbnail description that may accompany your book cover photo on a website, Blog, or storefront. Fifty words distill the work down to its most essential elements.

3. Medium Synopsis (100 words) A medium synopsis allows for additional detail. This length is more like a movie trailer. You can choose the most significant selling points for the book and describe what is in it for the reader.

4. Long Synopsis (400-600 words) Your long synopsis gives readers a good overview of the book, the storyline, or the marketing

niche if it is nonfiction. At the end, list any accolades, quotes from reviewers, or endorsements.

If you are writing a novel, you can use many creative ways to describe your book. Of course, your approach will be different, but the goal is the same. Your website can be much more visual to reflect your story and personality. However, these varying synopses will still come in handy. They are an excellent exercise for you before you work on your brand.

Other items to consider:

After you write the synopses, we recommend you write at least five points of interest about the book and you. Next, crystalize your selling points and think about potential interview questions. Finally, consider what a media person might find most interesting about you and your book.

Next, write the backstory to why you wrote your book. This exercise can lead to an exciting section on your website and can be good material for interview questions.

What about you? You are your brand.

One of the first things we request from our clients is to have a professional photograph taken. You may be able to fool us with a photo taken from a phone, but you are only hurting yourself if the lighting is wrong or you forget to look at what is sitting behind you. The proper photographs help sell you, build trust with your website visitors, help sell your book, increase your appeal to media, and make it easier for any print reviews to use in their promotion.

Photographs should be in various sizes. Today it is more likely you will only need photos suitable for the web. They can be RGB, a type of color that is best for digital use. The dimensions can be 600 x 900 pixels. Or, if you want something to be used as a banner, you may wish to have the dimensions 1900 x 1080. Any graphic designer or web developer can help you with this. Or, if you are so inclined, there are youtube videos to teach about anything.

We ask people to have a professional headshot. A headshot should include your neck and some of your shoulders. This photo is not a glamor shot unless that is what you are selling. Save that for your significant others. Choose clothing that reflects your personality. If you are a flowy dress or T-shirt person, that is fine. Think about the energy you want to convey, as it is also part of your brand.

Your headshot is only one of the photos you can use on your website and social media. We always recommend environment shots that show you in places revealing more of your personality. For example, maybe include a photograph of you with your dog running in a field of wildflowers. Or you can take a good shot of yourself teaching a workshop. You can use these photographs throughout your website. While stock photos are suitable for filler, authentic images showing you and your personality are much better.

You will need your author bios and some other items to fill out your brand but now, let's discuss what your website should include.

WHAT YOU SHOULD INCLUDE ON YOUR AUTHOR WEBSITE

Your Pages

We will discuss how to optimize your website further in this chapter, but you should note that how you structure your website will help your ranking. In addition, some websites and blogs can help you dive deeper into the wondrous world of website and Search Engine Optimization. I will take you on a manageable tour so you do not become overwhelmed. When you understand these tools and how they work, they can be fun. However, they are complicated, and if you are not a detail person, they can be more than you want to do. Anything you do to help your platform is more than you had yesterday. So, start with some basics and grow into it.

Most author websites have several pages to spread out the content. You can also create a website with different sections on one page with a scroll down. We typically recommend you have the following pages in your navigation. Navigation is just the menu on top of the website that shows people what is where. An organized navigation menu helps the Google spiders search your website for relevant information. It is part of creating an overall structure. Here are the pages we recommend:

Home
About the Author
About the Book
Media Kit
Contact Us
Blog

We also recommend you create an email capture through something like Mailchimp, Constant Contact, Aweber, or any new email programs joining the market. Some of the more established email capture programs make it easier to set up because WordPress already had integrations with them. In addition, there are typically plugins, small pieces of code designed to add these things to your website. Make sure the plugin you choose is compatible with your website and version of WordPress. Other platforms may also have email capture built into their drag and drop features. As long as you can grow an email list, it doesn't matter how you create your author website.

This simple structure works well. Of course, if you want to use your website for other things, such as your work or spiritual practice, you can add to the menu with drop-downs and top navigation such as services. However, for your author platform, we suggest you include these items in an easy-to-find prominent fashion.

Home Page

The home page is crucial real estate. You want the person visiting your site to know why they are there. You can put teasers about your website's different sections with "see more." The advantage of that is it creates what is called an internal link to an interior page. Suffice it to say that is a good thing.

We like to put even a mock-up of the book. If you are building a platform for a book you hope to submit to traditional publishers, there is no reason you can't do a cover mock-up. Ultimately, you will promote your published title in the honor spot near the page's top.

Your home page should include a short synopsis of your book. This spot is where you can reuse your hook. You don't want to use this space for an overload of information. Do not hype, entice.

You may want to put your professional photograph on a banner or somewhere on the front page. You can use your short bio with a read more that will lead to your dedicated *About the Author* Page. I can't stress enough that your headshot needs to be professional, clear, and flattering. You may want to hire a professional design person to create the image for your website. They can fix lighting flaws and make it the optimum size.

About the Author

As you already know, the *About the Author* is not a resume or Curriculum Vitae. This section is an optimized description of you and why you are the authority to write your book or your Blog. The different length bios you wrote for your book proposal will be helpful for your website. You can use parts of your bio in various places, saving the longest one for your Author page. You will want to break up the text with subheadings to make a more extended bio easier to read. Also, consider if someone is introducing you on a radio show, television, or speaking engagement. What would interest you to know more? Some credentials are good if they are relevant, but don't overdo it, so it is boring. People do like to know things that are unusual about you. They even want to know about your pets. Your tone throughout your website should match the content of your book. A website about suicide prevention should not be all rainbows and lollipops as the style would be respectful, serious, uplifting, and informative.

About the Book

There are two purposes for this section. One is to be like a book blurb to entice agents or editors to want to look at your book for possible acquisition or to get your audience excited. Read book blurbs or think in terms of good movie trailers. Some give too much away, and some are too disjointed for anyone to want to see the film. As with your bio, you will use the different length descriptions in various parts of the website.

Some authors have a dedicated page for the story behind the book. You can make it a drop-down or have a space in your navigation if the story is exciting and unusual.

Media Kit

A media kit is an add-on. You can create a dedicated page for all the information a potential media person would need in preparation for an interview with you. Media people have very little time and sometimes don't read the books their guests have written. So you want to spoonfeed as much information as possible on this page. Some websites can host electronic press kits, or you can create a flipbook using software like InDesign. The simplest thing is to add items to your website that will help promote you and your book.

We like to include a Q and A section on author websites. Rather than using these as frequently asked questions, we use this for interview questions. We write out what we think would interest an interviewer and include questions and short answers. This section provides you the opportunity to control the conversation. You decide what you want to discuss about your book. We recommend up to 15 questions. These can be teasers as you want to hold out some information for a potential interviewer. As always, keep in mind what will make you an interesting guest.

Contact Page

We recommend you have an email capture like Mailchimp, Constant Contact, or whatever new system is available, inexpensive, or at no cost. You can always upgrade. It is a missed opportunity if you do not create a mailing list of the people who visit your site. You can have a plugin with a sign-up that pops up when people visit. It may be annoying at first, but it is effective. If you are so inclined, you can do a monthly email blast. Or just something on occasion. If you do not keep up with sending emails when you do expect some unsubscribes. It is a good idea to keep testing your list to keep it fresh with the occasional "hello." However, if they sign up, they are legitimately part of your list, and that can be very valuable when you are ready to promote your book or other workshops and events.

We also recommend a dedicated email, even if it forwards to your regular personal email. Please do not use AOL. Many of us still have it, but it will immediately mark you as behind the times. Instead, either use a business email or something like Gmail.

Your Blog

Your Blog is where people typically say no way. But, this is how you will draw people to your site and the easiest and best way to use your keywords and key phrases. Blogging is the core of a content strategy because if you write consistently about your topics, you will raise your search engine ranking.

Blogging is not out of style. You may not become famous for your Blog, but that is not your goal here. Your goal is to bring people to your website because of what you have to say. Social media is a great way to build engagement. You can become a social media influencer. However, social media does not get you ranked in search engines.

Your overall strategy should be to have an optimized website with an optimized blog using keywords that you then share through your social media. Then, if people read your blogs, they can also share them. This method is how to build an organic platform.

WHAT IS SEO, AND WHY IS IT IMPORTANT?

Now on to the nitty-gritty. SEO refers to Search Engine Optimization. For your purposes, it is also the best way to find out how to bring your audience to your website. Your Blog will be about something. That something is potentially a word or phrase that a person using Google, Mozilla, or Bing might be typing into the search bar. For example, someone might be typing, "how do I know if I am psychic?" If that is a subject you are writing about, you can use that phrase as part of your content strategy. That is part of on-page optimization. The spiders crawl the pages people see on your website to find answers to the questions people pose in the search engines.

There is more to SEO than this and a definite technique for finding your magic keywords. People who are SEO experts can compare what you believe are your keywords and phrases with how many people are searching for that thing to determine how well you can rank for that subject. Believe it or not, you want to find words with fewer people searching for them with less competition rather than trying to rank for the most popular phrases. Some great websites can explain SEO to you if you want to try it. When you start your author branding, we recommend you begin with an SEO driven content strategy so you know through data and rank precisely who your readers are and how to reach them. People are looking for answers. If you are clear about what you can offer them and are true to your message, you can draw them to you by providing good information. This understanding of their needs is an essential step in gaining trust and engagement.

In the early days of websites, people looked at keywords and search terms as potential gold. They would flood their sites with irrelevant words just because they knew they would rank high and get noticed. There can be advertising dollars related to search engine ranking. Whenever there is potential money, people will try to cheat the system. The people behind the search engines are more intelligent than that and have created best practices. You are looking for your audience and don't want to bring people to your site or page under false pretenses. Not only will the search engines penalize you, but you will also live with a guilty conscience. We wouldn't want that, would we?

Keywords embedded in well-written content are part of your on-page optimization. The importance of on-page optimization is if someone visits your site, they will stay there and read what you provide for them. This reduces what is called the bounce rate. If people find your site and leave without visiting your pages or doing something like signing up for an email list, if they bounce, your ranking will be penalized. You want your site to not only be pretty with a good user experience, but you also want to have information that they will find informative, entertaining, or inspiring.

There are more factors to the on-page optimization that can become complicated. I am not trying to underestimate your willingness to learn, but I know enough to be dangerous. I am learning through blogs and by hiring people to optimize my sites.

In general, on-page optimization is based on how you design your pages and how easy it is for visitors and the search engines to navigate them. Some suggestions include a logical structure and easy-to-read content broken up by subheadings. Your Blog can draw your readers to you by providing rich content that answers their questions.

Unless you are techy or willing to learn about metadata, you might want to hire someone to do the backend digital marketing. It is another vital step to gaining traffic and building your platform, but there is a learning curve.

You can add plugins to your websites, such as Yoast or All in One SEO. I am not suggesting either of these as I don't know enough about how they compare to give you any certainty. They may also not be compatible with your website. But they do show you how to do your backend SEO.

In the back end of your website, there are places where you can add titles and keywords to help your website so the search engines see it. It is specialized. If you take anything from this section, at least you will know why on-page search engine optimization is a tool for you. You will be able to ask questions of anyone who claims to do SEO, so you will know if they know what they are recommending. I recommend you learn about this. It does make a difference. The search engines look for titles, keywords, headings, and how the content is written. I am not enough of an expert to explain how to do the back end.

So How do you Write a Blog?

Before they were called blogs, they were known as Weblogs. The earliest bloggers wrote online diaries, and companies used these weblogs as a new way to get customer feedback. Business authors primarily provided articles that would raise awareness of their work while educating readers about their specific techniques or perspectives.

Early blogs relied on interaction with the reader through open comments. Unfortunately, the comments are a sure way for hackers to invade your website. You will need to make sure you have security on your site or may want to make your blogs shareable without allowing comments. It is a shame, but hackers find new ways to be nefarious each year. I am not enough of an expert on web security to advise you on how to prevent this. I got frustrated with having to delete the spam no matter how much protection I had on my websites, so I opted to shut off comments entirely. If you make your blogs shareable, you will still be able to gauge people's interest in your topic and can evaluate the effectiveness of your writing.

Blogs have always been written in an informative but personal tone. Even large corporations have adopted this approach because it is what people expect. However, as with your book, you do not want to make your blogs so personal that you are writing for your entertainment. Instead, you will take the topics you have determined to interest your potential readers and write something that can benefit them.

Blogs are not rants. While some passionate statements about subjects that concern you are warranted, if you are disorganized and letting off steam, you risk alienating your readers. And things that are published on the internet stay there. Be purposeful and intentional with what you write. Pray or meditate before you write to bring in what is from your highest self.

I like to keep blogs to anywhere from 250 to 500 words. Some people recommend nothing shorter than 600 words. You will want to break up the text with images or subtitles. Most blog platforms will also allow you to separate quotes that will break up the text. Try to keep to one main topic and point in your Blog. Tight, easy-to-read writing is always the most effective.

Images are essential to your Blog. You should have a featured image that reflects the topic. You can get stock images from many places for little or no money, and Creative Commons images will not cost anything. When you look for images for a website, you do not need anything larger than 72 dpi, but it is easier to reduce a higher resolution image than the other way around. When you upload a photo to your site, you will want to compress it. I never realized that images could influence the loading speed of your website. That can have an impact on your ranking in the search engines. Look up image compression. I use something called compresspng.com, but there are likely others. It also works for other formats like jpeg. If you don't understand these terms, you will need someone to help you with your graphic design. I have been doing this for so long now that I forget what it was like the first time I looked at photoshop. It can be daunting. But it can also be a lot of fun and a new way of creative expression for you.

An important thing to remember when writing your blog articles, aside from using optimized titles and keywords, is to write authentically. Write with passion, conviction, and authority. You are the author writing a book that will change people's consciousness. Stand in your power and believe in yourself. Ask the Creator for help that you connect to your Divine inner spark. Then enjoy this remarkable way to communicate with people worldwide in ways never before possible.

Off-Page Optimization

The more you write articles for sites like Quora and Medium and whatever new platforms develop that link back to your site, the better. And make sure if you receive any media hits, you link them to your page. Off-page optimization is about promotion. It is how you bring people to your website by strategically sharing your content. This is where social media marketing comes in. Anything that brings your audience back to your website is a benefit. Google only ranks your website; it doesn't rank social media. But they all work in concert for an overall strategy

This information might be overwhelming but remember; you are a spiritual writer who wants your message to be received. The digital world has many tools and opportunities for you to make a difference. There is a learning curve, but if you can either align with the right professionals or take the time to embrace this new age of technological opportunity, you can level the playing field. You can build an online brand that will bring your audience to you.

A FEW WORDS ABOUT SOCIAL MEDIA MARKETING

Your website is your hub and where you can establish your identity and platform. However, social media is how you can build your tribe. You can connect with and interact with like-minded people on many groups and pages, and you do not need to be on all the social platforms to benefit from social media marketing. You should start small and build up. Think about the type of book you are writing and who your audience is to determine where they might congregate on the internet. If Self-Love is one of your lessons, take note. You can't be everything to everybody, and everybody can't like you. Do not look to your social media for personal validation. Social media is also a dangerous place for people with self-esteem issues. It is where you can feel that your life is not good enough. Keep in mind people show their best selves on social media. If you look at the postings on Facebook, most people will not show you how they look first thing in the morning before having coffee.

It is human nature to share happy things. Don't measure your insides by someone else's outsides, especially what they show you on social media. And as spiritual writers, don't be intimidated by what you perceive as someone else's better and bigger following. You only want to attract the people who resonate with you; if you are starting, it is always a slow build. Social media is a marathon, not a sprint. And any get more likes scheme will give you a lot of false numbers of nonengaged followers who will never convert into buyers.

Where do I Begin, and What do I do?

The first thing you need to have is a marketing mindset. Lose your fear of the computer, quit worrying about people seeing or knowing you, and determine a strategy to brand you as an author. Of course, you can keep your personal life separate and should not post anything you would not want your children or parents to see. However, if you post and comment calculatedly, you will build a means of networking that will translate into book buyers. People want to buy from authors they like. Your biggest challenge is to rise above the noise that is out there now in cyberspace. It would be best if you had a quality product and a blueprint. These are the leading players in social media marketing right now:

- Facebook
- Twitter
- LinkedIn
- Pinterest
- Instagram
- Youtube
- TikTok

How to Build a Facebook following

I recommend everyone start social media with Facebook. Of course, there are many newer and fancier platforms, but it is pretty easy to use. Social media, which began as a way to connect with friends and families and to exchange information or photographs, is a great way to build up a community and market your books. However, the best way to use social media is to stay on top of the interactions you have with others. You want to use good etiquette and respond when others comment on your postings or retweet something you post. You also want to be giving in the digital world. Therefore, like and comment on others' posts as well.

When approaching social media marketing, the first thing to consider is why you are doing it. This question is the same exercise when determining why you want to write a book in the first place. Think about what you want people to know about you and how you can explain your credentials or book in a nutshell. There are techniques you can utilize when you are ready to launch a book, but I would like to introduce the basics of starting an online presence using social media.

Facebook is still the best real estate for social networking on the internet. There are very stringent rules for self-promotion on Facebook, and I highly recommend you follow them. Even though you will develop relationships that can turn into business contacts or future readers on your home page, it is a personal page. Facebook does not encourage direct business use on the personal page. However, if you post consistently, you can build a following. You can set events to promote things you are doing and even advertise through Facebook if you want people to see something you are doing directly on their timelines.

The posts that get high rankings through Facebook are those that are engaging. If you pose some kind of question, so much the better. You can have up to 5,000 friends on your page. Business pages seem to be unlimited. People can subscribe to your page if you do not add them as friends or have reached your limit. If you are thinking, how would anyone get 5,000 Facebook friends? You would be surprised how quickly you can reach a critical mass if you use specific key terms on your page. I listed myself as "Spiritual" when I first set up my page, and one thing

led to another. I am often past my limit, so to follow my posts, you have to subscribe. If you want to connect on my page, know that although I am sure I would "like" you, you may only be able to follow. It is nothing personal. I will have a page for this book that you can also "like" to follow posts and interact with me.

Many people do not want a personal page because they do not like people being able to see their posts. You can set your page to only be for your friends and family, and they can be your real friends, so your numbers should be more reasonable. However, unless you have someone doing your social media for you, you will need a personal page to set up your fan page

Fan Pages

Fan pages are unlimited in how many people can "like" you. While you are not allowed to put a "like" button or graphic in your cover design, you can find ways to invite friends to your page. If you post consistently, you will gain followers. If you Blog or have a link to your fan page on your website, you will also get followers. This is the world that you are creating to build community. Offer things for free like your content. Remember not to be overly self-promoting. This advice may sound counter-intuitive. You can assume that the people who "like" your page are interested in you and what you have to offer. You can put some bio information in the appropriate places when you create the page.

You can automate your posts through such things as www.bufferapp.com where you can schedule posts ahead of time. You will then need to find a way to keep track of the responses to your posts. I do not have to write tomes to each person; however, a little acknowledgment goes a long way. Unfortunately, I am not always prompt with the follow-up.

I like www.Bufferapp.com because it is easy to follow several pages, and I can set up links from any page I think would be relevant to my followers. In addition, you can set up Google alerts to screen relevant articles you can curate throughout your social media platforms. This curation is a way to give something to your followers. You are giving them the information they might enjoy or need while sparing them the work to find it.

Twitter

When a young intern at our office first mentioned "Twitter" to me, I thought it was hilarious. What the heck is a "tweet," I responded. But, of course, "Twitter" is here to stay, at least for now, so it is wise for you to take advantage of it. Some social media people think it is old school, but they keep adding more options that make it relevant for specific markets.

When you "tweet" you are given 140 characters to send out a mini blog. You can "tweet" about all kinds of things. When it first became popular, people would "tweet" about everything and anything, but mostly everything. It became boring to know what people were eating or what they were wearing.

Of course, savvy marketers figured out ways to utilize "Twitter" to build brands, and you can also use it this way. When you automate your social media, you can set up your "twitter" page or pages and schedule your posts. You must be consistent and stay within your message if you are using "Twitter" for brand building on a particular topic. Stay engaged and use good "Twitter" etiquette. The best results will be to provide things people find provocative but within their mindset. In today's world, as with any social media, stay out of controversy unless that is your brand. Stay just a bit beyond neutral, or you can find yourself canceled. I thoroughly believe in the real freedom of speech, but you should pick your battles and stay close to your message. Choose to follow like-minded people, and you should be fine.

. Quotes are good, and so are links. You can use services such as www. bitly.com to shorten your links, although "Twitter" has its way of shortening links, so they do not interfere with your word count for your posts. Did I already say be consistent? If you are using Twitter to build a following, try to post regularly and retweet other people's posts. I don't always walk my talk, but I know it is effective. You will probably see more of me on social media now that I am not glued to my computer screen writing this book.

By the way, do not spam everyone with endless retweets to build your following. As far as I am concerned, that is bad Twitter etiquette, especially if you are trying to keep up with the people interested in you. You want to give content and build relationships. So be a good "Twitter" neighbor and retweet and compliment others on their posts without a shotgun approach.

Linked In

LinkedIn.com is a well-regarded professional social networking community where you can find people with like minds. LinkedIn is an excellent place to find thought leaders in various fields. It is a good place for you to build a platform. You may not find dancing cats videos on LinkedIn, but you can share your status and join many active groups. For example, there are many groups on Linked In about publishing. You can learn a great deal there aside from making contacts. Remember that you want to build relationships with people before you ask them for something. You can do this by joining in discussions and commenting on things people say. There is also a professional level Linked In membership.

Pinterest

Pinterest is an online bulletin board. I think of it as scrapbooking, where people will look at what you put together. I used to scrapbook as a child before it became popular. I never found anyone who wanted to look at them except me. I had my first boyfriend's guitar pick—a napkin from my first date. On Pinterest, you can "pin" photographs from throughout the internet on your boards. You can express yourself in many ways; others will follow your boards and repin what you have if they also enjoy the same things. They ask that if it is not your photograph that you include the URL, the web address, of the photograph. This way, you are not violating anyone's copyright.

Pinterest can be used for marketing just as any other platform can. If you catch on with Pinterest has accounts specifically for businesses. Your posts on Pinterest are graphics instead of words. You can add words in the comments or descriptions, and you can even add a video. Pinterest is fun to do, which is why it is so successful. Remember that all of this has an element of fun, which is why people do it.

Instagram

With its highly visual and immediate interaction, Instagram has created an explosion of influencers. Instagramming is now an official verb. Instagram is designed especially for smartphones, but the app has recently improved the desktop interface to appeal to other users. However, you can't add video and images from the desktop, making it only a place for lurking. Young people caught on with Instagram initially, but it is also good for book marketers. One of the best methods for gaining attention is using #hashtags, captions, and emojis. Instagram will also repost to other social networks like Twitter and Facebook giving you more options for your images.

We can't ignore video platforms. YouTube disrupted everything when people began to create their content. There are over 2 billion YouTube users and an average of over 38 million channels. If you create videos, they should be short and optimized with tags and descriptions. YouTube has instructions on how to set up a channel, and many resources explain how to write the descriptions to act as Search Engine Optimization.

TikTok is a fun platform that, although it seems to be the domain of young people who can dance or sing, can be utilized in a strategic marketing plan. Adults do use and watch TikTok videos, and I experienced this firsthand. My daughter @thejessadams is a TikTok and social media influencer. She is an actress/model and an early adopter of these platforms. Whenever I visit her, she puts me in an embarrassing video. Jess decided I needed my own TikTok account to embarrass me further. I am open to new experiences, but aside from when I was with her, I never thought I would use it.

I had been taking medication for many years that was instrumental in helping me with Crohn's disease. The drug was keeping me in remission from an aggressive form of the disease. I am sure I will hear from some of you with ideas for natural healing, and I am open to suggestions; however, I have chosen to use this medication, and it works. Unfortunately, after ten years and no issues, my insurance company decided it would no longer cover this medication. I had minimal warning before I was required to switch. They didn't give me a choice. Some bureaucrat decided my fate, and I became incensed. When I heard all my appeals, including a letter from my doctor, had been turned down, I took to TikTok. I did a short video about how unfair it was that my insurance company decided not to pay for my medication and posted it. I used a good title for the video. In about two hours, I had over 17000 views. People were responding with their own problems with insurance companies. This is the power of the platform. I didn't have any followers, but people found my video because of the topic and related to it. At that moment, I realized the advantages we have at our fingertips.

We have a calling. The internet is a way to bring us together in ways never anticipated. I am so happy that you, as spiritual writers, can utilize it to share your messages.

16

Your Role In Publicity And Promotion

*Y*our author brand and platform are different from your book launch strategy. Promoting your book is a partnership between you and your publisher. Or, if you are on your own or working with a hybrid publisher, you will be the one to support your book. No one, not even your publisher, knows your book as well as you do, and most publishers have limited resources to promote books. If you are under contract with a traditional publisher, your book promotion will be most active in the months immediately before and after your book's publication date. The publicist will send Advance Reader copies and media releases to reviewers in hopes of getting your book reviewed or otherwise mentioned in print. They may also send out releases to online magazines but may leave that to you and your book launch plan.

After the book is in the stores, your publisher may set up book signings at stores in your area or wherever you can travel. However, the changing climate of publishing and slashed promotion budgets means you may also need to do this yourself. If you arrange events or signings, your publishing house can help ensure books are available, but they will rarely go beyond this level of support.

If you are fortunate enough to have an initial publicity push for your book, you will want to keep the momentum going. Your book may not be in every bookstore. Still, if it is traditionally published, it will be available in various warehouses. You can contact bookstores to set up signings or book readings. Your well-crafted hook will help you prepare a package to submit to places you hope will host you for an event or signing can have a successful event if you have a topic that can attract an audience who may not know who you are. When you contact bookstores, present your book by the subject rather than only about you. You can set up a coordinated travel schedule and book-signing tour by contacting potential locations ahead of time to see if you can get yourself on their calendar. If you can tie your book to a topic that interests specific audiences, you can adjust the signing to be more than just reading your book.

Be creative. If you know anything about the history of the Chicken Soup for the Soul books, for which we were the agents, it was the teamwork of the authors that made it into the phenomenon it became. Mark Victor Hansen and Jack Canfield received a few dozen rejections, not the legendary hundreds before a small house signed it up. Health Communications was on the verge of bankruptcy and offered a modest advance. They paid a very modest advance that the authors leveraged into a phenomenon. Once the book was published, the authors would go to the malls and the bookstores and bring people in for signings. They pounded the pavement during a time before the internet. They were tireless and earned all of their success. Jack Canfield still conducts numerous programs to share his marketing secrets. But, the biggest secret that I am sharing with you here is the tireless work, passion, and complete manifestation of their dreams. They were responsible for the results, and you can be too. They set the publishing world on its ear, an example of innovation and faith in your work.

When you are on your own or with a traditionally published book, it is time to kick your creative energy into high gear. You are not promoting yourself; for those too shy to think of doing this, you are promoting your book. You do not need a hard sell. You need a quality product you believe in and many means to make readers aware of its existence.

One more reminder for those grappling with the Self-Love lesson. If your publisher limits what they do for you after they launch your book, they are not purposely abandoning you. They have to pay attention to next season's titles. They may love you, but you are only one of their children. We all want to be only children, but only God has room to love us each unconditionally

If you want your book to continue to move off the shelves, you must put on your publicity hat. If you have taken the time to build a platform, especially online, a book launch and follow-up promotion will be much easier for you. First, you will need a strong, easily recognizable brand message to gain attention for your book. Then ask followers, family members, and friends to help you get the word out. Finally, if you have been cultivating a following by providing good content, it is time to ask for a favor.

There is nothing wrong with offering perks to your friends and fans for helping you launch your new book. Social media is suited to this as it is immediate. You can create contests. You will need to research this as the rules change. Facebook required third-party apps in the past, but now you can create contests directly. Your contests should consider your topic. Make sure you remain appropriate to your message. You can offer people a signed copy of your book or other gifts. These don't need to be expensive. I had great results when naming my bookstore. People submitted ideas, and everyone got a small gift. The winner got a bigger gift. Sometimes people are happy with the recognition and a special shoutout, but prizes are always better. I don't think people ever outgrow them. I know I haven't.

Because the best advertising is word of mouth, you can generate buzz through speaking to groups and selling your book afterward. You can line up bookstore readings, query newspaper or magazine editors about reviews or features based on your book's facets, or arrange local television or radio appearances. Numerous online radio shows or podcasts are always looking for guests. You can even decide to do your own show or podcast through the many platforms available today, but setting up the interviews is the quickest way to publicize at first. You are raising your profile, but these efforts may not translate directly into book sales. However, the more you stay with it consistently, the greater the return.

Consider corporate sponsors for your book. If your topic is relevant to therapists, for example, you can find lists through websites like pyschologytoday.com, which will show you their specialty areas. Look for people who can benefit from your work and who can connect you with others who will benefit as well. As writers, we may only think of the traditional forms of promotion, but if you brainstorm, you may realize there are other ways to reach people. For example, if your book is about relationships, you can send a query and offer to send a copy of your book to couple's counselors. The idea is to get your book into as many hands as possible so it will inspire word-of-mouth recommendations.

Don't expect your traditional publisher to promote you past the first two months. I was under the illusion that front list books somehow would receive more attention. I am so grateful that I had the experience of writing a big book with a major publisher so I could see how little they do that is proactive after the first few months. *Member of the Family,* as of this writing, has over 1000, almost all five-star reviews on Amazon alone and equal or greater accolades on other platforms. But this is happening organically without effort by the publisher. My collaborator did the rounds of the major talk shows and morning news shows right after the book came out, but the documentaries we were in all came to us. The publicist did not arrange those. Although I do not have experience with million-copy bestselling authors, I imagine there is a formula for those books that keeps them at the highest ranking. I can't advise you on how to reach that status. All I know is becoming your own promoter and advocate is the best way for you to succeed.

When preparing a book launch, you want to ensure your book is visible on many platforms. Any publisher will list and sell your book to Amazon, so you should create a profile on Author Central. You don't need to publish through Amazon directly to benefit from your Author Central profile. Go to https://author.amazon.com/ to set one up. Your Author Central profile is a hub where you can add a bio and a link to any of your books. You can add up to eight photographs, so choose a headshot and other environmental shots that show who you are and what is interesting about you. You can add up to eight videos, but they should not be long. Although they can be up to ten minutes, it is rare anyone will want a video longer than three minutes. You can also link your Blog to your Author Central page. You can see the advantages. Like many spiritual writers, we don't love business behemoths, but Amazon doesn't seem to be leaving us soon. Even major publishers have realized it is one of the best book sales and marketing platforms.

Another place to join is Goodreads. Goodreads is the largest platform for bringing writers and readers together in one place. As you have learned about the importance of engagement, Goodreads takes us back to the good old days of word-of-mouth recommendations. There are so many books available that it is overwhelming. Readers don't want to listen to the hype provided by publisher ads. They want to know if someone has read a book. They want someone who can give them a good idea if the book is worth their time and money.

If you set up a profile on Goodreads, use it to connect with people who share your interests. Unfortunately, I do not fully utilize this great resource, but I am thankful that readers recommended the *Member of the Family* book to each other. I saw the power of the platform in action. The last time I checked, we had 5,732, almost all five-star ratings with 684 reviews. We didn't do anything to encourage that, but it proves that people will share information about a book they like. Imagine what a little proactive marketing can do for you when you utilize Goodreads's tools. Please forgive me for referring to this book. I am proud of it, but it was also the scariest thing I ever did. I had no idea that I could write a book of that caliber. And every day when I got into my writing room, my prayer was not nearly as lofty as the one I recommend for you. It was more like, "Almighty God, please don't let me @#$% this up."

I encourage you to stretch beyond anything you think you can do when Spirit hands you opportunities to make your dreams come true. I am sure I brought in that chance, but I am not kidding when I say I didn't know if I could pull it off. When you write from your heart about something meaningful to you, it will be frightening. And promoting it will be terrifying.

However, you will gain confidence beyond your wildest expectations when you see people resonating with your message through these online groups. God will always be stretching you toward your highest potential. I have only given you a smattering of the tools available to you. Start with my recommendations, and then ask God and your Guides to show you the rest of the way.

Epilogue

Your Choices as a Professional Spiritual Writer

Spirituality, for many, is a competitive business. Therefore, spiritual people compete against others for a greater sense of importance. This attitude can be prevalent in publishing when certain books become lucrative. Some spiritual messengers have become the prophets of our day through the best-selling status of their books, and this is attractive to people who want all the material things this earth has to offer. However, I see a shift. I am not sure, but it appears the day of the iconic guru has passed. There is room for you and your message as publishing becomes more diffuse.

We also don't have the major talk shows which build celebrities in the new thought arena. Although people might choose to follow a particular author, they are looking for more than one voice to show them the path. I believe the most sustaining messengers are those who do not forget the information comes from the Source. If they have been raising their vibrations through the Seven Lessons, Spirit guides them to their audience.

I said at the beginning of the book that I do not wish to discuss the concept of "the last days." However, it doesn't take a mystic to see we are in very turbulent times. It took a lot of Soul searching for me to take the time and the many hours of worry and restless sleep to rewrite this book essentially. There were a few things I retained from the original, but not much. Think about the technological changes that have occurred in the past two decades. And indeed, I have a lot more miles behind me than I had at that time.

The most amusing thing is how God reminded me about the Seven Lessons each time I described one of them. I gave you some recent illustrations of how the lessons influence my life to show you they are real. Even though I hope my Soul has matured, until we leave this earth, we will never be beyond refinement and spiritual growth.

I am working on other projects as I always am, but this book is from my heart. It always has been. I hope you study the Seven Lessons, journal them, and take them into your heart. Your calling to write is no accident. Your voice is extraordinary and essential to the larger picture. We all have our place. Maintain your integrity as you persist on your path. If you accept your writer's journey with gratitude and humility, you will have achieved success.

You will encounter obstacles on your path to publication, just as any writer. But know everything is perfect for your experience and be glad they are there. Trying situations force you to reach for your inner resources; the most annoying situations or people can be the ones that help you grow the most. By trusting what is in front of you, you will see that you are on the right path and not alone.

Book publishing and the spiritual path have their methods. There are many things we can't control in either arena and shouldn't try. But there are many things we can control and influence with our choices and by listening to the answers our Guides give us. The answers are everywhere in equal proportion to the questions.

You have learned to connect to your inner Spirit. Trust that and move ahead! As you spread your wings and begin your journey toward publication, do not forget why you started. You are called to write because there is a higher calling that you must satisfy. If you try to ignore it, you will be forever filled with a sense of something yet undone. It will haunt you.

Whether or not anyone reads what you write, you need your gift of writing to learn your truth. So try not to allow the race toward publication to cloud the process. Instead, allow yourself to be enriched and share with those who can bask in the glow of your inner light.

There is so much to do! You have a role in the process of our collective awakening to higher truth. Writers have influence. Good writers—those who allow their message to outweigh their need for personal recognition—can change the world. Take pride in your work and glory in your achievements, but don't forget that all spiritual writing comes from the same source. You are a collaborator who we pray will remember to thank your co-creator.

May the creative force of the universe light your way so you can fulfill your destiny.

Bonus:

Memoir as
a Spiritual Journey

Many spiritual writers are called to share their personal stories. While memoirs are challenging to sell to traditional publishers if you are not a celebrity, a well-structured, well-written personal story can appeal to the right agent or editor. If it does not rise to the level of the traditional publishing avenues, it can still find an audience that will appreciate the work. Writing a memoir is a beautiful exercise in self-awareness. I think everyone should write one to have a high-level perspective of the life path. The connections you will see when you look at your life as a story are amazing. As you will see in this guest essay by my colleague Wendy Dale, the basic structure of a memoir is typically in three acts. First, like in a novel, a protagonist, you, has some triggering event that creates the conflict or problem that moves the story along.

It is like what you see in a film logline: something happens to the main character: this is the inciting incident. Then what follows are the protagonist's goals and conflicts that lead to the resolution. Of course, twists and turns in between make up the story, but the critical thing to remember in writing a memoir is not what details you put in but what you leave out. When we write our personal stories, we mine our memories for details that bring them to life. It is good to think of all the senses when you picture events. However, in the final memoir, you will find too many details are not necessary. Like in a film, if lipstick is on a burning cigarette in an ashtray, it is only a significant detail if it belongs to the killer. You only want to include details that move the story along, form descriptions of key characters, or are significant to the events.

In a memoir, you are writing about yourself, but it is in the form of a persona. You are a character in your book, just like anyone you include. As you would in a novel, you want to know about your characters, such as background, history, and personality quirks. You will want to know what they look like and maybe even what their dreams and unrealized goals might be. Understanding the characters you choose to include in your story will bring it to life. It will be the ingredient that helps you write three-dimensionally using the best techniques of creative nonfiction.

In the addenda material, I have added a list of questions you can consider when writing character profiles of the essential people in your story. You may not use all the characters or refer to any or all of the descriptive material. However, when you write, you will see your story in an expansive way that will make it ring true to your reader.

Memoirs are typically written from the first-person point of view. I have seen books written in the present tense, but I think this is very difficult to maintain. In my opinion, it is better to write in the past tense. No matter what you choose, you need to be consistent. Writing in first-person lets you have an internal dialog, giving you many opportunities for observation and reflection.

You can use dialog and scene-setting in your first-person memoir if you remember you cannot know what is inside someone else's head. You can make assumptions about what they may be feeling through observing body language or knowing a lot about the person, but you can't know what they think unless you can read minds. Many of you can, but it won't work in your memoir.

You can use background information in your memoir in the form of exposition. But you want to avoid long data dump explanations. Instead, try to work with information in limited ways so it doesn't interfere with the flow of the story. You, as your protagonist, can explain things that you would know. For example, if you have a relative who worked at a department store when you were a child, you can explain in a short paragraph the history or description of the store if it is relevant to the atmosphere of your narrative.

When you write your memoir, it is tempting to write a chronological story without any structure or story arc. So I invited Wendy Dale to share an essay on memoir structure. When I was editing a memoir for a client, I felt I was in over my head. The book had great bones, but the material was a mixed-up batch and over 600 pages. I am not one to shy away from a challenge, but I am also not too proud to reach out for help when needed.

I honestly don't remember how I stumbled upon Wendy. I credit my Angels for trying to prevent me from having an emotional meltdown. I reviewed some of Wendy's videos, and they made sense. Then I reached out to her and established a friendship of mutual admiration. Wendy is an American who lives in Peru. Her personal story is fascinating. Wendy has a background in engineering, which I believe gives her one of the most organized ways to approach memoir structure I have ever seen. With her guidance, the memoir I am editing will ultimately be a respectable 350 pages when finished. Still, more importantly, I would highly recommend Wendy's videos to help spiritual writers organize their stories into exceptional memoirs.

Wendy and I plan to do some webinars together, but for now, enjoy her essay on basic memoir structure and check out the free videos she set up for my special spiritual readers. And please do make sure to join writersnetworking.com and the spiritual writer's group, as that is where we will be announcing future classes and online workshops. Your voices need to be heard, and your stories need to be told. Our jobs are fulfilled if we can help you do it in a professional way that will reach your audience.

Your Memoir Should Not Read Like A Diary: The Basics Of Memoir Structure

By Wendy Dale

As a writing teacher, one of the most common errors I come across is the attempt to make a memoir resemble a diary. On the surface, this seems like a smart decision to make. After all, both of these vehicles recount true events from your life.

However, a diary has one huge flaw that prevents it from holding a reader's attention for very long: A diary is a collection of disjointed stories pasted together. And telling someone a bunch of random things that happened to you does not create a plot.

One of the hardest aspects of writing a memoir is getting your structure right. (Structure is basically synonymous with plot.) If your structure is off, your book won't work—even if you have stellar prose and good stories. Memoirs with structural problems tend to be boring and often confusing. Most importantly, without the right structure, you won't create that key ingredient that's necessary for a reader to keep turning the pages: suspense.

Connect Your Scenes to Create Plot

Memoir structure can be distilled down to a very simple concept: "connected events." In other words, the key to creating a plot is to take your scenes and link them together for your reader. When you do this, you've created a cohesive story—in short, you've crafted a memoir and not a diary. However, actually achieving this is one of the most challenging aspects of writing a great book.

One way to connect your events, to link one scene to the next, is to use causality. This is how novelists and screenwriters create a plot. When one event *brings about* the next one — voilà!—you have structure.

Let me give you an example that should illustrate how causality works.

Below are four events that you might write about in your memoir:
- I get in a car wreck.
- I go to the hospital.
- My sister comes to visit me.
- We reconcile after not talking for seven years.

Here, each of these four events has a causal relationship. One event *causes* the next one to occur. One event can't exist without the previous one.

For instance, my sister would not have visited me had I not wound up in the hospital. And I would not be in the hospital had I not gotten into a car crash in the first place.

If you have causality in your book, you have structure. You have created a single storyline.

Another Way of Creating Structure

While causality is a fabulous way of creating a plot, it can sometimes be tough to achieve in a memoir, mostly because of the fact that so many of the experiences you've lived through will not be connected in this way. It's much easier to rely on causality in fiction, where you can simply invent your plot.

Fortunately, there exists another option for connecting your stories: using a chapter premise. In this case, you come up with a single idea that all of your events have in common.

Let's say you're working with these events:
- My sister calls to tell me she's getting a divorce.
- My brother visits and informs me he's lost 80 pounds.
- My dog goes missing.
- I take a trip to the Bahamas.

Here you have four different scenes, which on the surface are completely unrelated. So how do you combine these disconnected scenes so that they tell a single story in your memoir?

Start by thinking of a concept that all of these events share. In this example, the idea of separation comes to mind.

If I decide that separation is the premise I'll use to structure my chapter, I'll refer to this idea time and time again as a way of connecting my scenes.

I might start the chapter by discussing the impact of separation in my life, mentioning the sense of separation I've sometimes felt from my family members. Then I include my first scene: My sister calls, and it turns out she's going through a divorce. So, I conclude the scene with new reflections: My sister is going through her own separation, one that actually winds up bringing us closer together.

When I see my brother and realize he's lost 80 pounds, I see both integration and separation going on in his life. He's achieved something huge, separating himself from a weight that held him down for decades. At the same time, his identity is in flux, and he sometimes feels distant from the person he's always thought himself to be.

Then my dog goes missing. Suddenly, I'm separated from the companion that's been with me for the past seven years. To recover from the loss, I decide to escape to the Bahamas. There I take a break from the routine of daily life, a separation from the worries that define my day-to-day existence.

What have I just done there? I took four events that had nothing to do with one another and used an idea to connect them, to turn them into a single story.

The key to keeping a reader's attention is to create a plot. And the key to creating a plot is by connecting your events. Keep this important concept in mind, and you'll craft a memoir that works, a story that compels a reader to keep turning the pages.

Wendy Dale is the author of *Avoiding Prison and Other Noble Vacation Goals* and the creator of Memoir Writing for Geniuses. To receive her free video class "Seven Steps to Structure," visit www.memoirwritingforgeniuses.com/freeclassdh

The Challenges of the Spiritual Writer
Reprinted with permission from Jeff Herman

About twenty years ago, I wrote an essay for my husband, Jeff Herman's book *Jeff Herman's Guide to Book Publishers, Editors, and Literary Agents,* titled *The Challenges of the Spiritual Writer* (reprinted with permission with a few changes.) Each time there is a new edition, he includes the essay as is, and over the years, we have received letters from people who say it was a surprise in such a nuts-and-bolts book and that it made them feel seen. So I am sharing it here because it is meant for you. It may repeat some of what I include in the book in various ways, but I hope you will feel the messages bear repeating.

When you pursue writing as a career instead of a longing or a dream, you might focus on the goal instead of the process. For example, when you have a great book idea, you may envision yourself on a book-signing tour or as a guest on a talk show before you've written a single word.

It's human nature to look into your future, but too much projection can get in the way of the writing experience. The process of writing is like a wondrous journey that can help you cross a bridge to the treasures hidden within your Soul. It is a way for you to link with God and the collective storehouse of all wisdom and truth, as it has existed since the beginning of time.

Many methods of writing bring unique rewards. Some people can produce exceptional prose using their intellect and mastery of the writing craft. They use research and analytical skills to help them create works of great importance and merit.

Then some have learned to tap into the wellspring from which all genius flows. These writers are the inspired ones who write with the intensity of a passionate lover. They are the spiritual writers who write because they have to. They may not want to or know how to, but something inside them is begging to be let out. It gnaws away at them until they find a way to set it free. Although they may not realize it, spiritual writers are engaged in a more significant spiritual journey toward ultimate self-mastery and unification with God.

Spiritual writers often feel as if they're taking dictation. Spiritual writing has an otherworldly feeling and can teach writers things they would otherwise not have known. It is not uncommon to read something after a session in "the zone" and question if indeed you had written it.

Writing opens you up to new perspectives, much like self-induced psychotherapy. Although journals are the most direct route for self-evaluation, fiction and nonfiction also serve as vehicles for a writer's growth. Writing helps the mind expand to the limits of the imagination.

One can become a spiritual writer; among the many benefits is Soul development. More practically, writing with flow and fervor is much less challenging than being bound by logic and analysis limitations. If you tap into the universal Source, there is no end to your potential creativity.

The most significant barrier to becoming a spiritual writer is the human ego. We treat our words as if they were our children—only we tend to be neurotic parents. Parents do not own their children. Children must be loved, guided, and nurtured until they can carry on, on their own.

The same is true for our words. If we try to own and control them like property, our vision will limit them. We will overprotect them and will not be able to see when we may be taking them in the wrong direction for their ultimate well-being. Another ego problem that creates a barrier to creativity is our hunger for constant approval and our tendency toward perfectionism. We may feel the tug toward free expression but will erect blockades to ensure appropriate style and structure. We write with a "schoolmarm" hanging over our shoulders, waiting to tell us what we are doing wrong.

The ultimate presentation's style and structure are important, but that is what editing is for. Ideas and concepts may flow like water in a running stream. The best way to become a spiritual writer is to relax and have fun. If you are relaxed and pray for guidance, you'll be open to intuition and higher truth. However, writers tend to take themselves too seriously, which causes anxiety, which exacerbates fear, which causes insecurity, which diminishes our self-confidence, and ultimately leads to mounds of crumpled papers, deleted text, and lost inspiration. You are worthy. Do not let insecurity prevent you from getting started and following through.

If you have faith in a Supreme Being, the best way to begin a spiritual writing session is with the following writer's prayer:

Almighty God (Jesus, Allah, Great Spirit, Buddha, Shiva, etc.), Creator of the Universe, help me become a vehicle for your wisdom so that what I write is of the highest purpose and will serve the greatest good. I humbly place my (pen/keyboard/digital recorder) in your hands so that you may guide me.

Prayer helps to connect you to the universal Source. It empties the mind of trash, noise, and potential writer's blocks. If you are uncomfortable with formal prayer, a few minutes of meditation will serve the same purpose. Just some silence off the grid is fine. You don't need to study meditation techniques unless you enjoy it. A conscious effort to quiet the mind will help you prepare for your writing session.

Spiritual writing as a process does not necessarily lead to a sale. The fact is that some people have more commercial potential than others. Knowledge of the writing business will help you make a career in it. If you combine this with the spiritual process, it can also bring you gratification and inner peace. If you trust the writing process and make room for the journey, you will grow and achieve far beyond your expectations.

Keep in mind that you are not merely a conduit. You are to be commended and should take pride in allowing yourself to be a vessel for the Divine. You are the one who is taking the complex steps in a world full of obstacles and challenges. You are the one who is sometimes so pushed to the edge that you have no idea how you go on. But you do. You maintain your faith and know there is a reason for everything. You may not know what it is, but you have an innate sense that all your experiences are part of some bigger plan. At a minimum, they create good material for your book.

To be a messenger of the Divine, you must be a vessel willing to get out of the way. You must be courageous and steadfast in your beliefs because God's truth is your truth. When you find that your inner truth does not match that of others, this lesson teaches you to be strong enough to stay true to yourself. Your Soul, that inner spark that connects you to all creation, is your only reliable guide. You will receive pressure from everywhere. But your relationship with your creator is as personal as your DNA. You will be a house divided if you accept things other people tell you to please them while sensing that it does not resonate with your Spirit.

When you find your inner truth, your next challenge is to make sure you do not become the person trying to tell everyone else what to believe. When a spiritual writer touches that moment of epiphany, it is easy to become God-intoxicated. There is no more incredible bliss than to be transformed by a connection to the Source of all Creation. Though people try to describe it, it is individual. Spiritual writers are called upon to protect this experience for the other seekers. The role of a spiritual messenger who manifests their mission through the written word is to guide a person to the threshold of awakening. Bring them to the gate but allow God to take them the rest of the way. Your job is to make the introduction. From there, the relationship is no longer your responsibility. Your task is to shine the light brightly for some other seeker to find it.

It is challenging to believe strongly in something while not finding anyone to listen to you. If you try too hard, you might find that others will drain your energy and life force while giving nothing in return. They may ridicule you and cause you to step away from your path. You do not have to change the world by yourself. You can do your part. Whether visible or as simple as helping someone know you care, you are participating in elevating the world for the better.

Some people like it exactly as it is. Some thrive on chaos and the diseases of the Soul. Your job as a spiritual writer is to protect your Spirit as you would your child. Please do not give away your energy; make it available to those who genuinely want it and will appreciate it. When you write, expect nothing in return. While following the protocols of the business world, do not set your goal too high such as reaching everyone. If you do this, you will elevate your responsibility beyond the capability of simple humans. If you do the groundwork, God will do the rest.

The world of the spiritual writer can be a very lonely place. It is easier to love God, creation, and humanity than to feel worthy of receiving the love in return. Making a difference through writing is a gift and a reward for our goodness, faith, and love. It is a two-way street. What we offer, we can also receive. It maintains the balance. It replenishes our energy so we can continue growing and fulfilling our destinies. We are all loved unconditionally. God knows everything we have ever thought, done, or even thought about doing. We judge ourselves far more harshly than God ever would. We come into this world to learn; we only do this through object lessons. We have free will. Sometimes we must burn our hands on the stove several times before we understand that it is too hot to handle. I have lived with the two-by-four-on-the-head method, and I do not recommend it. It is the only way I have been able to learn some of my more difficult lessons.

I have often considered wearing a helmet.

When we connect with our inner truth, we can become intoxicated with our greatness. Writing is very heady, especially if we can see our name in print. If we have people listening to what we say, we can believe that we are the message and forget that we are merely the messenger. Spiritual writers benefit from starting every day praying for humility. If we don't, and there is a danger that we will put ourselves before the purity of Divine truth, we will not be able to be the pure vessel we had hoped to become. The universe has methods of protecting itself. We will experience humiliation to knock us down a few pegs to allow us to get over ourselves. I have experienced many instances of humorous humiliation, such as feeling so amazed with myself only to splat on my face by tripping over the air—no injury, except to my inflated pride. God has a sense of humor.

On a more serious note, spiritual messengers are vulnerable to negativity if taken in by their egos. The information they convey becomes deceiving and can divert people from their paths. This potential pitfall is why I recommend spiritual writers always begin each session with a prayer to be a vessel for the highest of the high and the greater good. While readers have the choice to discern the wheat from the chaff, in this time of rapid spiritual growth, it is essential to help seekers stay as close to their paths as possible. There is no time for significant detours. We all have a lot of work to do.

We are all here to improve the lives of each other. We are blessed with living in an information age where we can communicate quickly and clearly in real-time. However, technology also serves to make us separate. We all cling to our ideas without necessarily respecting the paths of one another. We are all headed to the same place, the center of the maze, where there is nothing and everything all at once. It is where pure love binds us all together. We don't want to get caught up with trivial arguments about who is right and who is wrong. Especially now.

When I wrote this essay over twenty years ago, I could not have imagined the level of divisiveness. It feels unprecedented, but I know from history that it is not. As you will see through this new edition, I purposely do not focus on the idea of "end times." From what I have studied, it seems almost every generation has considered themselves at the end. I know it is up to God, and I do not want to disparage anyone's belief system. Perhaps a sense of urgency is in God's plan for us so we do not become apathetic. However, I encourage our focus as spiritual messengers to foster everyone's path to higher truth. Whether or not we are in the so-called end times, I do not promote fear but rather the incentive to be the best humans we can be. We, as spiritual messengers, can help people become whole and healed and make this world a better place for God. We share what we have so others can find it without wasting time arguing the point to win them to our side. Too many battles are happening in our world over who is the most right. We all come from the same Source.

When it comes down to it, spiritual writers are the prophets of today. We are here to give God direct access to our world in ways we can understand. The essence of the message is more important than focusing on who is the greater prophet. In the business of writing, there is no sin in profit. But in the writing mission, one must not forget that we all answer to the same boss and serve the same master.

You are also a messenger. When you agree to be a spiritual writer, you also agree to bring light into the world. This choice is no small commitment. Remember to keep your ego out of it. While learning to promote and support your work is essential, you must not forget that you are the messenger, not the message. I will repeat this mantra for you Ad nauseum (a legal term for: to a sickening or excessive degree) throughout this book so you do not forget it. If you keep this at the center of your heart and remember that you serve the greater good, you are a true spiritual writer honoring the call. May God bless you and guide you always.

The Writer's Journey and the Spiritual Path are One.

Resources For Spiritual Writers

There are many excellent editors and consultants for all of your needs. Here are some other resources to help you succeed in your writing journey. Make sure to write if you have further questions not answered in this book. If I can't answer them, I know I can find many of my colleagues who can. This list is not comprehensive as websites, magazines, and resources change quickly. Please write to me at Soulodysseybooks.com to update or recommend resources to share. You can also connect on Facebook @ Soulodysseymedia

Some Books to Get You Started:

Jeff Herman's Guide to Book Publishers, Editors, and Literary Agents: What they want and how to Win them Over By Jeff Herman www.Jeffherman.com

Making the Perfect Pitch: How To Catch a Literary Agent's Eye By Katharine Sands (Apr 1, 2004)

On Writing Well, 30th Anniversary Edition: The Classic Guide to Writing Nonfiction By William Knowlton Zinsser (May 9, 2006)

1001 Ways to Market Your Books (1001 Ways to Market Your Books: For Authors and Publishers) By John Kremer (May 26, 2006)

Sell More Books!: Book Marketing and Publishing for Low Profile and Debut Authors: Rethinking Book Publicity after the Digital Revolutions By J. Steve Miller, Blythe Daniel, Stephanie Richards, and John Kremer (Jun 8, 2011)

Write the Perfect Book Proposal: Ten Proposals that Worked and Why By Jeff Herman and Deborah Levine Herman (

Websites And Online Directories

American Book Trade Directory

http://books.infotoday.com/directories/American-Book-Trade-Directory.shtml

Lists wholesalers and sales representatives for self-published books. Published by R. R. Bowker; available at most libraries.

The Association of Authors' Representatives, Inc.
http://www.aaronline.org/.
AAR is a not-for-profit membership organization active in all areas of publishing. 676-A 9th Ave, Suite 312 New York, NY 10036

The Christian Writer's Market Guide http://www.stuartmarket.com/
Writer's guidelines and submission procedures for
all Christian publishing houses that accept unsolicited manuscripts. Sally Stuard, founder of the Christian Writer's Market Guide also has many other resources on her website.

Literary Market Place www.LiteraryMarketPlace.com
Subtitled The Directory of the American Book Publishing Industry with Industry Yellow Pages. Lists U.S. and Canadian publishers, agents, printers, and editorial services, including contact and submission information as well as geographical indexes. U.S. publishers are categorized by types and subjects of books. Published annually by R. R. Bowker; available in the reference section at most libraries brings the power of automated searching to the world's largest, most complete database of the book publishing industry.

PMA, the Independent Book Publisher Association
PMA is a cooperative association of 4.000 independent publishers across the USA, specializing in trade, and non-fiction books (i.e. business, computers, psychology, self-help, health, new age/metaphysical, religious/spiritual etc).

Publishers Global: Publishers Directory Religion Publisher's Directory:
http://www.publishersglobal.com/directory/subject/religion-publishers/
Lists 480 Religion Publishing Companies

Web Sites

The invention of the Internet truly blesses spiritual writers. The World Wide Web provides writers the opportunity to explore every aspect of the publishing world: the industry, writing resources, connecting with other writers, and even finding sources of funding for certain types of projects. You may also explore the innumerable sites on spirituality and connect with like-minded people. Everything eventually connects to itself. So, who knows? What first seems like something irrelevant could wind up bringing you to your destiny.

This annotated list of sites offers descriptions of some of the most useful sites for writers. For your convenience, I grouped the sites in resource categories.

Media

PR Web www.prweb.com

By PR professionals for PR professionals. A press-release distribution Service where you can set up an account for free, but setting up releases is where you spend the money. PRWeb, claims to have the the highest-rated SEO press release service, which means higher ratings in the search engines. This is a good thing to build into your marketing budget.

Radio Online www.radioonline.com

This website is for the radio industry and is a very useful resource for determining how to conduct a radio book tour. A comprehensive resource of up-to-the-minute radio information.

Talkers Magazine Online www.talkers.com

"The Bible of Talk Radio and the New Talk Media." This website is a trade publication serving the talk-radio industry.

Writing And Publishing

Book Marketing Bestsellers

Book Marketing and Book Promotion by the author of *1001 Ways to Market Your Books* www.bookmarket.com

This site offers a book-marketing newsletter, consulting services, and book-marketing updates.

American Booksellers Association www.bookweb.org

The American Booksellers Association is a trade organization representing independent bookstores nationwide. The site links members to recent articles about the industry and features "Idea Exchange" discussion forums.

Association of American Publishers, Inc. www.publishers.org

Association of American Publishers "is the principal trade association of the book publishing industry." The site includes information and registration for annual meetings and conferences, industry news, info about book publishing, industry stats and issues, and copyright data.

Association of Authors' Representatives, Inc. www.aaronline.org

The Association of Authors' Representatives, Inc, is "an organization of independent literary and dramatic agents." It is a member-only site that offers information about finding an agent, Internet links, a newsletter, and a canon of ethics.

Authorlink www.authorlink.com

Authorlink is the award-winning online news, information, and marketing service for editors, agents, producers, writers, and readers. We serve more than one million unique visitors per year. It is among the longest-running and largest publishing and writing communities on the Internet.

The Authors Guild www.authorsguild.org

The Authors Guild has been the published writer's advocate for effective copyright, fair contracts, and free expression since 1912.

Beliefnet www.beliefnet.com

This is a site to gain inspiration and access to other spiritual writers. It also takes editorial submissions. It is unaffiliated with any spiritual organization or movement. "Our mission is to help people like you find, and walk, a spiritual path that will bring comfort, hope, clarity, strength, and happiness."

Booklist online www.booklistonline.com

In the site is a current selection of reviews, feature articles, and a searchable cumulative index. Review topics include books for youth, adult books, media, and reference materials. The site also includes press releases, the best-books list, and subscription information.

Bookreporter

www.bookreporter.com/ Bookreporter offers book reviews and a perspectives section that deals with topics such as when a book becomes a movie. It features a daily quote by a famous author

Booktalk www.booktalk.com

Booktalk is an online booklovers' community composed of many of today's bestselling and popular authors. Personalized author home pages are complete with excerpts from bestselling novels as well as information about upcoming releases, author notes and personal hobbies and interests as well as publisher, literary agent and book industry information. Writing related articles by Booktalk authors and others in the writing community and upcoming literary events are also included on Booktalk pages. This is a good place to see what readers like.

Bookwire www.bookwire.com

Bookwire makes it easier for people to discover, evaluate, order, and experience books. Powered by Bowker's Books in Print® database, Bookwire makes it easy to search and discover over 20 million book titles, including print, e-books, audiobooks, and more. Bookwire™ is a service provided by Bowker, the world's leading provider of bibliographic information management solutions designed to help publishers, booksellers, and libraries better serve their customers.

Christian Storyteller http://www.christianstoryteller.com

This is a listing and marketing resource for Christian books. Whether traditionally published or self-published, they will help promote and advertise your book for a relatively small fee.

Editorial Freelancers Association http://www.the-efa.org/

This free online freelancer directory offers clients instant access to the diverse assortment of skilled publishing professionals who make up EFA membership.

Debsbookparadise.com This is my dream store. It exists as an online store with new books published by Micro Publishing Media and our imprints. You can also find a lifetime collection of unusual and hard-to-find gently used books; most are like new. Of course, my store weighs heavily in the spirituality and self-help genres. But you can find almost anything. Eventually, my dream is to create Deb's Book Paradise in a physical location. I plan to have it in a house with a cat and room to have book clubs and spiritual sessions. What do you think?

Other Deborah Herman Websites:
Soulodysseybooks.com
www.micropublishingmedia.com
www.authorbrandingsolutions.com
www.writersnetworking.com

Forwriters.com www.forwriters.com

This site provides numerous links to writing resources of all kinds. It lists conferences, markets, agents, commercial services, and more. It seems a bit dated, but not always up to date.

Independent Book Publishers Association https://www.ibpa-online.org/
IBPA's mission is to lead and serve the independent publishing community through advocacy, education, and tools for success. They publish an informative magazine and hold contests for independent authors offering prestigious recognition.

Literary Market Place www.literarymarketplace.com
LMP offers information about publishers, categorized by U.S. book publishers, Canadian book publishers, independent presses, and literary agents, including illustration and lecture agents. The site also offers trade services and resources. Limited information is free; the full information found in the book is available to subscribers.

Midwest Book Review www.midwestbookreview.com
This site has book reviews, resources, and advice for writers and publishers.

The National Writers Union www.nwu.org
NWU is the trade union for freelance writers of all genres. The website links various union services, including grievance resolution, insurance, job information, and databases.

Pen American Center www.pen.org
Pen is an international "membership organization of prominent literary writers and editors. As a major voice of the literary community, the organization seeks to defend the freedom of expression wherever it may be threatened, and to promote and encourage the recognition and reading of contemporary literature." The site links to information about several Pen-sponsored initiatives, including literary awards.

Preditors and Editors www.pred-ed.com
This is a great site to educate yourself about the Industry and to learn about potential fraudulent companies. Do not accept everything without discernment. Some complaints may be from disgruntled writers whose work was and probably should be rejected.

Publishers Weekly Online www.publishersweekly.com
Publishers Weekly offers news about the publishing industry in general, as well as special features. You've found it if you want to know where the editors and agents get their information. You can get into the minds of the

industry and can develop ideas by looking at the trends. You will also learn about the business side of things.

Reedsy https://blog.reedsy.com
Reedsy is an innovative site with a great many resources. They have a blog that covers a lot of good information about publishing.

R. R. Bowker www.bowker.com
This site offers a listing of books in print, books out of print, a directory of the book-publishing industry, a data-collection center for R. R. Bowker publications, and a directory of vendors to the publishing community.

Self Growth.com www.selfgrowth.com
This self-improvement site allows you to set yourself up with your profile and page. Then, you can become an expert in your area and build your platform.

Sensible Solutions for Getting Happily Published www.happilypublished.com
This site is "designed to help writers, publishers, self-publishers, and everyone else who cares about reaching readers, including editors, agents, booksellers, reviewers, industry observers and talk show hosts." It includes information about finding a publisher, ways for publishers to raise revenues, the self-publishing option, how to boost a book's sales, and sensible solutions for reaching readers.

Social Media Marketing Examiner https://www.socialmediaexaminer.com/
This is more than a website; it is a community focused entirely on social media marketing. There are many creative ideas to be found on the site.

United States Copyright Office lcweb.loc.gov/copyright
The U.S. Copyright Office offers valuable information about copyright procedures and other basics. In addition, the user can download publications and forms and link to information about international copyright laws.

Wow! Women On Writing www.wow-womenonwriting.com
This is a lively website with great information for women who write. It has a regular newsletter and archives of blogs and articles to help you learn about the publishing industry and social media marketing.

Writers Networking, formerly Writers, Agents and Editors Network
https://www.writersnetworking.com

Co-founded by Jeff and Deborah Herman, this is a comprehensive social network bringing content and innovative features through the vision of veteran literary Agents. It has groups for every genre and interest and aims to be a 24-hour writer's conference bringing industry insiders and writers together in a comfortable and friendly setting.

Writers on the Net www.writers.com

"Writers.com has been offering writing classes on the internet in all genres since 1995. It has been a pioneer in writer education. Published writers and experienced writing teachers teach the classes.

Writerspace www.writerspace.com

Founded in 1998, Writerspace is the home for over 550 authors, primarily romance and mystery, of the best fiction on the market today. Writerspace communities are familiar places for readers to gather, talk to each other, learn about releases and communicate with authors.

The Writer's Retreat www.writersretreat.com

This is a comprehensive and searchable site to find writer's retreats and workshops. It has a step-by-step guide to setting up and operating a writer's retreat. There may be a spiritual writer's retreat in the future. Sign up for my email list.

https://www.writtenwordmedia.com/

According to their website, they: "empower authors and publishers to reach their audience through our book promotion sites. We have five reader-facing brands that allow authors and publishers to reach the right readers. Each of these brands caters to a different reader profile and demographic. The audience for each site is built using our specialized and proprietary data-driven marketing techniques."

You will need to investigate, price, and use due diligence for their paid services. However, I liked their blog posts, and I recommend you check them out.

POETRY

Here are some sites that may prove helpful to the aspiring spiritual poet.

Poetry Society of America www.poetrysociety.org

Includes information about the newest developments in the Poetry in Motion project, which posts poetry to seven million subway and bus riders in New York City, Chicago, Baltimore, Portland (Oregon), and Boston. It also includes news about poetry awards, seminars, tributes in libraries, poetry in public, and poetry festivals.

Poets & Writers www.pw.org

This online resource for creative writers includes publishing advice, message forums, contests, a directory of writers, literary links, information on grants and awards, news from the writing world, trivia, and workshops.

Children's Books

There is a small but solid market for spiritual work for children and young adults. Here's a sample of online resources. Many aren't explicitly geared to spiritual material. These resources may help.

The Children's Book Council www.cbcbooks.org

"CBC Online is the Web site of the Children's Book Council— encouraging reading since 1945." It provides a list of articles geared toward publishers, teachers, librarians, booksellers, parents, authors, and illustrators—all those who are interested in the children's book field.

The Society of Children's Book Writers and Illustrators www.scbwi.org

This Web site "has a dual purpose: It exists as a service to our members, as well as offering information about the children's publishing industry and our organization to nonmembers." It features a listing of events, awards and grants, publications, information for members, information on how to become a member, and a site map.

Spiritual Magazines

This list is intended to give you a sense of the range of subjects covered by spiritual magazines, though it is impossible to be truly representative. It would take several lifetimes to exhaust the list of these sites, especially since new ones are added daily. I have tried to check all the links but also found that some magazines fold without warning. Please email my website with further recommendations of your favorite magazines, especially if they offer freelance opportunities to spiritual writers.

No matter how obscure your interest is, you will find that there are always people who share it. Magazines can offer spiritual writers freelance opportunities to build up a portfolio of clippings. If you are published in your book's subject, such articles improve your credibility. While freelancing can give many intangible rewards that make it worth pursuing. It is a great way to build your platform. Many magazines are now using an online edition only. Make sure to continue checking the most updated information as to the status of your favorite magazine. Here is a sampling.

Awareness Magazine www.awarenessmag.com
Southern California's guide to Conscious Living. This publication reaches individuals concerned with many issues that involve the environment, spirituality, holistic health, natural health products, fitness, and personal growth.

Christian Book.com www.christianbook.com
This site lists Christian Magazines. Examples include *Men of Integrity, Leadership, Christianity Today,. Homecoming.* It is also an E-commerce site for homeschooling supplies, Bibles and other Christian books. It may be a good place to research popular titles.

Focus Magazine www.focusmagazine.org
Christianity Magazine recently combined forces with Focus Magazine. "Scriptural insights for thoughtful disciples of Jesus.

Hinduism Today www.hinduismtoday.com
In print and online. A news magazine articulating Indian spirituality. "Hindu news and wisdom for your family and spiritual life."

New Leaf Distributing https://newleafdist.com/
New Leaf is an established and large distributor of books and other informational materials that foster learning, personal awakening, spiritual growth, and healing. "New Leaf has a sacred intention: to play an active role in fostering individual and collective spiritual awakening by being the nexus of trading partners for commerce in conscious books and other products yielding prosperity for all.

According to their website, their goal is: "To best serve our retailer customers, our priorities are to be a 'one-stop' source carrying a wide selection of quality, saleable books and products that serve our intention, to provide the highest level of service and to offer effective support to build their sales and help more people. To best serve our vendor customers, our priorities are to effectively stock and deliver their products and to provide effective marketing programs for them to reach our retailer customers and their end-user customers.

I include them here for you to review their listings to see trends, and it is possible if you are on your own, you can try to get them to distribute your book.

Parabola: Myth, Tradition, and the Search for Meaning www.parabola. org

A magazine published by members of The Society for the Study of Myth and Tradition, a not-for-profit organization devoted to disseminating and exploring materials relating to the myths, symbols, rituals, and art of the world's religious and cultural traditions. To this end, the Society is the publisher of *Parabola Magazine*.

Retailing Insight (Formerly New Age Retailer) http://www. retailinginsight.com

"A Trade magazine for the mindful retailer." *Retailing Insight* is the only trade magazine published exclusively for retail store owners, managers, and buyers in the body-mind-Spirit industry. You may get ideas, and you could also attend trade shows if they are still offering them.

GLOSSARY

ADVANCE

Money paid (usually in installments) to an author by a publisher before publication. The advance is paid against royalties; if an author is given a $5,000 advance, the author will collect royalties only after the royalty moneys due exceed $5,000. A good contract protects the advance if it should exceed the royalties ultimately due from sales.

ADVANCE ORDERS

Orders received any time before a book's official publication date.

AGENT

The person who acts on behalf of the author to handle the sale and negotiations of the author's work. Agents are paid on a percentage basis from the money owed to their author clients.

AMERICAN BOOKSELLERS ASSOCIATION (ABA)

The national trade association for independent booksellers— since 1900. ABA offers education, services and products, advocacy, and relevant business information. The major trade organization for chain and independent retail booksellers.

AUTHOR'S COPIES/AUTHOR'S DISCOUNT

Author's copies are the free copies of the book that the author receives from the publisher; the exact number is negotiated before the contract is signed— usually at least ten. The author's discount allows the author to purchase additional copies (usually at a 40 percent discount from the retail price) and resell them at readings, lectures, and other public engagements.

AUTHOR TOUR

A series of appearances by an author to promote and publicize their book.

BACKLIST

Titles published before the current season and still in print. Such books often represent the publisher's cash-flow mainstays. Although many backlist titles may be difficult to find in bookstores, they can be ordered through a local bookseller or directly from the publisher. Compare frontlist.

BACK MATTER

Elements of a book that follow the text. Back matter may include the appendix, notes, glossary, bibliography, resources, index, author biography, list of additional books from the author and publisher, and colophon.

BEST-SELLER

Those titles that move in the largest quantities, based on sales or orders by bookstores, wholesalers, and distributors. Lists of bestsellers can be local (as in metropolitan newspapers), regional (as in geographically keyed trade or consumer periodicals), or national (as in USA Today, Publishers Weekly, or the New York Times), as well as international. Fiction and nonfiction are usually listed separately, as are hardcover and paperback.

BIBLIOGRAPHY

A list of books, articles, and other sources used in the research and writing of the book's text.

BLURB

Written copy or an extracted quotation used for publicity and promotional purposes, as on a flyer, in a catalog, or in an advertisement. See cover blurbs.

BOOK CLUB

A book-marketing operation that ships selected titles to subscribing members on a regular basis, sometimes at greatly reduced prices. Sales to book clubs are negotiated through the publisher's subsidiary-rights department. (In the case of a best-seller or other work that has gained acclaim, these rights can be auctioned off.) Terms vary, but the split of royalties between author and publisher is often 50-50. This is not the same as local book clubs.

BOOK EXPO AMERICA

(commonly referred to within the book publishing industry as BEA) was the largest annual book trade show in theUnited States. BEA was almost always held in a major city over four days in late May and/or early June. Nearly all significant book publishers in the United States, and many from abroad, had booths and exhibits at BEA, and used the trade show as an opportunity to showcase upcoming titles, sell current books, socialize with colleagues from other publishing houses, and sell and buy subsidiary rights and international rights.

BOOK PRODUCER OR BOOK PACKAGER

Someone who conceives an idea for a book (most often nonfiction) or series, brings together the professionals (including the writer) needed to produce the book(s), sells the project to a publisher, and takes the project through to manufactured product—or performs any selection of those functions, as commissioned by the publisher or other client. The book producer may negotiate separate contracts with the publisher and with the writers, editors, and illustrators who contribute to the book.

BOOK REVIEW

A critical appraisal of a book that evaluates such aspects as organization and writing style, possible market appeal, and cultural, political, or literary significance. A positive review from a respected book-trade journal such as Publishers Weekly, Library Journal, or Booklist will encourage booksellers to order the book. Copies of these raves will be used for promotion and publicity by the publisher and will encourage reviewers nationwide to review the book.

BOOKS IN PRINT

Listings, published by R. R. Bowker, of books currently in print. These yearly volumes (along with periodic supplements such as Forthcoming Books in Print) provide ordering information including title, author, ISBN, price, publisher, and whether the book is available in hardcover or paperback or with library binding. Listings are provided alphabetically by author, title, and subject area. This can be found in libraries and some bookstores. It is available digitally at www.booksinprint.com

BOUND GALLEYS

Copies of uncorrected typesetter's page proofs or printouts of electronically produced mechanicals that are bound together to distribute to potential reviewers before a book's publication. Bound galleys also called Advance Reader Copies are sent to trade journals as well as to a limited number of reviewers who require long lead times. Many now accept PDFs.

BULK SALES

The sale at a set discount of many copies of a single title— the greater the number of books, the larger the discount.

BYLINE

The name of the author of a given piece, identifying him or her as the author of a book or article. Ghostwriters, by definition, do not receive bylines.

CHRISTIAN

A category of books and writing in which Christian theology, dogma, and strictures is integral, not incidental, to the core message.

CO-AUTHOR

One who shares authorship of a work. Co-authors have bylines and share royalties based on their contributions to the book. Compare ghostwriter.

COLLABORATION

A term denoting the working relationship that occurs when a writer wishes to work with another person to produce books outside the writer's own area of expertise. (For example, a writer with an interest in antiques may collaborate with a historian to increase the scope of a book.) The writer may be billed as a co-author or as a ghostwriter. Royalties are shared, based on respective contributions to the book, including expertise, promotional abilities, and actual writing of the book.

COLOPHON

A publisher's logo, although the term also applies to a listing of the fonts and materials used in the book production and credits for the design, composition, and production of the book. Such colophons are usually included in the back matter or as part of the copyright page.

COMMERCIAL BOOKS

Books that appeal to a broad, nonacademic audience.

CONCEPT

A general statement of the idea behind a book.

CONTRACT

A legally binding document between author and publisher that sets the terms for the advance, royalties, subsidiary rights, advertising, promotion, publicity, and many other contingencies and responsibilities.

COOPERATIVE ADVERTISING, OR CO-OP.

An advertising agreement between a publisher and a bookstore. The publisher's book is featured in an ad for the bookstore (often in conjunction with an author appearance), and the publisher contributes to the cost of the ad.

COPY EDITOR

An editor responsible for the final polishing of a manuscript, who reads primarily in terms of appropriate word usage and grammar, with an eye toward clarity and coherence, factual errors and inconsistencies, spelling, and punctuation. Also called line editor. See also editor.

COPYRIGHT

The legal proprietary right to reproduce, publish, and sell copies of literary, musical, and other artistic works. The rights to literary properties reside in the author from the time the work is produced, regardless of whether or not a formal copyright registration is obtained. However, for legal recourse in the event of plagiarism or other infringement, the work must be registered with the U.S. Copyright Office, and all copies of the work must bear the copyright notice.

COVER BLURBS

Endorsing quotes from other writers, celebrities, or experts in a book's subject area. On the cover or dust jacket, they enhance the book's point-of-purchase appeal.

DEADLINE

The author's due date for delivery of the completed manuscript to the publisher. It can be as much as a full year before official publication date.

DELIVERY

Submission of the completed manuscript to the editor or publisher.

DIRECT MARKETING

Advertising that involves a "direct response" (which is an equivalent term) from a consumer—for instance, order forms, coupons, or mailings directed at buyers presumed to hold a special interest in a particular book.

DISPLAY TITLES

Books designed to be eye-catching to the casual shopper in a bookstore setting often with the intention of piquing book-buyer excitement about the store's stock in general. Many display titles with attractive cover art are stacked on their own freestanding racks; sometimes broad tables are laden with these items. A book shelved with its front cover showing on racks along with diverse other titles is technically a display title. Promotional or premium titles are likely to be display items, as are mass-market paperbacks and hardbacks with best-seller potential.

DISTRIBUTION

The method of getting books from the production stage into the reader's hands. Distribution is traditionally through bookstores, but it can also include such means as telemarketing and mail-order sales, special-interest outlets such as health-food or New Age venues, sports and fitness emporiums, or gift shops. Publishers use their own sales forces as well as independent salespeople, wholesalers, and distributors. Many large and some small publishers distribute for other publishers.

DISTRIBUTOR.

An agent or business that buys books from a publisher to resell, at a higher cost, to wholesalers, retailers, or individuals. Distribution houses are often excellent marketing enterprises because of their sales representatives, publicity and promotion personnel, and house catalogs. Skillful use of distribution networks can give a small publisher considerable national visibility.

DUST JACKET

The wrapper that covers hardcover books, designed by the publisher's art department or a freelance artist. Dust jackets were originally conceived to protect the book during shipping, but now their function is primarily to entice the browser with graphics and promotional copy to pick up the book.

DUST-JACKET COPY

Descriptive text printed on the dust-jacket flaps that is written by the book's editor, in-house copywriters, or freelance specialists. Quotable praise the author has received from other writers, experts, and celebrities often appears on the jacket. See also blurb.

EDITOR

Editorial responsibilities and titles vary from house to house, often being less strictly defined in smaller houses. The duties of the editor in chief or executive editor are primarily administrative: managing personnel, scheduling, budgeting, and defining the editorial personality of the firm or imprint. Senior editors and acquisitions editors acquire manuscripts (and authors), conceive project ideas and find writers to carry them out, and may oversee the writing and rewriting of manuscripts. Managing editors coordinate and schedule the book through the various phases of production. Associate and assistant editors are involved in much of the rewriting and reshaping of the manuscript and may also have acquisitions duties. Copy editors style the manuscript for punctuation, grammar, spelling, headings and subheadings, and so forth. Editorial assistants, in addition to general office work, perform some editorial duties as well—often as springboards to senior editorial positions.

ENDNOTES

Explanatory notes and source citations that appear either at the end of individual chapters or at the end of a book's text, usually in scholarly works. Compare footnotes.

EPILOGUE

The final segment of a book that offers commentary or further information but does not bear directly on the book's central design. footnotes. Explanatory notes and source citations that appear at the bottom of a page. Footnotes are rare in general-interest books; instead
such information is contained in endnotes or worked into the text or listed in the bibliography.

FOREIGN AGENTS

People who work with their U.S. counterparts to acquire rights for books from the United States for publication abroad. They can also represent U.S. publishers directly.

FOREIGN MARKET

Any foreign entity, such as a publisher or broadcast medium, that buys rights. Authors either share royalties with whoever negotiates the deal or keep 100 percent if they do their own negotiating.

FOREIGN RIGHTS

Translation or reprint rights that can be sold to other countries. Foreign rights belong to the author but can be sold either country-by-country or as world rights. Often the U.S. publisher will own world rights, and the author will be entitled to anywhere from 50 to 85 percent of these revenues.

FOREWORD

An introductory piece usually written by someone other than the author, such as an expert in the given field. If written by a celebrity or well-respected authority, the foreword can be a strong selling point for a prospective author and the book itself. Contrast introduction.

FRANKFURT BOOK FAIR

The largest international publishing exhibition, with a five-hundred-year history. This annual event in Frankfurt, Germany, provides an opportunity for thousands of publishers, agents, and writers from all over the world to negotiate, network, and buy and sell rights.

FREIGHT PASS THROUGH

The bookseller's freight cost (the cost of getting the book from the publisher to the bookseller). It is added to the basic invoice price the publisher charges the bookseller.

FRONT- LIST

New titles published in a given season by a publisher. Front list titles usually receive priority exposure in the front of the sales catalog— as opposed to backlist titles, which are usually found at the back of the catalog. Compare backlist.

FRONT MATTER

The elements that precede the text of the work, including the title page, copyright page, dedication, table of contents, foreword, preface, acknowledgments, and introduction.

FULFILLMENT HOUSE

A firm commissioned to fulfill orders for a publisher. Services may include warehousing, shipping, receiving returns, and mail-order and direct-marketing functions. Although more common for magazine publishers, fulfillment houses also serve book publishers.

GALLEYS OR GALLEY PROOFS

Printouts from the typesetter of the electronically produced setup of the book's interior—the author's last chance to check for typos and make (usually minimal) revisions or additions to the copy. See also bound galleys.

GHOSTWRITER

A writer without a byline, often without the remuneration and recognition that credited authors receive. Ghostwriters often get flat fees for their work instead of royalties. Compare co-author.

HARDCOVER

Books bound in a format that conventionally includes thick, sturdy binding, a cover made usually of cloth spine and finished binding paper, and a dust jacket for a wrapper. See also dust jacket.

HOOK

A term denoting the distinctive concept or theme of a work that sets it apart as being fresh, new, or different from others in its field. A hook can be an author's special point of view, often encapsulated in a catchy or provocative phrase intended to attract or pique the interest of a reader, editor, or agent and turn the work into an exciting, commercially attractive package.

IMPRINT

A separate line of product within a publishing house. Houses can have imprints composed of one or two series to those offering full-fledged and diversified lists. Imprints vary in their autonomy from the parent company. An imprint may have its own editorial department (perhaps consisting of just one editor), or house acquisitions editors may assign titles for release on appropriate specialized imprints. An individual imprint's categories often overlap with other imprints or with the publisher's core list, but some imprints maintain a small house feel within an otherwise enormous conglomerate. The imprint can offer the distinct advantages of a personalized editorial approach while availing itself of the larger company's production, publicity, marketing, sales, and advertising resources.

INDEX

An alphabetical directory at the end of a book that references names and subjects discussed in the book and the pages where such mentions can be found.

INSPIRATIONAL

A category of books characterized by their inspiring and uplifting content, often containing stories of triumph over tragedy, frequently given as gifts.

INTRODUCTION

Preliminary remarks pertaining to a book. An introduction can be written by the author or an appropriate authority on the subject. If a book has both a foreword and an introduction, the foreword will be written by someone other than the author; the introduction will be written by the book's author and will be more closely tied to the text. Contrast foreword.

ISBN (International Standard Book Number).

A ten-digit or thirteen-digit number that identifies the title and publisher of a book. It is used for ordering and cataloging the book and appears on the dust jacket, the back cover, and the copyright page.

ISSN (International Standard Serial Number).

An eight-digit cataloging and ordering number that identifies all U.S. and foreign periodicals.

LIBRARY OF CONGRESS.

The largest library in the world, located in Washington, D.C. The LOC can supply a writer with up-to-date sources and bibliographies in all fields, from arts and humanities to science and technology. For more information, write to the Library of Congress, Central Services Division, Washington, DC 20540.

LIBRARY OF CONGRESS CATALOG CARD NUMBER

An identifying number issued by the Library of Congress to books it has accepted for its collection. The publication of those books, which are submitted by the publisher, are announced by the Library of Congress to libraries, which use Library of Congress numbers for their own ordering and cataloging purposes.

LIST

A publishing house's collection of books published, further refined as the frontlist and backlist to distinguish new titles from older ones.

LITERARY MARKET PLACE (LMP)

An annual directory of the publishing industry that contains a comprehensive list of publishers with their addresses, phone numbers, some personnel, and the types of books they publish. Other listings include literary agencies, writers' conferences and competitions, and editorial and distribution services. LMP is published by R. R. Bowker and is available in most public libraries. www.literarymarketplace.com

MARKETING PLAN

The strategy for selling a book, including its publicity, promotion, sales, and advertising. Now should also include digital marketing and social media.

MASS-MARKET PAPERBACK

Less-expensive smaller-format paperbacks sold from racks in supermarkets, variety stores, drugstores, and specialty shops, as well as in bookstores. Also called rack (or rack-sized) editions. Compare trade books.

MIDLIST

Books that traditionally form the bulk of a large publisher's list—nowadays often by default rather than intent. Midlist books are expected to be commercially viable but not explosive bestsellers.

MULTIPLE CONTRACT

A book contract that includes a provisional agreement for a future book or books. See also option clause.

MULTIPLE SUBMISSION

The submission of the same material to more than one publisher or agents at once. Although multiple submission is a common practice, publishers should always be made aware that it is being done.

NET RECEIPTS

The amount of money a publisher receives for sales of a book: the retail price minus the bookseller's discount or other discount. Once the cost of distribution and the number of returned copies is factored in, the net amount received per book is even lower. Royalties are usually figured on these net amounts rather than on the retail price of the book.

NEW AGE

A category of books covering transformation, meditation, channeling, pyramids, ancient mysticism, shamanism, Native American, spirituality, crystals, alternative health, energy work, and spiritualism. occult. Having to do with esoteric, mysterious, or supernatural spiritual practices such as tarot cards, divination, Wicca, psychic phenomena, mediumship, astrology, dousing, or astral projection.

OPTION CLAUSE

A clause in a book contract which stipulates that the publisher will have the exclusive right to consider and make an offer for the author's next book. However, the publisher is under no obligation to publish the book, and in most variations of the clause the author may opt for publication elsewhere. Also called right of first refusal. See also multiple contract

OUTLINE

A hierarchical listing of a book's topics that provides the writer (and the proposal reader) with an overview of the ideas in a book in the order in which they are to be presented. Compare synopsis.

OUT-OF-PRINT BOOKS

Books no longer available from the publisher; rights usually revert to the author. See also out of stock indefinitely. Some publishers now have clauses for print on demand books. They can sometimes keep books technically in print even though they have not done a print run.

OUT OF STOCK INDEFINITELY

Another term for out-of-print books intended to soften the finality of the more common term. See also out-of-print books.

PACKAGE

The book itself

PACKAGER.

See book producer.

PAGE PROOF

The final typeset copy of the book, in page-layout form, before it is sent to the printer. See also galleys.

PAPERBACK

Books bound with a flexible, stress-resistant, paper covering.

PERMISSIONS.

The right to quote or reprint previously published material, obtained by the author early in the publishing process from the copyright holder.

PLAGIARISM

The false presentation of someone else's writing as one's own. In the case of copyrighted work, plagiarism is illegal.

PREFACE

An element of a book's front matter. In it, the author may discuss the purpose behind the format of the book, the type of research upon which it is based, its genesis, or its underlying philosophy.

PREMIUM

Books sold at a reduced price as part of a special promotion. Premiums can be sold to a bookseller, who in turn sells them to the book buyer (as with a line of modestly priced art books). Alternatively, such books may be produced as part of a broader marketing package. For instance, an organization may acquire books for use in personnel training and as giveaways to clients. See also special sales.

PRESS KIT (See also media kit)

A promotional package that includes a book's press release, author biography and photograph, reviews, and other pertinent information. The press kit can be created by the publisher's publicity department or an independent publicist and sent with a review copy of the book to potential reviewers and to media professionals who book author appearances. Many authors upload their own press kits on their websites as part of an overall digital marketing plan.

PRICE

There are two prices for a book: the amount the publisher charges the bookseller is the invoice price; the amount the consumer pays is the retail, cover, or list price.

PROPOSAL

A detailed presentation of the book's concept that includes such elements as a marketing plan, the author's credentials, and an analysis of competitive titles. It is used to gain the interest and services of an agent and to sell the project to a publisher.

PUBLICATION DATE OR PUB DATE

A book's official date of publication, customarily set by the publisher to fall four to six weeks after completed bound books are delivered from the printer. The publication date is used to plan the title's promotional activities so that books will have had adequate time to arrive in stores to coincide with the appearance of advertising and publicity.

PUBLICIST

The publicity professional who handles press releases for new books and arranges the author's publicity tours, interviews, speaking engagements, and book-signings.

PUBLISHER'S CATALOG

A seasonal sales catalog that lists and describes a publisher's new books and backlist titles. It is usually sent to potential buyers. Catalogs range from the basic to the glitzy and often include information on the authors, on print quantities, and on the publicity and promotion budget. Now many catalogs are often found only online.

PUBLISHER'S DISCOUNT

The percentage by which a publisher discounts the retail price of a book to a bookseller, often partially based on the number of copies purchased.

PUBLISHERS' TRADE LIST ANNUAL

A collection of current and backlist catalogs arranged alphabetically by publisher, available in many libraries.

PUBLISHERS WEEKLY (PW)

The publishing industry's chief trade journal. PW carries announcements of upcoming books, respected book reviews, interviews with authors and publishing-industry professionals, special reports on various book categories, and trade news (such as mergers, rights sales, and personnel changes). The online *Publisher's Marketplace* is an excellent resource for watching publishing trends.

QUERY LETTER

A brief written presentation to an agent or editor designed to pitch both the author and the book idea

RELIGIOUS

A category of books characterized by research-heavy text about major world religions.

REMAINDERS

Unsold book stock purchased from the publisher at a large discount and resold to the public.

REPRINT

A subsequent edition of a book already in print, especially publication in a different format (for example, the paperback reprint of a hardcover).

RETURNS

Unsold books a bookstore returns to a publisher, for which the store may receive full or partial credit (depending on the publisher's policy, the age of the book, and other factors).

REVERSION-OF-RIGHTS CLAUSE

A clause in the book contract which states that if the book goes out of print or the publisher fails to reprint the book within a stipulated length of time, all rights revert to the author. These clauses now need to consider issues of print on demand and book sales to determine reversion.

REVIEW COPY

A free copy of a book that the publisher sends to print and electronic media which review books for their audiences.

ROYALTY

The percentage of the retail cost of a book that is paid to the author for each copy sold after the author's advance has been recouped. Some publishers structure royalties as a percentage payment against net receipts.

SALES CONFERENCE

A meeting of a publisher's editorial, sales, promotion, and publicity departments that covers the upcoming season's new books and marketing strategies for each.

SALES REPRESENTATIVE OR SALES REP

A member of the publisher's sales force or an independent contractor who sells books to retailers in a certain territory.

SASE (self-addressed, stamped envelope)

This is an essential element for an author who sends physical queries and submissions by mail. Many editors and agents do not reply if a writer has neglected to enclose a SASE or has failed to provide the correct amount of postage. Agents and editors are under no obligation to respond if it is an unsolicited query, meaning they have not asked for it. But this will increase the chances of a response. Most agents and editors now have a mechanism to receive most query letters by email. Please check their websites or profiles in *Jeff Herman's Guide to Book, Publishers, Editors, and Literary Agents* to determine their specific policies.

SATISFACTORY CLAUSE

A clause in the book contract that enables the publisher to refuse publication of a manuscript which is not deemed satisfactory. The specific criteria for publisher satisfaction should be set forth in the contract to protect the author from being forced to pay back the publisher's advance should the work be deemed unsatisfactory. season. The time in which publishers introduce their new line of books. Most publishers announce books for the spring and fall seasons.

SELF-PUBLISHING

A publishing project wherein an author pays for the costs of manufacturing and selling his or her own book. For the most part print runs are not necessary, due to print on demand options. This is much easier today than in the past. It can be highly profitable when combined with speaking engagements or imaginative marketing techniques. Compare hybrid publishing.

SERIAL RIGHTS

Reprint rights sold to periodicals. First serial rights include the right to publish the material before any other publication (generally before the book is released or coinciding with the book's pub date). Second serial rights cover material already published, either in a book or another periodical.

SERIES

Books published as a group either because of their related subject matter or authorship

SHELF LIFE

The length of time a book remains on the bookstore shelf before it is pulled to make room for newer incoming stock.

SIGNATURE

A group of book pages printed together on one large sheet of paper that is then folded and cut in preparation for being bound, along with the book's other signatures, into the final product.

SIMULTANEOUS PUBLICATION

The simultaneous issuing of more than one edition of a work, such as in hardcover and trade paperback. Simultaneous releases can be expanded to include gift editions as well as mass-market paper versions. Audio versions of books most often coincide with the release of the first print edition.

SIMULTANEOUS SUBMISSION. See multiple submission

SLUSH PILE

Unsolicited manuscripts at a publishing house or literary agency awaiting review. Some publishers or agencies do not maintain slush piles per se but instead return unsolicited manuscripts without review (if an SASE is included). Querying a targeted publisher or agent before submitting a manuscript is an excellent way of avoiding the slush pile.

SPECIAL SALES

Sales of a book to appropriate retailers other than bookstores (for example, wine guides to liquor stores). This classification also includes books sold as premiums (see premiums) or for other promotional purposes. Depending on volume, per-unit costs can be very low, and the book can be custom-designed.

SUBSIDIARY RIGHTS

The reprint, serial, movie and television, and audiotape and videotape rights deriving from a book. The publisher and author negotiate the division of profits from the sales of these rights.

SYNOPSIS

A book summary in paragraph form, rather than in outline format, that serves as an important part of a book proposal. For fiction, the synopsis succinctly and dramatically describes the highlights of story line and plot. For nonfiction, the synopsis describes the thrust and content of the successive chapters of the manuscript.

TABLE OF CONTENTS

A listing of a book's chapters and other sections (such as the front matter, appendix, bibliography, and index) with respective beginning page numbers in the order in which they appear.

TERMS

The financial conditions agreed to in a book contract.

TIP SHEET

An information sheet on a single book that presents general publication information (publication date, editor, ISBN, etc.), a brief synopsis of the book, information on competing titles, and other pertinent marketing data such as author profile and advance blurbs. The tip sheet is given to the sales and publicity departments.

TITLE PAGE

The page at the front of a book that lists the title, subtitle, author (and other contributors, such as translator or illustrator), as well as the publishing house and sometimes its logo.

TRADE BOOKS

Books distributed through the book trade—meaning bookstores and major book clubs—as opposed to, for example, mass-market paperbacks, which are often sold at magazine racks, newsstands, and supermarkets as well.

TRADE DISCOUNT

The discount from the cover or list price that a publisher gives the bookseller. It is usually proportional to the number of books ordered (the larger the order, the greater the discount) and typically varies between 40 and 50 percent.

TRADE PUBLISHER

A publisher of books for a general readership—that is, nonprofessional, nonacademic books that are distributed primarily through bookstores.

UNSOLICITED MANUSCRIPT

A manuscript sent to an editor or agent without being requested.

vanity press. A publisher that prints books only at the author's expense—and will generally agree to publish virtually anything that is submitted and paid for. See also self-publishing, subsidy publishing.

WORD COUNT

The number of words in a given document. When noted on a manuscript, the word count is usually rounded off to the nearest one hundred words.

WORK-FOR-HIRE

Writing done for an employer, or writing commissioned by a publisher or book packager who retains ownership of, and all rights pertaining to, the written material

INDEX